THE LANGUAGE OF
GERARD MANLEY HOPKINS

THE LANGUAGE LIBRARY

EDITED BY ERIC PARTRIDGE

James Milroy

THE LANGUAGE OF GERARD MANLEY HOPKINS

ANDRE DEUTSCH

First published 1977 by
André Deutsch Limited
105 Great Russell Street London WC1

Copyright © 1977 by James Milroy
all rights reserved

Printed in Great Britain
by W & J Mackay Limited, Chatham

ISBN 0 233 96916 0

Distributed in the United States and Canada
by Westview Press, 1898 Flatiron Court,
Boulder, Colorado 80301, USA

821.09
POETRY
ENGLISH LITERATURE
LITERARY CRITICISM
GERARD MANLEY HOPKINS

In Memoriam
My Parents

Contents

𒀭𒀭𒀭𒀭𒀭𒀭

Abbreviations used in the Text

𝕾𝕾𝕾𝕾𝕾𝕾

I HOPKINS'S WORKS

Poems   W. H. Gardner and N. H. MacKenzie (eds), *The Poems of Gerard Manley Hopkins*, 4th edition, London, 1967, reprinted with corrections in 1970, 1972, 1975.

JP   Humphry House (ed.), *The Journals and Papers of Gerard Manley Hopkins*, completed by Graham Storey, London, 1959.

LB   C. C. Abbott (ed.), *The Letters of Gerard Manley Hopkins to Robert Bridges*, London, 1935.

CD   C. C. Abbott (ed.), *The Correspondence of Gerard Manley Hopkins and Richard Watson Dixon*, London, 1935.

FL   C. C. Abbott (ed.), *Further Letters of Gerard Manley Hopkins including his Correspondence with Coventry Patmore*, 2nd edition, revised and enlarged, London, 1956.

SD   Christopher Devlin, S.J. (ed.), *The Sermons and Devotional Writings of Gerard Manley Hopkins*, London, 1959.

Letters, notes and other prose-writings are referred to by page-number (e.g. *JP*, 123) and occasionally by date. Poems are referred to by number (e.g. No. 61) or by (abbreviated) name, except that stanzas of 'The Wreck of the Deutschland' are referred to by the abbreviation 'Deutschland' and the stanza number.

etym.   etymology, etymological
Fr.   French
Gk   Greek
Gmc   Germanic
IE   Indo-European
imit.   imitative
Lat.   Latin
ME   Middle English
OE   Old English
OF   Old French
ON   Old Norse
Scand. Scandinavian
St.E   Standard English

III DICTIONARIES, REFERENCES USED IN COMMENTARY

BARNES William Barnes, *Outline of English Speech-Craft*, London, 1878.

BREMER see Bibliography.

EDD *English Dialect Dictionary* (see also Wright).

MACKENZIE see Bibliography.

MARIANI see Bibliography.

MILROY see Bibliography.

MILWARD see Bibliography.

MÜLLER, *Lectures* I Max Müller, *Lectures on the Science of Language*, First Series, London, 1861.

OED *Oxford English Dictionary*.

OGILVIE John Ogilvie, *The Imperial Dictionary*, Glasgow, 1851–5.

ONIONS C. T. Onions, *The Oxford Dictionary of English Etymology*, with the assistance of G. W. S. Friedrichsen and R. W. Burchfield, Oxford, 1966.

PARTRIDGE Eric Partridge, *Origins: A Short Etymological Dictionary of Modern English*, 4th ed., London, 1966.

RICHARDSON Charles Richardson, *A New Dictionary of the English Language*, London, 1838.

RICHARDSON, *Philology* Charles Richardson, *Illustrations of English Philology*, London, 1815.

SCHODER see Bibliography.

TODD H. J. Todd, *Samuel Johnson, A Dictionary of the English Language . . . with numerous corrections. . . .* London, 1818.

WARD Alan Ward, 'Philological Notes' in Humphry House, *Journals and Papers of Gerard Manley Hopkins*, pp. 499ff.

WEDGWOOD Hensleigh Wedgwood, *Dictionary of English Etymology*, London, 1859–65.

WRIGHT Joseph Wright, *English Dialect Dictionary*.

Preface

FROM time to time in the history of English poetry, a notable innovation in poetic language takes place. Gerard Manley Hopkins, like certain others before him (including Spenser and Wordsworth) was an innovator. Like Wordsworth, he rejected an established tradition and sought to reform poetic diction by appealing to the norms of ordinary speech. But he differed from Wordsworth in two important respects. First, he lived at a time in which the investigation of linguistic change and variation was a major scholarly concern; he was aware of this research. Second this interest in 'simple' speech did not lead, for Hopkins, to a simple poetic diction. On the contrary, many have found his language dense, elliptical and difficult. The purpose of this book is to help to resolve this apparent contradiction. Its aim is thus to explain his language rather than to evaluate it. To this end we invoke Hopkin's declaration that the poetical language of an age should be *the current language heightened*. In the first part of the book, we consider in detail Hopkin's notion of *current language* in the light of his linguistic interests. In the second part, we focus on the methods used by the poet to *heighten* this language in his poetry. The main concern, therefore, is with the general configurations of Hopkin's language, and passages from his work are used chiefly to illustrate particular points. Nevertheless, the book contains a good deal of incidental comment and explanation on the poems and is equipped with a Commentary on words used by the poet in unfamiliar ways.

This book owes a great deal to the patience, kindness and encouragement given by the General Editor, Professor Simeon Potter, who, before his death in 1976, commented carefully on several chapters. I should like to record my appreciation here. I am also very grateful to Professor John Braidwood and to my wife, Lesley, for reading the text and suggesting improvements. My

xii

small sons, David, Andrew and Richard, have also been helpful. Finally, I should like to thank Irene Dempster and Karen Johnston for their careful typing. For any imperfections which remain I am, of course, solely responsible.

JAMES MILROY
Queen's University of Belfast
March 1977

Acknowledgements

ꙮꙮꙮꙮꙮ

I am grateful to Oxford University Press for permission to reprint quotations from *Fiction for the Working Man 1830–1850*; to Nirad Chaudhuri and Messrs Chatto and Windus for permission to quote from *Scholar Extraordinary: The Life of ... Max Müller*; to Basil Blackwell for permission to quote from *Gerard Manley Hopkins: A Critical Essay towards the Understanding of his Poetry*, by W. A. M. Peters, S.J. (2nd edition 1970; first published by the Oxford University Press). Quotations from J. D. Connor *Phonetics* (1973), pp. 197–8, 238–9, are reprinted by permission of Penguin Books Ltd., and the author. I am greatly indebted to all those other scholars and critics whose work I have commented on in any way (even where there is disagreement), and I hope that they will accept this general acknowledgement as an expression of my gratitude to them.

Copyright material from Hopkins's Work is reprinted by permission of O.U.P. on behalf of the Society of Jesus, as follows: *The Poems of Gerard Manley Hopkins*, 4th ed., edited by W. H. Gardner and N. H. MacKenzie (1967); *The Journals and Papers of Gerard Manley Hopkins*, edited by Humphry House and Graham Storey (1959); *The Letters of Gerard Manley Hopkins to Robert Bridges*, edited by Claude Colleer Abbott (1935); *The Correspondence of Gerard Manley Hopkins and Richard Watson Dixon . . .*, edited by Claude Colleer Abbott (1956); *The Sermons and Devotional Writings of Gerard Manley Hopkins*, edited by Christopher Devlin, S.J. (1959).

Brief quotations from the works of Dylan Thomas appear by permission of J. M. Dent and Sons on behalf of the Trustees for the Copyright of the late Dylan Thomas (*Collected Poems of Dylan Thomas*, 1952) and by permission of the New Directions Publishing Corporation (*The Poems of Dylan Thomas*, 1946).

Brief quotations from the works of George Orwell appear by permission of Mrs Sonia Brownwell Orwell ('Politics and the English Language' in *Shooting an Elephant an Other Essays*, published by Martin Secker and Warburg).

Part 1

'CURRENT LANGUAGE'

❧❧❧❧❧❧

CHAPTER I

'Continuous Literary Decorum':
Hopkins and the Tradition

𝕊𝕊𝕊𝕊𝕊𝕊

GERARD MANLEY HOPKINS died in 1889, and when – nearly thirty years after his death – his complete poems were published at last, they were not immediately received with enthusiasm. The hostile criticism (and much of it was hostile) was based almost wholly on the difficulty and unconventionality of his language. The *New Statesman*, for example, commented that 'Hopkins rhythmical peculiarity was only one expression of a general and pervading eccentricity', and went on to attack his diction:

> His adjectives not only at first reading but also at the tenth or twentieth, distract the mind altogether from their meaning by their strangeness. *Silk-sack clouds, azurous hung hills, majestic as a stallion stalwart, very-violet-sweet, mild night's blear-all black* and the like are traps for the attention, not aids to visualization.

The *TLS* reviewer, in an otherwise good review, condemned Hopkins for his plays on sound:

> His worst trick is that of passing from one word to another . . . merely because they are alike in sound. This at its worst produces the effect almost of idiocy, of speech without sense and prolonged merely by echoes . . . a bad habit, like stuttering, except that he did not strive against it.

Indeed, Sturge Moore in 1930 was so offended by Hopkins's echo-words that he rewrote the opening lines of 'The Leaden Echo'. These are his opening lines:

> How to keep beauty? is there any way?
> Is there nowhere any means to have it stay?
> Will no bow or brooch or braid

Brace or lace
Latch or catch
Or key to lock the door lend aid . . . ?

The last line is a fine example of near-meaninglessness masquerad-
ing as elegance or good taste. What else is a key for but 'to lock
the door', and what excuse is there for 'lend aid' apart from metre
and rhyme? So great was the care that Hopkins bestowed on
every word he wrote that this rewriting seems almost sacrilege.[1]

Even Hopkins's close friend, Robert Bridges, who had lovingly
preserved the manuscripts and who sent Hopkins's poems forth
into the world with a dedicatory sonnet, felt it necessary to
apologize for the oddity, obscurity and mannerism of the language.
Readers were warned that they might find certain 'faults', 'extrava-
gances' and 'blemishes'. Some of these, Bridges felt, might be hard
to forgive:

> For these blemishes in the poet's style are of such quality and
> magnitude as to deny him even a hearing from those who love a
> continuous literary decorum and are grown to be intolerant of
> its absence.[2]

Hopkins's metaphors, said Bridges, were often affected, his
grammar elliptical (often wilfully so), his rhymes 'childish' or even
'hideous'. But, at the same time, Bridges thought the poetry well
worth commending to the world, and besought his readers to
persevere and 'search out the rare masterly beauties that distinguish
his work'. Although Bridges was no doubt sincere in many of his
criticisms, it looks very much as if he wished also to forestall and
disarm the much more hostile criticism that his friend's poetry was
bound to provoke from a conservative literary establishment.
That he was aware of its excellences is suggested by the fact that
he published it at all and by the last two lines of his dedicatory
sonnet:

> Go forth: amidst our chaffinch flock display
> Thy plumage of far wonder and heavenward flight!

Hopkins's 'rare masterly beauties' have since that time been much
more fully appreciated. The small literary output of that earnest
priest, unknown and unappreciated in his lifetime, holds an
honoured place in English poetry. Although serious critics admire

Hopkins and speak of him as a major poet, his is the kind of poetry which because of its distinctiveness may also attract less critical enthusiasts and devotees. It is not now unreasonable to speak of a Hopkins 'cult' or 'industry', as Dr Leavis did in a recent lecture. Few single poems have been the subject of so many academic articles as 'The Windhover', and few single poets are the subject of so many student theses and dissertations.[3] Hopkins shares with Chaucer, Shakespeare, Dickens and Joyce the distinction of having an academic journal (*The Hopkins Quarterly*) devoted to the study of his work and its background. There is a Hopkins Society, based in London, which issues an excellent annual bulletin and sponsors each year a Hopkins Lecture and a Hopkins Sermon, given by distinguished scholars and churchmen. There is even a Hopkins Society of Japan. Recently, on the centenary of the disaster that led to the composition of 'The Wreck of the Deutschland', Hopkins was accorded the greatest accolade England can award to a poet – membership of Poets' Corner in Westminster Abbey. Those readers who are devotees of Hopkins will know how easy it is to forgive Hopkins his 'blemishes' (if they admit that there are any at all), and how striking and memorable his best poems are.

Although Hopkins still has his detractors, his work now generally occupies a position of high esteem. It did not rise to this position without the help of able and enthusiastic defenders, and it is well to be reminded that, just as the early detractors had attacked the 'oddity' and 'obscurity' of his language, so it was the vigour and originality of his *language* that these defenders praised. It was F. R. Leavis in 1932 who did most to draw attention to his excellences. 'What Dr Bridges calls "blemishes" are essential to Hopkins's aim and achievement,' says Leavis; he goes on to explain that Hopkins 'aimed to get out of words as much as possible unhampered by the rules of grammar, syntax and common usage . . . the peculiarities of his technique appeal for sanction to the spirit of the language; his innovations accentuate and develop bents it exhibits in living use and, above all, in the writings of the greatest master who ever used it . . . Paradoxical as it may sound to say so, his strength was that he brought poetry much closer to living speech.' Although Leavis compares Hopkins very fully with Shakespeare and the Metaphysical poets, he goes out of his way to insist that there is no necessary connection, and that Hopkins based his techniques on the sounds and rhythms of 'living' English rather than on any literary tradition. To nine-teenth-century poetic diction, adds Leavis, he owes nothing, and – in a now famous conclusion: 'He is likely to prove, for our time and the future, the only influential poet of the Victorian age, and he seems to me the greatest.'[4]

The work of explaining and appreciating Hopkins was carried out over the succeeding decades, much helped by the appearance of editions of Hopkins's letters, journals and sermons, and the best of this explanatory work has continued to discuss the poet's distinctive language. Perhaps the most 'linguistic' of the many books that have appeared is that of W. A. M. Peters, which is sub-titled: 'A Critical Essay towards the Understanding of his Poetry'. Father Peters makes full use of many passages in Hopkins's letters and journals that throw light on his poetic techniques, emphasizes Hopkins's notion that 'the poetical language of an age should be the current language heightened', and points out that, to Hopkins, not only natural objects but words also have their 'inscape' and 'instress'. In much valuable commentary on Hopkins's language he goes on to discuss details of the sounds and syntax of particular lines and particular poems. Rhythm, rather than grammar, is the subject of Walter Ong's fine essay in *Immortal Diamond* – an essay which shows Hopkins's 'sprung rhythm' as the offspring of a long but submerged tradition in English poetry, having its origins in the natural rhythms of the ordinary language. J. Hillis Miller has for his theme the principle of rhyme – in natural creation as in language. Hopkins was obsessed with the principle of rhyme – vowel and consonant rhyme, end-rhyme, initial rhyme and internal rhyme, the idea that one word can echo another and even that the word can 'rhyme' with the thing it stands for – and, as Miller shows, particularly in an admirable analysis of 'Pied Beauty', rhyming can be found everywhere in Hopkins's nature, just as it is in his language. In recent years, as a by-product of his editorial labours, Norman MacKenzie has called for more attention to Hopkins's own statements about language and to his early interests in dialect and philology as clues to his use of language.[5]

No amount of scholarly explanation, however, can alter the fact that, to the uninitiated, Hopkins's poems do present uncommon difficulties. Most of the critics of 1919 seem to have admired 'continuous literary decorum' and were 'intolerant of its absence'. They found his poetry odd because it did not conform to the expected conventions, and even 'silk-sack clouds' became part of the 'general and pervading eccentricity' that made his work difficult to accept. Bridges was right in his presupposition that this 'continuous literary decorum' was absent from Hopkins, for Hopkins owed virtually nothing to nineteenth-century conventions of poetic diction. His language is original and has its own 'selfhood'. As he wrote in a letter to Bridges on 15 February 1879, Hopkins was well aware that the distinctiveness of his poetry might lead to oddness:

> No doubt my poetry errs on the side of oddness. I hope in time to have a more balanced and Miltonic style. But as air, melody, is what strikes me most of all in music and design in painting, so design, pattern or what I am in the habit of calling 'inscape' is what I above all aim at in poetry. Now it is the virtue of design, pattern or inscape to be distinctive and it is the vice of distinctiveness to become queer. This vice I cannot have escaped.

So, in 1879, before he had written 'Binsey Poplars' and not long after he had written 'The Loss of the Eurydice', we find Hopkins admitting that his language is sometimes *odd* and explaining why this has to be so. Many years later, also in a letter to Bridges (6 November 1887), we find him grappling with the problem of *obscurity*:

> Plainly, if it is possible to express a sub(t)le and recondite thought on a subtle and recondite subject in a subtle and recondite way and with great felicity and perfection, in the end, something must be sacrificed, with so trying a task, in the process, and this may be the being at once, nay perhaps even the being without explanation at all, intelligible.

If the thought is difficult, then the language in which it is expressed will also be difficult, and perhaps unintelligible. Moreover, to Hopkins, it is a matter of honesty or 'in-earnestness' that this should be so. Everything in the world of nature has its own 'selfhood' – its individuality – and each word has its own flavour and distinctiveness. To use the ready cliché instead of the language that most aptly captures the 'inscape' of the thing (however complicated), is to over-generalize, to simplify, to falsify and mislead.

In the poems written between 1875 and 1879 there are a few passages that could be described as difficult, but for the most part the charge of 'obscurity' is less relevant to these than to later poems. But by the standards of a 'continuous literary decorum', the language is often highly unconventional. If it is odd, it seems to us odd in a fresh and appealing way, and its effects and associations stir the emotions and imagination. The figurative language that Bridges condemned as 'mannerism' and that so offended the *New Statesman* critic seems to us now only strikingly original and appropriate:

And the azurous hung hills are his world-wielding shoulder
Majestic – as a stallion stalwart, very-violet-sweet!   (No. 38)

The hills are strong and enduring, but also beautiful in the blue haze; characteristically, different sense-impressions are brought together in the imagery. Hopkins's figurative language is usually quite dissimilar to the imagery of most nineteenth century verse, and multiplicity of sense impression is one of its hallmarks. The sense of *touch* is particularly important:

Over again I feel thy finger and find thee.
('Deutschland', st. 1)

and as Geoffrey Hartman has pointed out, 'the sense of pressure or stress is the sixth and radical sense in the experience of Hopkins'.[6] In both early and late poems, it is hard to say whether the early critics would be most surprised by this rich imagery or by what they would regard as the grammatical liberties that accompanied it. They would see that in 'rope-over thigh', Harry Ploughman's thighs were somehow being likened to rope, but surely, to be strictly 'grammatical', it should be 'roped-over'? Similarly, it is difficult to say whether 'there must/the sour scythe cringe' involves a difficulty of imagery or a difficulty of grammar. The scythe does not 'cringe', but the creatures it cuts down may. Hopkins appears to be using an *intransitive* verb as a *causative* with an implied object. Thus, apart from difficulties of imagery and subject-matter, passages must have seemed wanting in literary taste or in some way defective in language.

In vocabulary alone, some of the words Hopkins uses must have seemed at best 'unpoetic' and at worst incomprehensible:

The rash smart *sloggering* brine   ('Deutschland', st. 19)

7

The *down-dugged*, ground-hugged grey . . . pied and *peeled* May
('Deutschland', st. 26)

Look, look: a May-*mess*, like on orchard boughs! (32)

. . . *messes* of mortals ('Eurydice', 40)

Such words, and many more, were not in keeping with Victorian literary decorum. Some of his compound words and other coinages would have seemed brilliantly successful, while others might have seemed too strange to be acceptable, especially when they came in droves:

> Double-naturèd name,
> The heaven-flung, heart-fleshed, maiden-furled
> Miracle-in-Mary-of-flame ('Deutschland', st. 34)

Keats, himself a master of the compound word, would never have dared anything like this. Many of Hopkins's syntactic inversions and parenthetical constructions, even if reasonably comprehensible, must have seemed wilfully and deliberately eccentric:

And frightful a nightfall folded rueful a day
('Deutschland', st. 15)

No not uncomforted: lovely-felicitous Providence
Finger of a tender of, O of a feathery delicacy, the breast of the
  Maiden could obey so, be a bell to, ring of it, and
Startle the poor sheep back!
('Deutschland', st. 31)

His verbless or incomplete sentences and sentences interrupted by passionate questions and exclamations must have seemed 'ungrammatical', and therefore unacceptable, to many.

> O unteachably after evil, but uttering truth,
> Why, tears! is it? tears; such a melting, a madrigal start!
> ('Deutschland', st. 18)

> But how shall I . . . make me room there:
> Reach me a . . . Fancy, come faster –
> Strike you the sight of it? ('Deutschland', st. 28)

His long or unconventional pre-modifying phrases must also have seemed strange, and objectionable to the grammatical purist. The 'unshapeable shock night' ('Deutschland', st. 29) for example, not only uses as modifier a noun that is not usually a modifier, but is also – strictly speaking – grammatically ambiguous, as all such phrases are. Is it the 'unshapeable shock' or the 'unshapeable night' or both? The last line of the 'Deutschland' is even more difficult to unravel:

> Our hearts' charity's hearth's fire, our thought's chivalry's
>   throng's Lord.   ('Deutschland', st. 35)

We shall have more to say about such structures in our chapter on Hopkins's grammar. For the moment it is sufficient to note that since they are unconventional they would strike early readers as adding to the poet's oddity, and since such pre-modified phrases are actually more difficult to understand[7] than, say, 'The hearth's fire of the charity of our hearts', they would also be felt as obscure.

In the Preface to the original (1918) edition Bridges cited two main grammatical causes of Hopkins's obscurity: his habit of omitting the relative pronoun even when it is nominative ('O hero savest', No. 41, for 'O hero *that* savest'), and his delight in placing words in positions where their grammatical function is ambiguous or obscure.

> English swarms with words that have one identical form for substantive, adjective, and verb; and such a word should never be so placed as to allow of any doubt as to what part of speech it is used for; because such ambiguity or momentary uncertainty destroys the force of the sentence.

Hopkins, of course, took such a positive joy in these ambiguous placings of words that the habit must be counted as one of the guiding principles of his art. The 'obscurity' is not lessened by the tendency to leave out small 'grammatical' words which act as markers of nouns or verbs – not only the relative pronouns, but also definite and indefinite articles, conjunctions and even auxiliary verbs.

In Hopkins's later poems, the grammatical 'liberties' are more prominent than in the earlier ones, and several types are sometimes found within the same sentence: long parenthesis, ambiguous word-class, omission of 'grammatical' words, and so on:

        's cheek crimsons; curls
Wag or crossbridle, in a wind lifted, windlaced –
See his wind-lilylocks-laced;   (No. 71)

        lustily he his low lot (feel
That ne'er need hunger, Tom; Tom seldom sick,
Seldomer heartsore; that treads through, prickproof, thick
Thousands of thorns, thoughts) swings though.   (No. 70)

In the second quotation three lines of parenthesis intervene between object ('lot') and verb ('swings') and the syntactic relations of *prickproof*, *thick*, *thorns* and *thoughts* have to be carefully worked out by the reader.

Thus, Hopkins's breach of 'continuous literary decorum' is seen to be very largely a breach of the lexical and *syntactic* conventions that had become usual in nineteenth-century poetry. In other words it is a kind of 'linguistic' decorum that Hopkins breaks, and it is this breach of language conventions that forms the substance of Bridges's complaints and creates the most obvious difficulties for the reader. No one actually speaks or writes in the elliptical and parenthetical style of 'Tom's Garland' or 'Harry Ploughman'. These poems are the summits, the show-pieces, of Hopkins's highly individualized style in which he has striven most to 'rhyme' sound and sense – to make us feel and see in the texture of the language itself Harry's muscles, Tom's trudging. In a letter to Dixon (*CD*, 153), he described them as 'works of infinite, of over great contrivance'.

In the years since 1918, as we have seen, Hopkins's work has achieved a higher and higher reputation. The difficulties that undoubtedly exist in his poetry have been played down and its beauties appreciated. But there remains one notable detractor, many of whose criticisms are based on language attitudes. To Yvor Winters, Hopkins's poetry is vague and emotional, lacking in rational development, and unfavourably compared in these respects with the work of Donne and Bridges. It is no service to Hopkins to treat him with uncritical adulation, and there may be some respects in which Winters is right. But what is noticeable in the present connection is that Winters is a true inheritor of the linguistic complaints of Bridges. Indeed, he goes much further. Whereas Bridges condemned the confusion of parts of speech because it might lead – perhaps only momentarily – to difficulty in reading, Winters quite cheerfully subscribes to a full-blown and crude prescriptivism. First, he prescribes rigid semantic rules. Without quoting any authority, he states that words are fixed concepts with identities that can be 'impaired' (and Hopkins by implication impairs them). Any semanticist or lexicographer knows that words vary semantically in their use or application from sentence to sentence and have changed in the course of history. The relation of word to concept is never static or clear, much as we might wish it to be: hence many of the misunderstandings of ordinary life, the need for legal, technical or *ad hoc* definitions of meanings, and much of the rich suggestiveness of poetry, either by Donne or Bridges or by anyone else.

This cheerful *ipsedixitism* is further developed in a number of grammatical prescriptions, of which the chief motivation seems to be a horror of what Winters calls ambiguity. The possible omission of the definite article in the phrase 'shook foil' ('God's Grandeur') is the chief butt of his criticism.

> . . . if we assume that the second line is *grammatically correct* [my italics], then *foil* is a quantitative word and refers to tin-foil or gold-leaf, or to something of that nature, and we have what amounts, in effect, to an image of a mad man . . . brandishing a metal bouquet; if the foil in question, however, is a fencing foil, then *the grammar is defective* [my italics], for the article is omitted.

In fact there is no necessary ambiguity here anyway. The tinfoil put out to scare away the birds is a perfectly familiar country sight – and it may well have been in Hopkins's day too. It does flap in the wind and glint in the sun. But it is the narrowness and triviality of Winters's grammatical prescription that is disturbing. He is in fact denying to any poet the right to deviate slightly (for whatever purpose) from a 'grammatical' prescription the authority for which is not stated. If it is reasonable for Winters to do this, why should we not go through the work of Hopkins blue-pencilling and changing, seeking out split infinitives, prepositions at the ends of sentences, ambiguities and redundancies, much in the manner of the eighteenth-century correctors of Milton and Shakespeare? There is nothing truly 'ungrammatical' about the omission of the article in English when it is done with a clear semantic purpose, when it is successful in its effects, and when it conforms (as Hopkins's many such omissions may be said to conform) with deep-lying rules of English grammar. One cannot judge the language of an innovating poet by criteria that he himself rejected, especially when they are as narrow and weak and irrelevant to poetry as the superficial rules of schoolboy grammar; it does not speak well for the linguistic sophistication of critics that they do not more frequently expose the narrowness of such approaches. Hopkins thought long and deeply about language and observed it carefully; the springs of his poetic diction lay much deeper than the 'rules' of school grammar. To accuse him of mere carelessness, as Winters does, is ludicrous. 'No one', Bridges recalled, 'wrote words with more critical deliberation than G. Hopkins.'

Judged by any standards and in any age, Hopkins is an innovating poet, and in the diction of his mature poetry he sought effects that were entirely new, and which seemed to him to capture precisely his own observation of nature. To this end, he cut himself off as far as possible from the literary tradition (since this might interpose a prefabricated kind of language between observer and observed) and considered schoolboy grammar of relatively slight importance. He attempted to construct a new diction on the basis of 'current language' – the language of ordinary speech as he heard it around him in all its complexity and variety. The effect of reading masterpieces, he averred, was to make him 'admire and do otherwise'. Critics have often claimed to hear echoes of Shakespeare, Milton, Donne and others in Hopkins's work. It is Shakespeare in the sestet of no. 65.

> O the mind, mind has mountains; cliffs of fall
> Frightful, sheer, no-man-fathomed . . .
> . . . Here! creep,
> Wretch, under a comfort serves in a whirlwind: all
> Life death does end and each day dies with sleep.

To the oft-noted similarities to *King Lear* we may add the Shakespearean ring of the last line – partly created by the monosyllabism, a frequent Shakespearean trick in the final line:

> So long lives this and this gives life to thee.
>
> (Sonnet 18)

There is also some general similarity between Hopkins's late sonnets and the Metaphysicals, and the occasional verbal reminiscence of Milton. But what is really important about Hopkins is the extent to which this is *not* so – the extent to which it is merely beside the point to mention that 'Binsey Poplars' reminds one of Cowper's 'The poplars are felled, farewell to the shade', or that the 'bone-house' of 'The Caged Skylark' is like *Beowulf*. Hopkins's language in its most generalized features – those of rhythm, sound and grammatical pattern, departs radically from that of all his predecessors; even his vocabulary is partly drawn from sources that few before him would have used, and exploited to an extent that no one before him (not excluding Shakespeare) had contemplated. In order to understand the springs of his poetic language it is far more important to understand Hopkins's linguistic attitudes and interests in general than to investigate his links with literary tradition. Fortunately, these interests can be conveniently studied in his undergraduate diaries (1863–6), which are full of linguistic notes, his Journal (1866–75), his essays and lecture-notes, and his letters.

It is remarkable that critics have paid so little attention to the early diaries and journals. It is one of the aims of this book to show how revealing these are; the next two chapters are devoted largely to analysis and discussion of the language notes in the diary and journals. Hopkins's better-known statements about poetic diction are, it seems to me, fully understood only in the light of his general interests in language. Many of these better-known statements are made in his letters – some of them in the midst of critiques of other men's poems or in explanations of his own. Other statements, particularly those in his lecture-notes on 'Rhythm and Other structural Parts of Rhetoric' (probably 1873–4), are quite technical, and set forth in some detail views on prosody, rhyme, alliteration and other matters of diction. Probably the best known, and certainly most widely quoted, are the views he expresses in his letters to Bridges: that a perfect poetic style should be 'of its age', and should be 'the current language heightened':

> . . . I cut myself off from the use of *ere, o'er, wellnigh, what time, say not* (for *do not say*), because, though dignified, they neither belong to nor ever cd. arise from, or be the elevation of, ordinary modern speech. For it seems to me that the poetical language of an age should be the current language heightened, to any degree heightened and unlike itself, but not (I mean

normally: passing freaks and graces are another thing) an obsolete one. This is Shakespeare's and Milton's practice and the want of it will be fatal to Tennyson's Idylls and plays, to Swinburne, and perhaps to Morris. (*LB*, 89)

Years later, he returns to a similar theme in remarks that recall his condemnation of inversions (which he avoids because they weaken and destroy the 'earnestness or in-earnestness of the utterance') in the 1879 letter:

> I hold that by archaism a thing is sicklied o'er as by blight. Some little flavours, but much spoils, and always for the same reason – it destroys earnest: we do not speak that way; therefore if a man speaks that way he is not serious, he is at something else than the seeming matter in hand, *non hoc agit, aliud agit*.
>
> (*LB*, 218)

Critics have discussed Hopkins's notion of 'current language' and the idea of heightening – but never fully satisfactorily. There remain many problems: how to reconcile Hopkins's own use of inversions with his rejection of inversion and how to reconcile his usu of apparently obsolete words with his rejection of archaism – but what is lacking above all is a clear understanding of what Hopkins *meant* by 'current language heightened'. In particular, it has not been thought necessary to consider in much detail what he meant by 'current language' (*before* it is heightened). Accordingly, much of this book is devoted to explaining how rich his concept of 'current language' was; for it is clearly necessary to appreciate this before one can explain anything else. One thing is plain: 'current language' was *not* the normal diction of nineteenth-century poetry – and this is what we shall consider first.

It is very well known that Hopkins repeatedly declared his contempt for and rejection of Victorian poetic diction and its chief practitioners. 'Hopkins' complaints about his fellow poets', says Alison Sulloway, 'centered upon their thoroughly outmoded treatment of outmoded subjects. But it was largely their style, the symbol of spiritual laziness, that engaged his criticism.'[8] As Dr Sulloway perceives, there is a close relation between subject-matter and style, and so Hopkins's subject-matter, being in many respects different from that of other Victorians, clearly required its own appropriate style.

Now, Hopkins's insistent rejection of archaism really amounts to a rejection of what had become the standard poetic diction, and is bound up with his partial rejection of traditional metre, his views on the language of ordinary speech, his interest in dialect and Anglo-Saxon purism and his desire to capture individualities in language. But it should be observed here that it is by no means obvious that a poetic language *should* reject archaism and be based on 'ordinary modern speech'. Indeed, poetic language is normally handed down by tradition and is normally inclined to use words and syntax that are not found in ordinary speech. Sometimes it will use words current in speech, but in different (perhaps obsolete) senses. This archaizing tendency is not confined to the literary circles of Victorian England, but is found in the oral poetry of non-literate societies, in which archaic language sanctified by tradition may be thought a considerable grace by the listeners. Clearly, this must also have been so in classical and early medieval poetry. The Old English language, which Hopkins in 1882 described as a much superior thing to what we have today, had a large vocabulary of poetic words that were obsolete in prose (and presumably speech also) and a large stock of traditional formulaic expressions. Old Icelandic poetry, which Hopkins used in his lecture-notes to demonstrate various principles of rhyme and alliteration, had a similar repertoire of traditional poetic words, and these were needed to enable the poets to meet the considerable technical demands of their art. That archaism in syntax and vocabulary is common in English poetry (and some prose) from the sixteenth century onwards needs no demonstration here. Spenser, like Hopkins, used dialect words, but also many archaisms and quasi-archaisms. It is probably true to say that any writer at any time who has wished – with Holofernes – that the epithets should be 'sweetly varied' will have sometimes found it convenient to use language not current in ordinary speech, and may often have done this with pleasing and successful effects:

> The full-juiced apple, *waxing* over-mellow
> Drops in a silent autumn night
> > (Tennyson, 'The Lotus Eaters')

To *wax* in the sense of 'grow, become', has been archaic for some time, except in reference to the moon. But it is obvious that to substitute *growing* or *becoming* would destroy the effect of these lines. The use of *waxing* actually adds something to the visualization, perhaps because of its association with the moon (roundness or fullness) or the accidental association with beeswax (waxiness of the skin).

That archaism can in certain circumstances be considered a grace by literate and sensitive people is well illustrated by the critical reception of the New English Bible of 1970. Many sensitive critics have declared their preference for the King James Version, the language of which was deliberately archaic even in its own time.

But the archaism of the Bible is a rather different matter from the archaism of nineteenth-century poetic diction. What the two have in common is the need for dignity and elevation. The difference is that, whereas the Bible is in itself fixed and complete (whatever model it may provide for prose-writers or preachers), Victorian poetic diction is an abstract underlying *model* which can be used by literally thousands of poets and versifiers to produce reams of hackneyed and uninspired work. The compelling power of the model can even prevent the writer from perceiving what there is to write about (only 'elevated topics', that are at some distance from ordinary life, are suitable), and may deny him the language in which he can express himself in the appropriate way. This, I think, is well seen amongst the lower-class poets of Hopkins's own day, discussed in an excellent study by Louis James. Apart from some eighteenth-century features, these poets are Romantic 'having the conception of the poet writing in an "exalted" mood, using emotionally charged words and sentiments . . . If we turn to these poems hoping to find the fresh observation of talents unspoilt by learning, we will be disappointed – these poets were all the more anxious to show that though working class they had a full poetic education'. It is a pity, adds James, that these poets 'did not turn more often to the life in which they found themselves, and, on the occasions that they did, that the results are so trite and conventional.

> Sweet child! departed day-star of my soul!
> The light is gone, I'm lonely on my way,
> Like ship on ocean when the storm doth roll . . .'[9]

The 'obsolete' diction of the Victorians, therefore, was objectionable to Hopkins in that it 'destroyed earnest'. It blinded one to the importance of life around one, suppressed freedom in language and dulled perception. It led to cliché in language and situation, and bad verse by major as well as minor poets. At best, archaisms confer dignity – in the Bible, in *Beowulf*, in traditional poetry; at worst, they pad out the lines. Well used, a poetic tradition gives a framework that can be exploited by good poets; badly used, it enables a poet to churn out his poems almost mechanically, with no thought and no originality. At worst – to quote Orwell on later misuse of language – such verse consists, not of words, but of ready-made *phrases* 'tacked together like the sections of a prefabricated henhouse'.[10]

This 'Standard Model' of poetic diction was not simply a matter of interlacing one's text with the occasional *whenas* or *perchance*, or inverting subject and verb for metrical purposes, or padding the line out with archaic verbal endings (*-eth* for *-s*) and auxiliary *do* and *doth*. This kind of usage was conditioned by more general requirements. First, the subject-matter of nineteenth-century poetry was itself often archaic: medieval legend or romance and classical story. Second, whatever incidental variation might be found in the rhythm, it was almost universally a syllable-timed metre in which the syllables, rather than stresses, had to be counted, and this goes back to the imitation of French models in the twelfth century.[11]

If we consider the subject-matter first, it will be obvious that it is wholly reasonable to use an archaic language (or a quasi-archaic one) to capture the essence of a long-past time. It is reasonable to argue that Hopkins's 'earnestness' or the fact that 'we do not speak that way' may in such circumstances be quite irrelevant. No one would suggest that Keats's 'Eve of St Agnes' is a truly bad poem or that its language as a whole is inappropriate, despite the fact that the first two lines alone (ignoring the rest) set the tone in archaizing diction:

> St. Agnes' Eve – Ah, bitter chill it was!
> The owl, for all his feathers, was a-cold . . .

Apart from inversion (read: *'it was* bitter chill'), and the feeling that we might not easily find *for* (='despite') in the standard prose of the period, there are two archaizing expressions in these two lines. The second one (*a-cold*), which conveniently provides the extra syllable needed for the iambic pentameter, is a genuine literary archaism which was known to Keats from earlier writers (e.g. 'Poor Tom's a-cold' in *King Lear*, III.iv.57). Hopkins, of course, might well have avoided the expression for the very reason that it would have appeared to be a borrowing from the literary tradition, despite the fact that he could also have encountered it as a living form in West Country dialect such as his favourite, William Barnes, might have used. And he would not have needed the excrescent syllable in 'sprung rhythm' anyway. Keats's *bitter chill* seems to be a spurious archaism (like *uprist* in 'The Ancient Mariner'). While one might encounter in speech *bitter chill* as a noun phrase, or *chill wind*, with *chill* as an attributive adjective (but hardly a *bitter chill* wind), the predicate adjectival expression has always been *bitter cold* (most memorably in *Hamlet*, I.i.8: ''Tis bitter cold, and I am sick at heart').

The Victorian flight to the Middle Ages – in Carlyle, Tennyson, Morris, following as it did the Romantic medievalists – is too well known to require comment. Hopkins knew about this medievalism and was interested. In his undergraduate diaries he records his intention to read the pre-Raphaelites and German 'medievalists' such as Tieck and the Schlegels. Morris, of course, found his ideal in Germanic antiquity, yet his long poem *Sigurd the Volsung* (1876) in which one might reasonably have expected experiments in recapturing the Germanic stress metre, is written in a mixed syllabic metre (with occasional 'dumb' beats), and the regularity of the rhythm becomes tedious at length, despite its success in the following:

> And they sing of the golden Sigurd and the face without a foe,
> And the lowly man exalted and the mighty brought alow:
> And they say, when the sun of the summer shall come aback
> to the land,
> It shall shine on the fields of the tiller that fears
> no heavy hand;
> That the sheaf shall be for the plougher, and the land for
> him that sowed,
> Through every furrowed acre where the Son of Sigmund rode.

If Morris thought of experimenting with stress-timed metres with varying numbers of syllables, his courage failed him here. All that we can see here that is Germanic is a tendency to alliteration, and even that does not follow the pattern of the Norse poetry he loved so well. Nor does it meet Hopkins's requirements about 'earnestness' and 'speaking that way'.

Some of the most extreme examples of medieval subjects wedded to archaic diction come in Morris's renderings of the Icelandic sagas into poeticizing prose. Morris cultivated this archaic language very consciously and very seriously. His collaborator, Eiríkur Magnusson, would provide a simple modern English rendering; then Morris would come along with his blue pencil and 'improve', putting it into his version of what early English might have been, but wasn't. Morris improves *much* to 'mickle'; *when* to 'whenas'; *whenever* to 'whenso'; *later* to 'sithence'; *happened* to 'betid'; *went* to 'fared'; *between* to 'betwixt'; *thought* to 'were minded'; *vowed* to 'yeasaid'. 'King Olaf then sailed west' becomes 'Then sailed King Olaf west', and compound words are revived or invented for *message* ('wordsending'), *war* ('unpeace'), *funeral* ('corpse-fare') and many others. But it has to be conceded that Morris's translations are by any standards splendid and memorable, more recent ones that concentrate on 'colloquial' and 'idiomatic' language often being poor by comparison:

> She answered in heavy mood from her seat, whereas she sat like unto swan on billow, having a sword in her hand, and a helm on her head, and being clad in a byrny, 'O Gunnar,' she says, 'speak not to me of such things; unless thou be the first and best of men; for then shalt thou slay those my wooers, if thou hast heart thereto . . .'

Morris translated *Volsunga Saga* in 1870.[12] There is no reason to believe that Hopkins had read this or any of his other translations, but there is reason to think that he might not have condemned this archaizing prose as fully as he condemned archaism in poetry. This kind of archaism is not associated with traditional metrical conventions and the need to supply empty 'weak' syllables to fill out the line, nor is it cliché; in Morris's case, it is associated with a movement that Hopkins is known to have admired: the Anglo-Saxon purist movement that sought to revive or coin pure Anglo-Saxon words to replace much of our 'vague' Latinate vocabulary. This background is important in understanding Hopkins's attitudes to language and we shall have more to say about it in Chapter 3.

The nineteenth-century poet who wrote on exotic subjects

might well have been able to justify an exotic language, decorated with archaic words. Hopkins, like Wordsworth, did not write on such subjects, and in his rejection of a 'standard' diction, he was to some extent like Wordsworth. Descriptions and celebrations of nature, odes on shipwrecks, descriptions of common soldiers or ploughmen, do not require an affectation of archaic language or manner to make them successful, any more than daffodils and solitary reapers require the elaborations of eighteenth-century diction. Indeed, if such subjects were 'translated' into Greek shepherds or landscapes, the result would be destruction rather than elevation. The essential 'thisness' of Hopkins's bird in flight or a plough in the furrow would be lost. Hopkins's language, to match his subject-matter, had to be rooted in the here and now. But, in his insistence on 'current language', Hopkins went much further than Wordsworth.

As Hopkins noted in an essay, Wordsworth had in the Preface to *Lyrical Ballads* made the following comments: 'that poetic diction scarcely differed or ought to differ from that of prose . . . The most interesting parts of the best poems will be found to be strictly the language of prose when prose is well written.' And Wordsworth, with Blake, and with Burns at his best, was able to treat apparently simple subjects in an apparently unadorned language that contrasted with the more ornate diction of the eighteenth century.

As Wordsworth rejected the clichés of eighteenth-century poetic diction, so Hopkins rejected the clichés of nineteenth-century poetic diction. But unlike Wordsworth he was capable of setting aside the rules of schoolbook grammar (as we have seen) and clearly considered them of slight relevance in his poetic diction. He also differed from Wordsworth in that the model for his language was not *prose*, but *speech*. Although he never fully explained what he meant by 'current language', it is plain from his journals and diaries, from his essays and lecture-notes and from his letters, that it had no more basis in standard literary prose than it had in the standard model of poetic diction.

Anyone who has given the matter much thought will realize quite well that speech and prose are not identical, nor necessarily always similar, and that it may even be reasonable to argue that poetry is nearer to speech than prose is. It is the poetic tradition (the one that Hopkins questioned) – with its regular number of syllables to a line and its predictable rhyme-schemes – that leads us to assume sometimes that speech, being apparently unmetrical and unrhymed, is more like prose. But literary prose, even if we do not go back to its various origins in the telling of folktales, in Greek oratory, in sermons, in historical and legal records, is in modern times something quite distant from speech. It has been cultivated in the development over the centuries of a powerful standard language, elaborated by the incorporation of a vast Latin vocabulary and much affected in its syntax by Latin prose. Where it is like speech, it is like the speech of explanation, of lectures and debates and serious commentary, and this kind of speech itself owes much to the development of standard written prose in a standard language. It is notorious that less able or less privileged people find it very difficult to master the rules of this 'spoken prose', which is, like written prose, designed to develop logical argument without reference to non-linguistic context, and which requires years of schooling for its mastery.[13]

The essence of 'ordinary speech' is quite otherwise. Unlike writing, or the delivery of formal speeches, it is a social activity, and best observed in conversation. It is context-tied – that is to say, it takes for granted the context in which it takes place and will be vague and inaccurate even about specifying objects referred to: George Smith may be merely 'he' or 'this fellow', and the table or chair may be 'that over there'. If speech is taken out of its context, it will often seem vague and ambiguous; in context, however, its potential ambiguities are resolved by the participants' prior understanding of the subject discussed and by a number of features known as 'paralinguistic': facial expression, tone of voice and gesture, for instance. If it is written down, it is deprived of intonation, rhythm, pause, tone and quality of voice (this is what makes the art of dialogue-writing so difficult). Its functions too are different from those of most written prose. It is by no means certain that the primary function of speech is to argue logically or to communicate 'ideas'. On the contrary, most conversation has little logic and few ideas, and is better described as passing the time of day or communicating attitudes.[14] Written prose, since it has to dispense with context, must labour to avoid ambiguity and to be precise without having the contextual advantages of speech. A prose tradition, therefore, must develop a set of prescriptive rules: rules of rhetoric and composition which determine the general form of a prose work, rules of word-order, syntax and sentence structure which are more rigid and invariable than the rules of speech, and rules of word-choice designed to ensure that the kind of vocabulary used will be as precise and unambiguous as possible. All this applies to ordinary serviceable prose, but the most artistic prose will additionally cultivate a pleasing effect by imposition of a 'prose rhythm'.

Those of us who conduct investigations into spoken English and make recordings of speech are keenly aware of the extent to which speech deviates from the prose tradition and how even the speech of highly literate people continually flouts the rules of 'correctness' that our prose tradition has inherited from the eighteenth century. Generally speaking, it is the language of lower-class people used in the most informal circumstances that deviates furthest from the standard English of literary prose – in grammar, in sounds and in vocabulary. Conversational language in the higher social classes approximates more closely to it – partly because it is influenced by the prose tradition anyway – but there are still many differences. Even this kind of conversation abounds in vague word-choice, context-tied references (which are not at all clear if listened to afterwards on a tape-recording), false starts, incomplete and interrupted sentences, words used in senses and functions not approved by authority, slang, abbreviations, trade 'jargon', and it is often ambiguous in a way that good prose is not but poetry may be (the potential misunderstandings of speech being resolved by the context of situation, by gestures and facial expressions, and by the subject-matter being discussed). Because of these complexities, speech is incomparably more difficult to describe accurately than either prose or poetry, and many scholars, particularly the American linguist, William Labov, have recently devoted considerable attention to devising suitable techniques for the elicitation and description of natural speech in informal environments. Only in the past few years have we begun to realize how great is the variety of speech – not only geographically and socially, but also in the varying speech-styles of one person.[15]

Not surprisingly, most literary critics have failed to take into account the complexity of spoken language in their discussions of the nature of prose and poetry. No serious attempt has been made by them to describe the kind of relation that might exist between ordinary speech and the languages of literature. We all tend to believe that we 'know' perfectly well what our own speech is like (unaware that we are – each of us – the least reliable reporters of the characteristics of our own speech), and the literary critics are no exception.

Dr Leavis tells us that Hopkins's techniques 'appeal for sanction to the spirit of the language' and that his innovations 'accentuate and develop bents it exhibits in living use . . .' He then goes on to show us how Shakespeare used the language, but the 'living use' of language (in speech) is to be taken for granted: Leavis does not give an account of this. John Wain praises 'Felix Randal' for its closeness to ordinary speech; yet he feels it necessary to comment that 'a colloquialism like "this seeing the sick endears them to us" would be quite normal in *educated* speech'[16] (my italics) as if Hopkins meant 'current language' to be *educated* current language. Mr Wain is one of Hopkins's most sensitive critics and probably knows full well that 'current language' is something much wider than *educated* speech. What is significant is that even he finds it natural to use the word 'educated', with all that implies in terms of 'spoken prose', when speaking of a poet known to have been deeply interested in *uneducated* speech. Into current language Mr Wain delves no deeper. As far as I am aware, the only critics (until very recently) who have made substantial attempts to devise a theoretical framework for the description of literature's relation to language are the critics of the Prague School. Of these we shall have something to say in a later chapter. But it must also be pointed out that in his diaries, Journal and letters Hopkins himself can be seen to be working out a poetic theory of his own, based, not on literature, but on *current language*. He was perfectly clear on the point that 'verse' was a form of *speech*.

His lecture-notes 'Rhythm and the Other Structural Parts of Rhetoric – Verse' begin thus:

> Mention of rhythm, 'number', as heard in periods, in prose, leads to treatment of rhythm and its belongings, the various shapes of speech called verse.
>
> Definition of verse – Verse is speech having a marked figure, order/of sounds independent of meaning and such as can be shifted from one word or words to others without changing. It is *figure of spoken sound*.

These notes go on to analyse in a very learned way the typical rhythms of different languages (contrasting English and French, for instance, as having stress accent and pitch accent respectively), and the different rhythms of different kinds of poetry. Early Latin Saturnian verse, *Piers Plowman* and popular weather saws are quoted as examples of stress metres with varying numbers of syllables to the foot. These lecture-notes repay careful reading, and we shall discuss them when we consider Hopkins's methods of 'heightening' current language.

In the Author's Preface to the *Poems*, Hopkins makes many of the same points. He clearly believed his 'sprung rhythm' to be based on the natural rhythms of English speech. It is 'the most natural of things'. It is 'the rhythm of common speech and of written prose when rhythm is perceived in them.' It is also the rhythm of music, of nursery rhymes and weather-saws; it occurs in Greek and Latin lyric and the 'old English verse seen in *Pierce Ploughman*', but has not been generally used by poets since Elizabethan times. Not far behind this (and behind similar comments made in his letters to Bridges in 1877) is the idea that the dominant syllable-timed metre of Tennyson, Swinburne and Morris is somehow less natural to English than is sprung rhythm.

In a letter to Dixon (5 October 1878), Hopkins demonstrates sprung rhythm by quoting nursery rhymes:

Díng dóng béll/Pússy's ín the wéll/;

but a principle like sprung rhythm is recognized by phoneticians as inherent in English speech. O'Connor[17] writes:

> Syllable length in English is . . . closely related to rhythm. Rhythm in English . . . is based on the stressed syllable. Utterances are broken up into groups of syllables each of which contains one and only one stressed syllable. For example compare *The man laughed* and *The manager laughed*; the syllables /mæn/ and /lɑːft/ are stressed in both, but the length of /mæn/ is very much shorter in 'manager' than in 'man', because there is a strong tendency for the syllables between stresses to be compressed into the same time; so we say the word *manager* in not much more time than *man* and therefore the syllable /mæn/ is very different in length in the two cases.

Again, in a comparison of *nine famous men, nine ignorant men, ninety famous men, nine terrifying men*, in which he explains the tendency for strongly stressed syllables to be shortened when extra weak stresses have to be accommodated, O'Connor could well be Hopkins expounding 'sprung rhythm':

> But the strong tendency to have the stresses occurring on a regular beat is certainly there; it has a considerable effect on the duration of sounds and syllables and it gives a very typical rhythmical character to the languages in which it operates.

Hopkins was right to describe his sprung rhythm as something inherent in English speech, and to recognize it as a principle of early English poetry. The rhythms of a stress-timed language such as English (in contrast to French) should give rise to a stress-timed metre: a metre based on the principle of nearly isochronous feet containing one stress but varying in the number of syllables to a foot. Old English verse was of this kind. There were four stresses to a line, and two or three of these had to be marked by alliteration, but the number of syllables and the placing of the stressed syllables varied (within limits) from line to line:

> Wodon þa wælwulfas, for wætere ne murnon
> wicinga werod west ofer Pantan
> ofer scir wæter scyldas wegon
> lidmen to lande linde bæron.
>
> (*The Battle of Maldon*, ll.96–9)

The alliterative tradition remained strong in English until well into the fifteenth century. Best known are the poems of the Alliterative Revival: a series of social and political poems from the West of England, the most famous of which is Langland's *Piers Plowman* (Hopkins read this in 1882 and thought it overrated); and a series of Romances from the North, represented by *Sir Gawain and the Green Knight* and the Alliterative *Morte Arthur*. The character of this native rhythm is well indicated by a fine short poem, 'The Blacksmiths' (early fifteenth century), in which the poet obviously uses the consonant pattern and rhythm for echoic effects, as Hopkins also attempted to do some centuries later:[18]

> Swarte smekyd smeþes smateryd wyth smoke
> Dryue me to deth wyth den of here dyntes.
> Swech noys on nyghtes he herd men neuer:

> What knauene cry and clateryng of knockes!
> Þe cammede kongons cryen after 'col, col!'
> And blowen here bellewys, þat al here brayn brestes.

Walter Ong[19] has shown how this tradition reappeared sporadically from the fifteenth century onwards – in Skelton and the Elizabethan drama and later, despite its general suppression by the Spenserian tradition.

> Hopkins found a tradition in English poetry which was older and stronger than the one in possession in his day. He found a rhythmic tradition which cut under and around the 'running' or 'common' rhythm of the nineteenth century, not because his new rhythm was the ancient rhythm of English – this would be a fact of no value in itself – but because it was a rhythm still inherent in the language and only suppressed by an artificially sustained tradition.

And, Father Ong insists, Hopkins *found* sprung rhythm in the language he heard spoken around him:

> But the rhythms of a language are already rooted when the poet arrives, and the real question to be answered concerning Hopkins' sprung rhythm is, What was this thing he was discovering all round him? or What is the life of this rhythm in the language, what are its claims on our speech?

Whereas the 'common' or 'running rhythm' of the 'Spenserian' tradition *imposes* an alternating beat on the natural rhythm of the language, as in:

> The curfew tolls the knell of parting day,

Hopkins's sprung rhythm *uses* the rhythm of speech *as its base*. It cannot be scanned in the manner of Gray's 'Elegy' with alternating weak and strong stresses. The stresses do not depend on the number of syllables:

> And the sea flint-flake, black-backed in the regular blow.

The stresses observed in this line are more natural to the language than those imposed by 'running' rhythm would be. Sprung rhythm can truly be said to be based on 'current language', that is, speech.

'Current language', as Hopkins used the term, certainly means the rejection of archaism and the use of a speech-based rhythm. It also seems to imply the use of informal and colloquial styles and varieties, the like of which will not be found in standard poetic diction or in standard literary prose. Speech, as we have seen, is much more variable than written prose, and it varies in different dimensions. First, and most obviously, it varies geographically – not only in pronunciation, but also in morphology, syntax and vocabulary. Hopkins never tired of observing regional varieties on all these levels. In his Journal on 30 April 1869 he has a long entry on the pronunciation of Latin by different priests and is particularly perceptive about the North Country tendency to lengthen long vowels:

> Fr Morris gives long *u* very full (*Luca*); he emphasizes the semi-consonant and the vowel before it where two vowels meet – *Pio* becomes *Pi-jo* and *tuam tu-vam* (that is *pee-yo* and *too-wam*) – but in *tuum* the vowel is simply repeated.

On 3 May 1866 he comments that Oxfordshire people pronounce '*weir* as if *wire*', and on 18 May 1870 makes notes on the pronunciation of a Br Gordon. In 1871 (*Journals*, p. 211), there is a long entry on Lancashire speech which includes speculation on the grammar of the omission of *the* in Northern England. There are many entries on local vocabulary: *nesh, whisket, clamp, road* (as in 'Felix Randal', meaning 'way'), and idiomatic expressions, and detailed accounts of the vocabulary of ploughing and haymaking. For language also varies in different trades and professions, and Hopkins was enormously interested in this too. As each trade has its 'gear and tackle and trim', it also has its language. We shall discuss these points fully in Chapter 3.

But these kinds of variability do not by any means exhaust the variability of language. It varies according to level of formality, according to social class, according to the degree to which it is public or private, ritualistic or intimate, and according to all the varied puposes for which it may be used – quite apart from literary ones.

Just as Hopkins used dialectal expressions from time to time to give what he thought was the right flavour to his poetry, so he also used very casual styles and deliberately disjointed syntax where he wanted to communicate immediacy of emotion. This colloquial and disjointed syntax, which is close to *speech* but very far from prose syntax, is a major feature of 'The Wreck of the Deutschland':

> The frown of his face
> Before me, the hurtle of hell
> Behind, *where, where was a, where was a* place? (st. 3)

> Is out with it! Oh,
> We lash with the best or worst
> Word last! How a lush-kept plush-capped sloe
> Will, mouthed to flesh-burst,
> Gush! (st. 8)

> O unteachably after evil, but uttering truth,
> Why tears! is it? tears; such a melting, a madrigal start!
> (st. 18)

And, as we have already noted, throughout the poem there are verb-less or subject-less sentences, sentences that start as questions and end as statements, or are interrupted by exclamations, sentences that contain incomplete constructions, and sentences that contain 'colloquial' repetitions:

> But how shall I . . . make me room there:
> Reach me a . . . Fancy, come faster –
> Strike you the sight of it? look at it loom there,
> Thing that she . . . There then! the Master,
> *Ipse*, the only one, Christ, King, Head: (st. 28)

The disjointed syntax of the 'Deutschland' is appropriate to the tumultuous emotions there expressed, but Hopkins's colloquial syntax is found throughout his poetry – in poems that are much 'easier' than the 'Deutschland' and in places where the emotions are less intense and dramatization absent.

It is well known that Hopkins's poetry is full of exclamations and that the words *Oh* and *Ah* are among his favourites:

> Look at the stars! look, look up at the skies!
> O look at all the fire-folk sitting in the air! (No. 32)

> Brute beauty and valour and act, oh, air, pride, plume, here
> Buckle! (No. 36)

The imperative verbs, used to urge or command, may be common in the dialogue of plays and novels, which imitates speech; they are not common in narrative, descriptive or persuasive *prose*. Hopkins's fondness for them adds to the immediacy and urgency of his poems and their closeness to speech – just as other kinds of exclamation add to the tone of *celebration* that is characteristic of many poems:

> . . . up above, what wind-walks! what lovely behaviour
> Of silk-sack clouds! (No. 38)

There is no verb in this; it does not report or state anything. It *celebrates*, just as in conversation we may celebrate good weather by saying 'What a lovely day!' The long parentheses that are so common in the 'Deutschland' are also found elsewhere. Whether the example in the first eight lines of 'The Bugler's First Communion' is truly characteristic of speech is perhaps disputable. While parenthesis is common enough in speech, such a long one is perhaps unlikely. But one feature – the *reprise* of the main verb – is certainly characteristic of speech:

> A bugler boy from barrack . . .
> This very very day *came* down . . .
> *Came*, I say, this day to it – to a First Communion.
> (No. 48)

So too is the explanatory repetition in the last line. The bugler came '*to it*'. To what? '*To a First Communion*'. This is one of Hopkins's favourite syntactic devices.

We shall discuss the poet's syntax in much greater detail in a later chapter. Here we wish to note only how close some of Hopkins's expressions are to ordinary speech. Indeed, expressions like 'The Eurydice: it concerned thee O Lord' are so close in their grammar to speech that it is hard to say whether they should be viewed as examples of 'current language *heightened*' or simply 'current language' without the heightening. This is a difficult question, which we shall discuss further in Chapter 4; but it is necessary to assert here that if some of these lines are to be seen as heightened language it is not by virtue of their deviation from normal grammar that they are heightened. Their grammar *is* normal, but it is the grammar of speech, not that of *prose* or the schoolbooks.

Fr Peters believes that the first line of 'Felix Randal' deviates from current language because it breaks the 'rules' of normal syntax by repeating the subject:

Felix Randal the farrier, O is he dead then?

The first half-line 'states' the subject of the sentence and of the poem, but it is not linked with a verb; instead, what appears to be a statement turns at the half-way point into a question and the subject is re-stated as the pronoun *he*. Several of Hopkins's poems begin in a broadly similar way:

The Eurydice – it concerned thee, O Lord: (No. 41)

This darksome burn, horseback brown,
His rollrock highroad roaring down,
In coop and in comb the fleece of his foam
Flutes and low to the lake falls home.   (No. 56)

In both cases the original subject is, as it were, left high and dry. Father Peters classes these as examples of psychological *heightening* in that the syntax departs from the 'logic of the system'. In other words the syntax is thought to be abnormal, and Hopkins is thought to have brought about a deviation from normal syntax, to have *broken its rules*. While it is true that some of the *disjointed* syntax of the 'Deutschland' reflects the breathless emotion of that poem, the examples that Peters discusses here do not deviate noticeably from *speech* and are heightened only if one compares them with *prose*. As he says himself: 'In affective speech this turn is very frequent'.[20]

They are not close to standard poetic diction either. If one compares the first line of 'Felix Randal' with the kind of language that might have been used in the 'high style' ('O weep for Felix Randal, O weep for he is dead!') its closeness to current language, and Hopkins's reasons for preferring it, become apparent. Above all, such a poem must be intimate and close to ordinary life; the high formality of the 'standard' elegy or lament would destroy that intimacy:

Yet once more, O ye laurels, and once more,
Ye myrtles brown, with ivy never sere . . .
                    (Milton, 'Lycidas', lines 1–2)

In 'Felix Randal' one can visualize clearly within the first line a scene in which the young priest has just received the news of the farrier's death; he turns to the speaker and replies musingly, for the death has not been unexpected: 'Felix Randal, did you say? So he's dead then . . .' The whole scene is homely, ordinary and natural, and the line is so close to current colloquial idiom that it seems at first sight not to have been 'heightened' at all. It *is* changed a little of course. Hopkins has to give us the information that Felix was a farrier, information that would not be necessary in conversation between intimates. But there is nothing in the *syntax* that deviates in the slightest degree from ordinary speech. In warmth and visual suggestiveness it far exceeds the poetic language used by many of Hopkins's contemporaries.

In dealing with *current language* and its *heightening*, therefore, we must recognize that Hopkins's attitude to these is bound up with his general attitudes to language and his rejection of what we have called the 'standard model'. He sought a basis for his diction in the language that he heard spoken around him and his interest in ordinary speech was greater than that of most poets of his time, carefully cultivated as it had been over a period of years. To be able to explain why and how 'he brought poetry . . . closer to living speech' (in Dr Leavis's words), we must try to appreciate the nature of living speech as keenly as Hopkins did. We must also try to appreciate the distinction between *current language* and the devices used by the poet for heightening this language.

Fr Peters's account of heightening is unsatisfactory because it does not clearly distinguish between these devices and the *effects* brought about by them, and because he assumes that the (under-lying) current language is a 'logical' language consisting of well-formed and carefully constructed sentences. In making such assumptions, we have suggested, critics are measuring Hopkins's heightened poetry against the language of *prose*, which is not *current language* at all. We shall therefore attempt to bear in mind throughout this book the distinction between the poet's art or artifice and the *effects* brought about in the finished poem, admitting that we shall not always succeed in maintaining such a difficult distinction. Nevertheless, some points are clear. First, we cannot say that heightening consists primarily of using *affective* or *emotive* language (semanticists are inclined to reject these terms because of their vagueness),[21] because we can equally say that much *current language* is 'affective'. Second, we must accept that many of Hopkins's innovations in diction (rhythmic, phonetic, syntactic or lexical) have their models in current language. In other words, many of the usages in which Hopkins broke the rules of 'continuous literary decorum' are directly based on the rules (not prescriptive ones) and norms of the various styles and registers of ordinary usage. Third, we must appreciate that all poetry involves *heightening*, even if it is not always a heightening of *current* language. All poetic language attempts to be distinctive and memorable in some way, seeks intensity and richness, and is 'affective'.

It appears, therefore, that what is really distinctive about Hopkins is his insistence on *current language* as the basis of his diction rather than the fact that he *heightened* it. To understand his concept of *current language* is an essential preliminary, a *sine qua non*, without which we cannot expect to understand the devices of *heightening*. In the following chapters, we address ourselves first to the poet's observation of, and attitudes to, ordinary language. We shall then consider what devices he used to achieve the rich verbal texture of his finished verse.

CHAPTER 2

The Wonder of Language: Hopkins and Victorian Philology

ꗚꗚꗚꗚꗚꗚ

POETS are normally interested in language as it is used around them in ordinary speech, and they observe – either effortlessly and intuitively or with conscious care and application – details of its use. Hopkins was exceptionally observant and exceptionally careful in recording his observations. His journals are notable for their exquisite and detailed descriptions of natural phenomena, but the entries on language are hardly less remarkable. There are entries on the local speech of various parts of England, sometimes analysed in considerable detail, and – in the undergraduate diaries – numerous entries on series of words that Hopkins believed to be related in etymology, or at least in general meaning and phonetic association: 'Twig (pinch), tweak, twitch, twit, to give one a wigging, earwig, wicker, twig (small branch), twist, twine, twire (?), twy, two . . .'. Sometimes he would record a word that he thought particularly apt for some literary purpose:

Altogether *peak* is a good word. For sunlight through shutter, locks of hair, rays in brass knobs etc. Meadows peaked with flowers   (*JP*, 47)

And, in the undergraduate diaries and later journals alike, he would often speculate on the figurative names of natural phenomena. Of 'snake's heads' (the fritillary) he had this to say: 'Like drops of blood. Buds pointed like snakes' heads, but the reason of name from mottling and scaly look'.

Already at an early age Hopkins is observing thoughtfully the links between language and nature, but, most obviously in his etymological notes, he is perceiving that language, like nature, has order and regularity. Miss Sulloway has emphasized that in his scrupulous observation of nature and his perception of regularity in it, Hopkins owed a great deal to Ruskin.[1] It is the argument of this chapter that in his attitudes to language, and in the use of it in his poetry, he owed just as much to quite another branch of nineteenth-century thought: the historical and comparative researches of nineteenth-century philology.

In this respect, Hopkins is exceptional amongst major nineteenth-century poets. Only William Barnes, who can hardly be ranked as a major poet, shares – and exceeds – Hopkins's philological interests, and a few (Barnes again included) share his interests in dialect. A great many of them, it is clear, have an interest in the history of vernacular (as against Classical) *literature*. These, starting with Keats, Hopkins (*CD*, 98) himself labels 'medievalists', and it is characteristic of these poets to use themes from Arthurian, early Italian or Nordic literature, and often to affect a pseudo-archaic style. They did not aim to model their language on the present, but fled to the past for language and theme alike. In his choice of theme, Hopkins has more in common with the lyrical subjects of the Lake poets, whom he identifies in a letter to Canon Dixon as a second school of poets. But it is clear in the same letter that he aligns himself with neither the Lake School nor the 'medieval' school, and one of the differences lies in his incomparably greater knowledge of and interest in the 'life' of language outside of literature and the literary tradition – an interest enlivened for him by a fascination with nineteenth-century language scholarship. No doubt, Hopkins could have written poetry without such knowledge, but it would have remained rooted in the tradition, as his schoolboy poems were. It is interesting to speculate what kind of poems he would then have produced. Nourished by Bridges, we may surmise, he might have produced poetry of a similar kind to Bridges. It would no doubt have been published and subjected to public criticism, and – if Hopkins had been able to stand up to that criticism – he would now be dimly remembered as a minor follower of Bridges. But Hopkins's language was in fact greatly influenced by the work of nineteenth-century language scholars, and this is the only contemporary work that could have helped him to achieve the freedom to break through narrow bounds of prescribed language use and 'continuous literary decorum'.

This has not been widely recognized. Notable among the few who have seen the importance of this background are E. R. August (whose excellent Ph.D. thesis is unfortunately not yet widely known) and N. H. MacKenzie, who has discussed a number of etymological points and whose forthcoming edition promises to take full account of Hopkins's interest in such matters. MacKenzie has pointed out – amongst other things – that the occurrence of *equal* in the first line of 'Spelt from Sibyl's Leaves' is illuminated by the knowledge that *even*, 'equal', and *even*, 'evening' were believed by early nineteenth-century lexicographers to be of the same origin. The implication that evening was a time of *equal* balance between day and night would undoubtedly appeal to Hopkins. It was of course possible for Hopkins to take this serious and scholarly interest in philology because of the immense strides which had been made in the subject by the 1850s and 1860s, and which continued to be made during the rest of his lifetime. If he had been born thirty years earlier, it is highly unlikely that he would have developed such interests.

Wordsworth, when he asked that poetic diction should be based on the language of prose and common speech, wrote at the end of a century whose main contribution to English language studies was to codify a standard language and to inculcate a strong sense of linguistic 'correctness' in prose and ordinary speech. Swift, in his famous *Proposal for Correcting, Improving and Ascertaining the English Tongue* (1712) clearly sought to fix the literary language in a form that would be comprehensible to future generations, and his ideals were the Classical languages, which had remained relatively constant in their literary forms for nearly two millennia. Swift was interested in polishing and refining the vernacular language to bring it up to the excellence of Greek and Latin and make it worthy of polite literature. In the second half of the eighteenth century, grammars of English appeared in large numbers; their tone was prescriptive, and they were based on the canons of logic and Latin grammar. They paid little attention to the flux and variability of ordinary speech; they were often hostile to dialect and 'low' words, and profoundly ignorant of the history of English. Bishop Lowth, for instance, whose grammar (1762) remained highly influential on school grammar for nearly two centuries, believed that the 'antient regular forms' of *swine* and *kine* were *sowen* (plural of 'sow') and *cowen*. The language, it was often believed, was a degenerate form of a pristine speech of great purity and regularity, which it was hoped to restore with the aid of classical and philosophical learning. The century's most remarkable piece of linguistic scholarship was Dr Johnson's *Dictionary* (1755), which, as codification of the vocabulary of English, ranked as an authority beside Lowth's codification of the grammar. Although Johnson's views on 'fixing' the language were moderate by eighteenth-century standards, he was fully conscious of his role as an authority and very careful to check such details as correct spelling by reference to the best authors. But by nineteenth-century standards, Johnson's dictionary has a literary air; it is weak on etymology, and strong on quotations from the best authors, 'the wells of English undefiled' in pre-Restoration literature. His comments on the kind of words excluded from his dictionary are in marked contrast to the views that inspired his successors a century later:

> Nor are all the words which are not found in the vocabulary, to be lamented as omissions. Of the laborious and mercantile part of the people, the diction is in a great measure casual and mutable; many of their terms are formed for some temporary or local convenience, and though current at certain times or places, are in others utterly unknown. This fugitive cant, which is always in a state of increase or decay, cannot be regarded as any part of the durable materials of a language, and therefore must be suffered to perish with other things unworthy of preservation.[2]

The views underlying these remarks are perfectly clear and perfectly typical. Johnson is concerned with Swift's 'politest part of the nation', and the most durable materials of a language are clearly those which are established in the written form and are thereby fixed and made available to future generations. These 'durable' forms will, moreover, help to regulate the spoken language. Such views are still influential: in the commonly held view that writing is somehow 'superior' to speech, or in the view that there is one, and only one, 'correct' form in spelling, pronunciation or usage. Disputes about the correctness of *it's me* or *it is I* or different *from*, different *to* or different *than*, are directly inherited from the eighteenth century, as is the common belief that dialects are degenerate forms of a 'correct' standard language. It is idle, of course, to protest that such attitudes to language are necessarily wrong or misconceived, as some modern linguists have insisted, but it is clear that such attitudes may be inimical to freedom, experiment and originality in poetic diction.

The relevant point is that the eighteenth century was concerned, consciously or unconsciously, with the cultivation of a standard language, regular and rich enough for written *prose*, much of it utilitarian rather than 'literary' in the narrowest modern sense.[3] English was replacing Latin as the language of treatises or dissertations on intellectual or scientific subjects; there was a rise in periodical literature and the beginnings of a popular press; there was a leisured, literate public large enough to create some considerable demand for literary prose, particularly novels; there was an expanding Empire requiring the dissemination of documents over wide areas and therefore needing an 'official' language. Standardization was needed, but the attitudes that accompanied it, being hostile to regionalism and colloquialism, did not favour the creation of new and original kinds of poetic diction. Wordsworth's innovations in diction take place within the context of a standard literary language; they take the form of a rejection of the elaborate clichés of eighteenth-century poetic diction and a substitution of plain and simple words suitable for plain and simple subjects. Apart from occasional Lakeland localisms, Wordwsorth's syntax and vocabulary are standard English. It could hardly have been otherwise, for the large-scale investigation of speech and non-standard dialect had hardly begun.

Nothing could contrast more markedly with eighteenth-century views than those that arose amongst nineteenth-century language scholars. The development of Sanskrit studies late in the eighteenth century led to the removal of Greek and Latin from exclusive status as Classical languages, and the realization that Sanskrit was related to Greek and Latin (showing a number of clear and regular correspondences that could not be explained as accidental or borrowed) led to the establishment of the new science of comparative philology. The Indo-European hypothesis, which was soon proposed, held that most European and some Asiatic languages were descended from a common ancestor (Indo-European or Aryan) through a process of slow change and dialectal divergence. Although earlier philologists still relied on their knowledge of the ancient tongues, it soon became essential to study more modern representatives of the Indo-European group, and regular correspondences in sound and grammar were established between different groups – most notably in Jacob Grimm's explanation of a series of regular consonantal correspondences between the Germanic languages on the one hand and Latin, Greek and Sanskrit on the other. Grimm's Law showed, amongst other things, that the sounds *f*, *th* and *h* in Gothic (or their counterparts in other Germanic languages, as in English *fish*, *three*, *horn*, German *Fisch*, *drei*, *Horn*) corresponded to *p*, *t* and *k* in Indo-European (cf. Latin *piscis*, *tres*, *cornu*). Although a good deal of work remained to be done in explaining apparent exceptions to this 'First Consonant Shift' in the various languages, it is obvious that such an advance in charting the regularities of linguistic change could give a great impetus to the study of etymology. Indeed, etymology could now become a relatively exact science.

But the rise of comparative philology carries with it a number of necessary implications that are relevant to our subject. First, although disputes about superiority or inferiority of one language to another could still be carried on, it became necessary for philological purposes to view them all objectively as varying manifestations of common originals. For some purposes, then, Latin, English, Albanian, Lithuanian and the other IE languages had to be regarded as equals. Second, the clear knowledge that all languages had undergone change, often of striking and far-reaching kinds, made it difficult to argue that a language could with any confidence be fixed in a permanent form. Nor could one be confident about 'correctness' since history showed this to be a relative and changing concept. The historical study of vernacular tongues soon became firmly entrenched, and by the end of the century it was generally assumed that linguistics was a historical discipline. To 'know' a word, one had to know its history, and the *Oxford English Dictionary* (1888–1924) was prepared on historical principles. Third, it became clear that linguistic change appeared primarily in the spoken language; indeed speech was simply the primary mode of language. William Barnes emphasizes this in his *Speech-Craft*: 'Speech was shapen of the breath-sounds of speakers, for the ears of hearers, and not from speech-tokens [letters] in books, for men's eyes . . .'4 Side by side with the study of the older forms of modern languages, there came about a great enthusiasm for the study of speech as it actually existed in current usage. A language was no longer something that could be confined between the covers of a grammar-book or dictionary; its immense variety was acknowledged and enthusiastically investigated. 'If a man would walk with me through our village', wrote Barnes, 'I could show him many things of which we want to speak every day, and for which we have words of which Johnson knew nothing.'[5] Phonetics became for the first time a highly developed branch of language study, and phonetic notations were invented for the purpose of recording dialectal pronunciation. Throughout the century amateur and professional language scholars devoted remarkable energy to the study of non-standard dialects, in France, Germany, Scandinavia and England.

From Hopkins's early diaries (1863–6) and Journal (1866–75), it is obvious that he pursued language study, informed by this background, with something of the same vigour and enthusiasm that was displayed by the experts. In writing of Hopkins, scholars have often referred scathingly to philology and have tended by implication to separate him from this vigorous philological movement. To McLuhan, Hopkins is the 'sole civilized fruit' of the 'brain-starved plodding' of professors of Anglo-Saxon; even Gardner speaks of Hopkins 'breathing poetic life into the *dry bones* of philological research' (my italics).[6] It is important to emphasize that Hopkins was in many ways *part of* this philological movement, displaying the same painstaking care in definition and description of words that was displayed by the lexicographers, and the same fascinated interest in the history and relationship of words. Only a generation of scholars spoiled by the foolish separation of 'language' and 'literature' studies (to the detriment of both) could seriously refer to Victorian philological research as 'dry' or 'brain-starved'. In the nineteenth century it was new, stimulating and full of wonder. Nor is it correct to say that it was Hopkins who breathed life into philology; on the contrary, it was philology that helped to breathe life into Hopkins's poetry. This needs no argument; the etymological notes and other linguistic comments in the undergraduate diaries are often well informed by mid-century standards; the dialectal notes in the journal, and his contributions to Joseph Wright's *English Dialect Dictionary* show him sharing the attitudes of the early students of dialect. His insistence that verse is a form of *speech*, a 'figure of spoken sound', that his poems should be read 'with the ear' and that the metre of the 'Deutschland' was born of a rhythm that had been haunting his ear, also show him as one sharing in the nineteenth-century philologist's insistence on the primacy of speech.

Clearly, there are further far-reaching implications in the attitudes of nineteenth-century philology, some of them obviously relevant to Hopkins. It had its rise in Germany, where it was associated on the one hand with medieval literary studies and on the other hand with myth and folklore research. Hopkins's early interest in medievalism is seen in various entries in the 1864 diary, where he records an intention to read the work of Tieck (a German Romantic medievalist) and the Schlegels (best known for their work on Sanskrit and Indian philosophy); he also makes various comments about pre-Raphaelitism and German and other Continental medievalists in art. As for myth and folklore, an 1864 entry records an intention to read Max Müller, who was as celebrated for his contributions to the study of myth as he was for his work on language; and a sustained interest in popular beliefs and stories is shown by several of Hopkins's entries in the later Journal. Indeed, the rise of philology can be clearly seen as related to the Romantic movement with all that implies with regard to interest in the past, interest in folk-culture, and the rise of nationalism. Already in 1772, in marked contrast to eighteenth-century Britain, Herder in Germany was able to emphasize the value of the folklore and medieval literature of his own country and admire his own mother-tongue: 'the combination of consonants gives it a certain measured pace; it does not rush forward, but walks with the firm carriage of a German'.[7] Very similar views – equally Romantic and nationalistic – are found in the writings of the most influential linguist-folklorist of the early nineteenth century, Jacob Grimm, and it was not long before this Teutonism was felt in England. Of the relevance of this to Hopkins's dialect interests we shall have something to say in the next chapter. Although the eyes of English scholars were in this way opened up to the vast riches of their own native tongue, the first important influence of Grimm's philology was on historical and editorial work. J. M. Kemble, who, with Richard Chenevix Trench, had studied in Germany, brought the principles of what he called Grimm's 'iron-bound system' to the editing of texts, notably *Beowulf* (1833). 'The laws of a language', he was able to say, 'ascertained by a wide and careful examination of all cognate tongues ... are like the laws of the Medes and Persians, and alter not.'[8] In other words, the comparatist discovery that there is nothing random or accidental about linguistic change, but that it conforms to rigid and describable patterns, was now introduced to English scholarship. Many scholars now devoted considerable energy to researches into the history of English and the Germanic languages and to the editing of medieval texts. Such a man as Thomas Wright, for example, who 'perfectly typifies the early Victorian antiquary scholar', contributed no fewer than one hundred and twenty-nine titles to the British Museum catalogue.[9] Most significantly, the Philological Society was founded in 1842, and work started under its auspices on the dictionary that was to become the great monument to Victorian language scholarship – the *Oxford English Dictionary*. One of that Society's members was Richard Chenevix Trench, whose two books, *On the Study of Words* (1851) and *English Past and Present* (1854) were extremely widely read and frequently reprinted, the first-named having reached its twentieth edition in 1888. Although the contribution of Victorian scholarship to language research was immense in a variety of fields, it is not unreasonable to argue that its greatest achievement was to establish on a sound footing the science of etymology.

Hopkins went up to Balliol in 1863, and his diary for the twelve months ending in September 1864 devotes as much space to speculation on the etymological and phonetic relationships of common English words as it does to any other single subject. Generally speaking, Hopkins is concerned with everyday English monosyllables like *horn*, *slip*, *flick* and series of words which seem to him to be related to them in consonantal structure and in meaning. The imaginative way in which he treats some of the words goes beyond strict etymology, and it is not always clear whether Hopkins believes all the words cited to be etymologically related.[10] Nevertheless, it is obvious that his knowledge of etymology and of language scholarship in general is well beyond the elementary stage. Moreover, this early interest is of great importance for his poetry. Already in his 1877 sonnets, there are some obvious instances of etymological play:

> Generations have *trod*, have *trod*, have *trod*
> And all is seared with *trade* . . .

In this, the etymological identity of the verb *tread* and the noun *trade* infuse a more concrete sense of *treading, walking to and fro*, into the paler, more abstract (and ultimately metaphorical) idea of *commerce*. Consider also this passage, cited by Bridges as an example of 'mannerism' (but surely an example of the essential Hopkins at his best):

> And the azurous hung hills are his world-wielding shoulder
> Majestic – as a stallion stalwart, very-violet-sweet!   (No. 38)

The collocation of *stallion* and *stalwart* could well have been suggested to Hopkins by a feeling that the words, being similar in sound, must be etymologically related. He would probably believe that *stall* (a place to stand) was the first element in both. Modern etymological opinion does in fact relate both words to the root represented in Latin by *sto, stare* (to stand); Partridge derives *stallion* from medieval Latin *stallum*, 'a stable', and *stalwart* from an OE word meaning 'firmly based'. Ogilvie's *Imperial Dictionary* (1851–5), however, while recognizing the connection of *stallion* with *stall*, mistakenly believed *stalwart* to be derived from roots meaning 'worthy of stealing', but Ogilvie was often wide of the mark.

In Hopkins's later poetry, the etymological play can often be very elaborate. In 'Spelt from Sibyl's Leaves', as Norman MacKenzie points out, Hopkins would probably believe that there was an etymological connection between *early* and *earl*, the latter having 'a basic notion of priority, and hence of seniority'. Although Richardson's *New Dictionary* (1836) supports this common etymology, modern dictionaries derive the two words from quite different medieval forms and describe *earl* as 'of unknown origin'. In

> her earliest stars, earlstars, stars principal . . .

Hopkins clearly plays on etymology, the middle term *earlstars* forming a transition between the outer terms, *earliest* and *principal*, and partaking of the meaning of both: 'prior in time' and 'prior in nobility or rank'. Indeed *stars principal* is almost a Latin gloss on the native *earlstars*. A similar etymological play is found in

> Sheer off, disseveral, a star . . .   (No. 72)

where one of the meanings of *sheer off* can be 'cut off', and the Latin (Romance) *sever* in *disseveral* is, amongst other things, a gloss on it. The pale, prose word *several* acquires a more concrete sense, and an image of violent separation is suggested.[11]

Hopkins lived at a time when the study of English etymology was advancing rapidly. In the previous century, Johnson's *Dictionary* had suffered in this respect from very limited knowledge, and Todd's revision of Johnson (1818), which Hopkins may have known, was hardly more advanced. Charles Richardson's *New Dictionary* (1836) had been preceded by a series of philological notes (1815), in which he declared his support for Horne Tooke's work on etymology and attacked Dr Johnson in a very lengthy critical examination of the *Dictionary*. Richardson's own dictionary still owed a great deal to Horne Tooke (it is prefaced by a series of Latinate words which Tooke had declared not to be English) and Tooke's highly speculative etymologies are often accepted. They are of this kind:

> *Asunder* is originally from Anglo-Saxon Sond; i.e. *Sand*...
> Junius and Skinner guide Johnson to the proper Anglo-Saxon verb for *Asunder*... but neither of them imagined that *Sand* was the origin of *Sunder*, *Asunder*.

No modern etymologist would dare to imagine this either – it is the sheerest speculation – but one cannot be entirely certain about Hopkins:

> I kiss my hand
> To the stars, lovely-asunder...
> ('Deutschland', st. 5)

The stars, after all, seem as numerous as grains of sand on the sea-shore: the comparison is commonplace. Hopkins was scholarly, but he was also imaginative. Richardson is credulous again, and poorly schooled in the history of English grammar, when he supports Horne Tooke's etymology of *birth*:

> It is according to Tooke, the third person singular of the present indicative of the verb to *bear*, from the Anglo-Saxon *bearan*.

Of course, although related, it is nothing of the kind.

Ogilvie's *Imperial Dictionary*, which is based on Webster, is rather more reliable than Richardson in its etymologies. It is the dictionary that Hopkins is most likely to have consulted, and

Ogilvie has certain characteristics that could have influenced Hopkins. He devotes much space to the *nautical* uses of words, like *drift, reeve, tackle, beam, brace*; and he is fond of citing an obsolete or 'original' use of a word as its 'proper signification'. In the case of *beam*, for example, before citing the word's various modern applications, he remarks: 'It properly signifies the stock or stem of a tree; that is the fixed, firm part'. Hopkins in his etymologies often speaks of 'original' meanings, and to many a language-historian of that period, the 'original' meaning was also the 'proper' meaning. But it must be emphasized that there is no clear proof as to Hopkins's use of English dictionaries. In his notes he mentions only Liddell and Scott's *Greek-English Lexicon*, and his reference to Ogilvie comes in a letter to Baillie in 1887, more than twenty years after his early diaries. And even the most recent of the main dictionaries, Ogilvie, had failed to take account of all the philological advances of the first half of the century; his association of English *sake, seek* with Latin *sequor*, for example, would have been prevented by a proper grasp of Grimm's First Consonant Shift. There was also a contemporary etymological dictionary that Hopkins might well have consulted; the first two volumes of it had appeared by 1862, and it was better informed than Ogilvie. This was the work of Hensleigh Wedgwood, a luminary of the Philological Society; it is a selective work avoiding Latin derivatives as far as possible and it contains long discussions of words that Wedgwood found interesting, somewhat in the manner of Hopkins's own notes. But wherever Hopkins might have derived his snippets of information, his etymologies show considerable sensitivity to the relationships of words, and he combines something of the bold speculation of early etymologists with the stricter methodology of the later ones. And there is much in the way he handles words – both in the notes and in the poetry – that is reminiscent of the lexicographers.

Many of Hopkins's etymological notes are concerned with series of words that begin with the same consonants or consonant clusters. A series in *gr- (grind, gride, gird . . .)* is followed by a series in *kr- (crook, crank, kranke . . .)*. Later, he briefly discusses a set in *sl-* and assumes a *dr- tr- thr* relationship in *drill, trill, thrill*. Then there is a long entry on *fl-* words, to which he returns, and in the following pages he discusses words in *h-, sk-, shl-, sp-, st-* and *tw-*. Apart from the long note on *horn* (to which we shall return), there are other shorter notes that do not quite fall into our initial-consonant category. At one point he expresses surprise that *earwig* corresponds to German *Ohrwurm* so that the syllable *ear* is not a particle but is indeed the word *ear*. This shows that he is already aware of the folk-etymology (e.g. *sparrowgrass* for 'asparagus') that particularly affects names of birds, plants and insects, and he has expected *earwig* to be an example of this. Elsewhere he wonders whether there is a connection between *lather* and Lat. *lavo* Gk λούω, notes that *than* and *then* have identical etymologies, lists river-names that are from Celtic, mentions some dialect usages ('*Duffer* in Cumberland means ass [literally]' . . . 'In Isle of Wight dialect to *gally* is to harry, annoy . . .), and, from Speke's *Journal of the Discovery of the Nile*, makes notes on the 'euphony' of an African language. It is difficult to understand why writers on Hopkins have made so little of these linguistic notes, and why, for example, they are excluded from John Pick's *Hopkins Reader*. They give such important insight into the way his mind worked at an early age, before his mature poetry, that it is surely impossible to achieve a full understanding of his linguistic attitudes and poetic practice without them.

Characteristically, he ascribes these sets of words associated by their initial consonants to 'original' roots with 'original' meanings. The notes repay careful examination since they not only give us a great deal of information about his knowledge of philology and attitudes to language, but also contain the paradigm of his later schemes of alliteration and vowel or consonant rhyme.

Sometimes the entries are brief: '*slip, slipper, slop, slabby* (muddy), *slide*, perhaps *slope*, but if *slope* is thus connected what are we to say of *slant*?' Although he does not say so, he seems to be associating this series with an 'original' meaning of slipperiness, just as he has given the *gr-* series an 'original' meaning' of striking and rubbing. *Slant* does not fit this meaning as well as the others: one may associate sliding or slipping with a 'slope' but not with a 'slant'. Had he gone on to treat this series in detail, he would no doubt have speculated on movements and curves and angles and would have added *slick, slug, slog* and others to his list. But this series does not seem to have interested him as much as some others, and, correspondingly, alliteration or other plays on *sl-* words are relatively rare in his poetry. The most memorable case is the 'rash, smart, *sloggering* brine' of 'The Deutschland', st. 19, and this usage is not fully anticipated by the etymological note.[12] It is the series in *fl-* that seems to have interested him most.

There are three successive entries on *fl-* words, and the first is worth quoting in full:

Flick, fillip, flip, fleck, flake
Flick means to touch or strike lightly as with the end of a whip, a finger, etc. To *fleck* is the next tone above flick, still meaning to touch or strike lightly (and leave a mark of the touch or stroke) but in a broader less slight manner. Hence substantively a fleck is a piece of light, colour, substance, etc. looking as though shaped or produced by such touches. *Flake* is a broad and decided *fleck*, a thin plate of something, the tone above it. Their connection is more clearly seen in the applications of the words to natural objects than in explanations. It would seem that *fillip* generally pronounced *flip* is a variation of *flick*, which however seems connected with *fly, flee, flit*, meaning to make fly off. Key to meaning of *flick, fleck* and *flake* is that of striking or cutting of the surface of a thing; in *flick* (as to flick off a fly) something little or light from the surface, while *flake* is a thin scale of surface. *Flay* is therefore connected, perhaps *flitch*.

The subsequent entries on *fl-* words suggest that Hopkins had in mind a basic meaning of *flying* or perhaps *flowing*. In one entry he speculates on *fly* and *flee*: 'No great difference can be shown, in spite of the purists, to exist between the verbs to *fly* and to *flee*.' These words he connects with *flit, fleet, flight, flutter, flitter*, and implies that the *fly – flit* variation is parallel to Latin *volare – volitare*. He connects *fluster* with *flutter*, and speculates that *flatter* may be 'to fan with applause, to flutter up – or else to inflate, blow out'. He also recognizes an 'original connection' of the series with *flow, blow, flare, flamma, float, flute* and others. In the final *fl-* entry, he discusses *flag*: '(droop, etc), *flaccere*, notion that of waving instead of rigidity, flowing (as we say of drapery). Hence *flag* the substantive.' He notes the connection of *fledge* to *fly, fled*, compares *fillip, flip* with *flap, flob*, and suggests a pattern of end-consonant relationships (velar to labial, although he does not use the terms) in *flag – flabby, flick – flip, flog – flap, flop*.

These observations on consonant correspondences and vowel variations in words of related sound and meaning are of the greatest importance for understanding his later poetic practice.

Hopkins's lines are full of internal vowel rhyme and assonance, but are also notable for the way in which they raise alliteration and medial or final *consonant* rhyme into an important principle. 'The Wreck of the Deutschland' is full of alliteration, sometimes confined to the line, sometimes binding whole sentences and stanzas together. Commonly the alliteration is on *fl-*:

> And *fled* with a *fling* of the heart . . .
> To *flash* from the *flame* to the *flame* . . .　　　(st. 3)

> And the sea *flint-flake* . . .　　　(st. 13)

> 'Some find me a sword; some
> The *flange* and the rail; *flame*,
> Fang, or *flood*' goes Death on drum . . .　　　(st. 11)

But it may be on other consonants or consonant clusters (some of which, like *st-* are discussed in these early etymologies):

> *Stroke* and a *stress* that *stars* and *storms* deliver . . .　(st. 6)

and not by any means confined to 'The Deutschland':

Flake-doves sent *floating* forth . . .　　　(No. 32)

. . . *long* and *lovely* and *lush* . . .　　　(No. 33)

O is there no frowning of these *wrinkles, rankèd wrinkles* deep . . . .
Will have the *waked* and have *waxed* and have *walked* with the
wind what *while* we slept . . . .　　　(No. 59)

It has in fact been difficult to find examples from Hopkins's poems that are simple alliterations. Usually the sound-patterns are much more complex, and the principles on which they are founded seem to be rather clearly foreshadowed in these early notes on *flick* and associated words. Final consonant rhyme and vowel gradation are highly developed as early as 'The Wreck of the Deutschland'

> Of the *Yore* flood, of the *year*'s fall . . .
> . . . *heeds* but *hides*, *bodes* but *abides*;　　　(st. 32)

In this case the vowel is varied within a stable consonant framework, as in Hopkins's discussion of the 'tone' variation in *flick, fleck, flake* and in his brief notes in words of the pattern: $h +$ vowel $+ l$, $sk + V + p$ and $sk + V + m$ which follow the *fl-* series. Sometimes, as in the famous image of the 'plush-capped sloe', the sound pattern is yet more complex, so that we can distinguish *vowel gradation* (vowelling-off), but also *internal vowel rhyme, vowel + consonant rhyme, initial consonant rhyme* (alliteration) and *final consonant rhyme*:

> We *lash* with the best or worst
> Word last! How a *lush*-kept *plush*-capped sloe
> Will, mouthed to *flesh*-burst
> *Gush*! – *flush* the man, being with it, sour or sweet,
> Brim, in a *flash*, full! (st. 8)

If we consider the *-sh* words alone, we can observe final C-rhyme in *lash, lush, plush, flesh, gush, flush* and *flash*. Some of these have V + C rhyme, others have gradation within the framework *l . . . sh* or *fl . . . sh*, while yet others have initial consonant rhyme. But this is not all. In addition, some members of this series have cross-alliterations and cross-rhymes with other words in the stanza: *lash* and *lush*, for example, 'reach out' to *last*. And there are subsidiary series of rhyme and gradation: *best, last, worst, burst* with consonant rhyme on *-st*, linking up also with *kept, capped* (which are themselves 'vowelled-off') with final *-t*.

Hopkins's principle of 'rhyme' is, I think, very clearly foreshadowed in these etymological notes, written long before he could have known much about Welsh or Germanic poetry, in which these schemes are used. There is also a clear acceptance in these notes that many of these common words are in some sense *echoic*. In one note he pauses to remark that 'the onomatopoetic theory has not had a fair chance', and in the *fl*-series, Hopkins clearly distinguishes a set such as *flick, flip, fleck, flit* that suggests light, sharp movement, from a set that has iterative implications (*flutter, flitter*) and a third set that suggests slower waving or flowing, which have so-called 'broad' vowels: *flag, flabby*, and so forth. That he retained a conscious interest in these vowel and consonant schemes is clearly shown not only by his later interest in the Welsh *cynghanedd*, but also in his lecture-notes on 'Rhythm and Other Structural Parts of Rhetoric'. Here he shows himself to be well informed about and highly observant of phonetic and phonological matters, and also demonstrates the principles of initial and final consonant rhyme in an Old Norse skaldic poem.

It has already been suggested that Hopkins's espousal of sprung rhythm is one of the controlling principles of his art. The principle of consonant rhyme is equally an innovation in terms of Victorian poetic diction, in which alliteration, for example, is an extra 'grace' rather than a principle, and in which the requirement of V(+C) end-rhyme is a considerable imposition on the phonological resources of the English language, which are quite different from those of Italian or French. Characteristically, Hopkins did not spare himself from the strict requirements of the traditional Italian rhyme-scheme in his sonnets, but he did allow himself end-rhymes that no one else would have dared. He found these permissible because of his emphasis on the 'current language', the phonological facts of current English, rather than the literary language ('continuous literary decorum'). He made use of the language's highly contrastive stress pattern and heavily consonantal structure, as no major poet had done for several hundred years.

The heavily consonantal structure of English justified his emphasis on consonant rhyme, which became one of his methods of heightening language, as it had been in early Germanic and early Welsh. We shall have a great deal more to say about Hopkins's methods of heightening in later chapters. For the moment let us return to the early notes on language to assess their further implications for his attitudes to language and the reading that lay behind these.

We have seen that there is no definite evidence about Hopkins's precise reading on philology, but he had learnt a good deal that an educated young man sixty years before could not possibly have known. Some of his etymologies are reasonably accurate (*horn* is cognate with Latin *cornu*; *kernel*, *granum*, *grain*, *corn* are related); he must have consulted the standard dictionaries of English and the Classical languages. But he seems to have known more than he would easily obtain from the standard dictionaries. In particular, his remark that the onomatopoeic theory had not had a fair chance suggests that he knew about this theory and further believed that it had been rejected. Hopkins's lifetime coincides with the heyday of English philology: he was born shortly after the founding of the Philological Society and died just after the publication of the first volume of that Society's great achievement – the *Oxford Dictionary*. It is possible that any intelligent and scholarly young man would have been likely to pick up information about this new and expanding subject, and it could be argued that we need not therefore trouble to track down the likely sources of Hopkins's interest. It is difficult for us today to recognize what an important subject philology was in the 1850s and 1860s. It was actually socially fashionable, and its chief exponent was Max Müller.

Müller's first series of lectures on 'The Science of Language' were delivered in 1861 at the Royal Institution in London. They were delivered to a distinguished audience of

> not only the intellectual but also the social élite of London. Among the distinguished hearers were the Duke of Argyll, Connop Thirwall, Milman, Stanley, F. D. Maurice, Faraday and John Stuart Mill. As the lectures proceeded the lecture-room became more and more crowded and Albemarle Street more and more blocked by the fine carriages of people who came to hear about Aryan roots . . . and the common Aryan home in Asia.

Müller's second series of lectures in 1863 was even better attended than the first, and before they were given Müller had been invited to Osborne House where he delivered a lecture to the Queen and her family.[13]

There is direct evidence that Hopkins probably read Müller's work after July 1864, by which time he had already made most of the etymological entries in his diary. Some time between 25 July and 7 September 1864, Hopkins makes a memo in his diary to read various works and authors, and includes Max Müller among them. The second series of Müller's *Lectures on the Science of Language* was published on 11 June 1864, and the familiarity of Hopkins's reference (no title is given) suggests that it was this recently published volume that he intended to read. If so, it is not unlikely that he had read the first volume before this date, and Müller could therefore have been one of the main formative influences on Hopkins's early language interests. A number of points support this probability. House and Storey (*JP*, 317) are quite certain that Hopkins read Max Müller, but they do not say when. Hopkins's father, however, is known to have sent Müller a copy of his book *Hawaii* in 1862, and Alan Ward (*JP*, 518) suggests that the first series of *Lectures on the Science of Language* may have influenced Hopkins's note on river names. But, in this respect, Hopkins's remark in his note on *grind*, etc., that the onomatopoetic theory has not had a fair chance suggests that in the autumn of 1863 Hopkins was already familiar with Müller's views, for Müller was the chief current opponent of the onomatopoetic theory of the origin of language. If Hopkins had confined himself to Wedgwood's introduction to his etymological dictionary, or to the books of William Barnes, he would have come away reasonably happy that such a theory had not been challenged. It was Müller who, by christening it the *Bow-wow* theory, made certain that his rejection of it would pass into the general consciousness, and this rejection was made public in 1861 in his first series of lectures. Apart from this, Müller's high reputation and popularity make it inevitable that Hopkins would have heard of his theories (as a modern counterpart might have heard of Chomsky or Lévi-Strauss) and almost certainly read his book. The etymologies show a knowledge of some fairly important philological principles, and Müller is by far the most likely immediate source of his knowledge.

Müller's chief argument is that linguistics is what he calls a *physical* science, by which is meant that it has more in common with the study of geology or biology than it has with the humanities, such as the history of art, morals or religion. He insists on speaking of 'the *growth* of language in contradistinction to the *history* of language' (my italics). It is not in the power of man, he argues, to produce or prevent change in language;[14] in an important sense, it is independent of man. This theme is returned to again and again in Müller's writing; the tone of this example from a lecture delivered in 1868 is typical:[15]

> We are bewildered by the variety of plants, of birds, and fishes, and insects, scattered with lavish prodigality over land and sea; but what is the living wealth of that Fauna as compared with the winged words which fill the air with unceasing music!

The idea that language study is part of what was then called natural history is by no means self-evident, nor has it ever been a particularly respectable view amongst professional language specialists. Max Müller was its chief exponent in the mid nineteenth century, and his declared views (inconsistent as they frequently were with his actual practice) were soon attacked by W. D. Whitney and others and superseded by the work of the German Neogrammarians. But it did find expression amongst the gentleman scholars of the day, many of whom devoted the same attention to seeking out specimens of language (usually of a rustic or archaic kind) as they might have devoted to collecting plants or insects or rock specimens. Müller's introductory chapter to his first series (entitled 'The Science of Language One of the Physical Sciences') describes linguistic science as having three stages – the empirical, the classificatory and the theoretical – and at all times he explicitly uses the analogy of physical sciences.

> There are two great divisions of human knowledge, which according to their subject-matter are called *physical* and *historical*. Physical science deals with the works of God, historical science with the works of man. (*Lectures*, I, p. 22)

Linguistics as a physical science deals with the collection and classification of specimens and the development of a body of theory to account for the observed phenomena, without the kind of value-judgements that might be part of a humanity or 'historical science'.

> In the science of language, languages are not treated as a means; language itself becomes the sole object of scientific inquiry. Dialects which have never produced any literature at all, the jargons of savage tribes, the clicks of the Hottentots, and the vocal modulations of the Indo-Chinese are as important, nay for the solution of some of our problems, more important, than the poetry of Homer, or the prose of Cicero. We do not want to know languages, we want to know language . . . its origin, its nature, its laws. (*Lectures*, I, p. 23)

In his own work, Müller never carried out these principles to the letter, and was as likely as anyone to let moral, social and historical considerations intrude. But his is the clearest exposition of language as a natural science that deals with the 'works of God'. The idea of language as something separate from man that must be studied to reveal its inner mysteries – that has its own 'behaviour' like the silk-sack clouds – is an idea surely implicit in the attitudes in Hopkins's diary. Language, like nature, has its laws, patterns and inscapes, which can be discovered and observed like natural phenomena. As he wrote:

> . . . although a leaf might have an outline on one side so irregular that no law could be traced in it, yet if the other side agreed exactly with it, you would say there was law or regularity about the leaf to make one side like the other. (*JP*, 90)

So too, as he gazed down on a theatre pit crowded with heads and shirt-fronts, he observed the design over all, yet separately each face, head and dress was individual. Although Ruskin is usually thought to be the inspiration of Hopkins's perception of law in the variety of nature, we may have to acknowledge that he owes as much or more to the study of the fundamental laws of language underlying its great variety.

However this may be, Hopkins collects and observes language specimens with much the same delight with which he observes the characteristic patterns of flowers, leaves, clouds and trees. For 3 May 1866, we find 'Yellow and green in the fields charming. Ferryman said "I can't justly tell you", and they call *weir* as if *wire*'. The observation of language is as natural to him as the observation of colour in the fields, and throughout nine years of the *Journal* we find more and more of these linguistic observations appearing cheek by jowl with, and often in the same paragraph as, his descriptions of nature. Sometimes it is the sound patterns that appeal to him, sometimes quaint or archaic dialect words or usages, sometimes the special terminology of country crafts like ploughing or haymaking. It is clear, I think, that he was sufficiently affected by the views expressed by Müller to consider all linguistic forms as equally worthy of respect (the details of euphony in African languages that he notes, an older more 'moralistic' view would have dismissed as savage grunts), equally worth treasuring for what is special about them. It is remarkable too how many of the sentiments that he later expressed about nature in his letters and poetry are equally applicable to the loving way in which he treasured and preserved the words of ordinary country people. Like 'the weeds and the wilderness', the living variety of language enriches the inscapes of the world.

The assumptions that underlie Hopkins's notes on *etymology* are also most easily elucidated by reference to Max Müller. The assumptions seem to be: first, that series of words that are related in meaning can be shown to be derived from a limited set of monosyllabic roots; second, that the meanings of words within these series are associated in a broadly metaphorical way, always going back to a root with a physical or 'sensible' meaning, no matter how abstract some of the derivative senses may be; third, that there is a connection between sound and sense, so that 'onomatopoetic' or 'echoic' theories about word-origins are found illuminating.

It is well known, and clearly established by etymological research carried out since about 1850, that a great many series of words in

English which do not seem at first sight to be related, are in fact related. Such series are usually common monosyllabic words of Germanic origin. It would not be intuitively clear to the layman that the words *sift* and *drift* (used by Hopkins) are derivatives of the same roots as *sieve* and *drive*, or that *shove* and *sheaf* are related. Some such relationships may involve quite extensive networks with many words associated; the word *stand*, for example, is related to *stead, steading, stool, state, stable, stance, stall, station*, and many more. The average speaker is obviously not conscious of these facts while he is actually speaking and does not necessarily think of the physical sense of 'standing' every time he uses a related word. These relationships have for the most part been 'discovered' and explained by philologists. Reference to any modern etymological dictionary will show how enormously productive the IE bases of such words as *stand* (bearing that simple physical sense) have been, not only in English but in other IE languages.

These words tend to be related within their series in a more or less regular way, and there is little doubt that Hopkins was aware of this regularity. There is for example a set of verbal nouns ending in *-ft*, like *drift, cleft* which are derivatives of verbs like *drive, cleave*, and hence there is a phonological (or morphophonemic) relationship between the so-called long *i* or long *e* of the verbs and the short vowels of the verbal nouns. As Chomsky and Halle have observed in their work on phonological theory, this kind of vowel relationship is an important principle in the phonology of English, and it is widespread throughout the language. There are also relationships between rounded and unrounded vowels (*loft* and *lift* are related), and between certain types of consonants. It would be normal in series of words to find *p* and *f* varying with *b* and *v* but not, for example, varying with *s* or *l*. Thus, a word like **dift* if it existed, could be related to *dive* but probably not to *dice*.[16]

In a general way, Hopkins seems to be aware of some of these phonological rules (except when he is obviously speculating about sound symbolism or echoism), and he is also aware of probable grammatical relationships. Nor surprisingly, in view of his knowledge of Latin, he thinks *fly* and *flit* may be related as Latin *volare* and *volitare* are (the second word presumably having an iterative or repetitive meaning), and he thinks that the relation between *fly* and *flick* may be causative ('meaning to make fly off'), as certain verbal relationships (*lie, lay*; *sit, set*; *fly, fledge*) in fact are. It is remarkable too that Hopkins chooses to describe the variations in *flick, fleck, flake* in terms of 'tones'. The idea of tone or pitch difference is part of the explanation usually offered for certain vowel differences that seemingly arose in IE and are handed down in the English strong verb system and elsewhere (*drink, drank, drunk*; *speak, spoke, spoken*). This kind of variation is known by Grimm's term *Ablaut* (or vowel-gradation); although Hopkins is applying the principle rather loosely to different words rather than forms of the same word, he may well have heard of it as an established philological theory.

Hopkins does seem to have accepted the currently dominant theory that IE roots were monosyllabic and limited in number. The notion was first developed around 1820 by Franz Bopp in his analytic work on the roots of Greek, Latin and Sanskrit. In these languages, Bopp maintained, the character of the roots 'is not to be determined by the number of letters, but by that of the syllables, of which they contain only one'.[17] Max Müller, in his first series of *Lectures* (1861), pauses in the midst of a dazzling exhibition of etymological virtuosity to maintain the same principle in a typically enthusiastic way:

> ... you will understand the marvellous power of language which out of a few simple elements has created a variety of names hardly surpassed by the unbounded variety of nature herself. I say 'out of a few simple elements' for the number of what we call full predicative roots, such as *ar*, to plough, or *spás*, to look, is indeed small. (*Lectures*, I, p. 249)

Müller further insists that 'a root is always monosyllabic', and goes on to classify types of 'predicative' root in terms of their vowel and consonant structure. He admits about five hundred such roots, which 'considering their fertility and pliancy, was (*sic*) more than was wanted for the dictionary of our primitive ancestors . . .'

> If they had a root expressive of light and splendour, that root might have formed the predicate in the names of sun, and moon, and stars, and heaven, day, morning, dawn, spring, gladness, joy, beauty, majesty, love, friend, gold, riches, etc.
> (*Lectures*, I, p. 254)

This kind of writing is obviously richly suggestive, and Müller is assuming that different senses and applications of an original root are developed through what can be loosely called metaphor or figurative usages. Hopkins clearly thinks in much the same way, especially in his note on *horn*, which explains the various transfers of meaning in related forms and similarly celebrates the richness of language.

But the idea that original roots were monosyllabic and restricted in number was not Müller's alone. The standard dictionaries tended to assume this without necessarily saying so, and also presented 'original' roots as denoting action or sense-impression or objects and things, rather than abstract notions. Hopkins had, however, read the dialect poetry of the Rev. William Barnes, and he might have seen or heard of a philological work by Barnes that was published in 1862, *Tiw; or a View of the Roots and Stems of the English as a Teutonic Tongue*. This is, by any standards, an eccentric work and could have had little general influence. The copy that I was able to obtain in a copyright library had all its pages still uncut after over a century. But Hopkins knew and admired Barnes's poetry and showed some sympathy for his excessive Anglo-Saxon purism. While we cannot prove that this philological work was read by Hopkins, its contents are of considerable interest. Not happy with 500 roots, Barnes reduces them to fifty, which, nevertheless, 'may yield 15,000 root forms and stems, of one or two vowel sounds, from which, again, an almost endless supply of words may be made by composition.'

Barnes's manner of discussing his roots and their meanings may be demonstrated from his root FL*NG. While the initial cluster remains constant, the -NG may alternate with other sounds such as -B, -K or -SH (which can be called -B stems, etc.). The stem may produce: *fling, flinch, flig* (*dial.* that can fly, as young birds), *flight, flag, flog, fleg* (*dial.* kick), *fledged, flack* (*dial.*), *flutter, fleck* (*dial*), *flick* (*dial.* to touch with a flying point, as a whip-lash), *fluck* (to flow about), *flock, flash* (what flies), *flush* (*dial.* that can fly, of young birds), *flush* (stream from mill-wheel), *flabby, flap, flop, flip*. And, 'with the meaning of flatness': *flange, flank, flag* (-stone), *flitch* (bacon), *fleck* (a spot), *flat, float, flood, flounder, floor*. With this root, as with others, Barnes distinguishes three related areas of meaning, the first of which seems to be the basic one:

(1) To go flyingly, as the air, or a body through the air, or flowingly, as a liquid. To fly, flee, spring about.

(2) Make flee, scare.
    Since the surface of a liquid is flat or level, it was taken as a
    type of what is –
(3) Flat, or level.
    This root, FL*NG, may be called the fluid root.

If Hopkins had known this in 1863, his etymological notes on
flick, etc. would probably have been more detailed, and some of
the associations made by Barnes (but not in Hopkins's note)
would have been discussed. The similarities to Hopkins's note,
therefore, and the similarity between Barnes's remarks and the
imagery of stanzas 3 and 4 of 'The Deutschland' ('I steady as a
water in a well . . .'), are probably coincidental. Barnes's philological theories, however, take the idea of the highly productive
monosyllabic root to its greatest extreme, and, like Hopkins's
notes, they do not insist on strict linguistic proof of relationship
between words. The implication that there is a necessary relationship between sound and sense is not far behind Barnes's views on
roots. There are certain truisms about Hopkins's grammar and
vocabulary to which this theory of monosyllabic roots is relevant.
Hopkins is often said to have preferred simple Germanic words to
Latinate ones, and these are often monosyllables. He is also
frequently accused of having ignored 'grammar' or of having
broken its rules.

The etymological notes show rather clearly that Hopkins
assumed that the roots were monosyllables. The words on which
he bases his speculations – *horn*, *grind*, *crook*, *slip*, *drill*, *flick* and so
on, are nearly all themselves Anglo-Saxon monosyllables, as are
most of the words he associates with them. The exceptions are
usually cognates or supposed parallels in Greek or Latin, which
being inflected languages are poor in monosyllables, or English
disyllables like *fluster*, *flutter* which Hopkins sees as derivatives of
the monosyllables. Hopkins does not usually mention his supposed
root, but it is rather obvious in such things as the belief that *mead*
and *meat* are 'active forms of the same root' that his primary roots
are assumed to be monosyllabic. Native Germanic words are more
likely to be monosyllabic than those borrowed from Latin (a fact
deplored by Swift in 1712), and are generally supposed to be
warmer and more emotive in meaning than borrowings: (home:
residence; child: *infant*; death: *mortality*). They also have a more

complex network of relationships within the language, as Hopkins perceived. But not the least of their virtues, from Hopkins's point of view, is their tendency to be neutral with regard to part of speech'. This is true of many of the words in his etymological series. Hopkins treats *flick* as a verb; *fleck* is treated as both verb and substantive; *flake* is a substantive. Clearly, all three can be either nouns or verbs, or in some uses modifiers, as in *flick-knife* or *flake-doves* (No. 32). The series *drill, trill, thrill* is similarly indifferent as to part of speech. So are *grind, grit, grate, greet, slip, slope, slide, slop, crook, crank, grunt* and many others. Hopkins is notoriously free in his manipulation of the traditional parts of speech, and makes full use of the tendency for English monosyllables to be ambiguous in this way:

> In him, all quail to the wallowing o' the plough: 's cheek
>   crimsons; curls
> Wag or crossbridle, in a wind lifted, . . .   (No. 71)

> . . . in pool and rutpeel parches
> Squandering ooze to squeezed dough, crust, dust; . . .
>   (No. 72)

And he is assisted by the ambiguity of the English plural inflection, which is identical with the third person singular of the verb:

> The glassy peartree *leaves* and *blooms*, they brush
> The descending blue; . . .   (No. 33)

The idea that the word itself is syntactically neutral, and may be developed for different grammatical functions, is surely suggested to Hopkins by his knowledge of IE roots theory. Monosyllabic and limited in number as they were thought to be, these 'predicative' roots were also neutral with respect to part of speech. 'We may say', says Müller, 'that no root was ever used as a noun or as a verb.' The huge battery of grammatical forms which gave to IE its highly inflected pattern and so made it possible to mark distinctions between nouns, verbs and so on, were believed to derive from a different set of roots – Müller's 'pronominal' roots (as distinct from the 'predicative' roots that were grammatically neutral but semantically full). Forms of these pronominal roots were presumed to have been added as prefixes, suffixes or infixes to mark syntactic functions. In the older IE languages, the markers of conjugation, class, tense, mood and so on had become fused into single 'synthetic' endings. Some languages outside the IE group, which were also inflected, had retained their grammatical inflections in more clearly separable forms; the most marked contrast with IE was not this type, but the 'isolative' type represented by Chinese.

Max Müller was very fond of referring to Chinese:

> In some languages, and particularly in Chinese, a predicative root may by itself be used as a noun, or a verb, or an adjective, or an adverb. Thus the Chinese sound *ta* means, without any change of form, great, greatness, and to be great . . . Thus *ta fu* means a great man . . . *fu ta* would mean the man is great . . . a noun is distinguished from a verb merely by its collocation in a sentence.
> (*Lectures*, I, p. 255)

Amongst this generation of linguists, there was still optimism about the possibility of finding out the 'original' forms of language. Although genetic relationship between IE and Chinese was certainly not claimed, there was a tendency to see Chinese as representing a 'primitive' state of language, such as IE must have been before it built up its complex inflectional systems. A later generation was to claim that English, by shedding most of its inflectional load, had moved a long way towards restoring this pristine purity, and English was often compared to Chinese. Hopkins in his etymologies clearly takes little account of the word-class of the associated words that he lists, and years later in his mature poetry he exploits the ambiguous class membership of Germanic monosyllables more than any other poet. At times, as many have noted, he seems to do away altogether with normal grammar. (But on this see Chapter 7.)

In his later poetry, Hopkins is particularly prone to tear a word out of its normal syntactic place and function, and the feeling is somehow communicated that the less grammatical binding a word has, the more its 'selfhood'. One gets the feeling that some at least of Hopkins's words are being set off independently of the sentence so that they can be savoured as themselves:

<blockquote>

                        (feel

That ne'er need hunger, Tom; Tom, seldom sick,

Seldomer heartsore; that treads through, prickproof, *thick*

Thousands of thorns, thoughts) . . .   (No. 70)

</blockquote>

Much simpler examples of transference or ambiguity of word-class can easily be found:

> . . . cliffs of *fall*
> Frightful, sheer, no-man-fathomed . . . (No. 65)

> This to hoard unheard,
> Heard unheeded, leaves me a lonely *began*. (No. 66)

> But ah, but O thou *terrible*, why wouldst thou *rude* on me
> Thy wring-world right foot rock? (No. 64)

Müller's discussion of roots and the example of Chinese may well have been the origin of this kind of syntactic freedom in Hopkins's work. He would not find freedom of the same order in the literary tradition.

In this optimistic age at the beginnings of comparative philology, Max Müller did more than anyone to impress his readers and hearers with a sense of the 'wonder' of language,[18] the fascinating facts about its nature, origin and growth that were there to be discovered and admired. It was with such a sense of wonder that Hopkins in his notebooks and his poems regarded cloud-formations, leaves, flowers, the flight of birds, God's mercy, and celebrated them in his poetry; but the wonder of language is there at the very beginning of his diaries (September–October 1863) almost before he went up to university.

> The various lights under which a horn may be looked at have given rise to a vast number of words in language. It may be regarded as a projection, a climax, a badge of strength, power or vigour, a tapering body, a spiral, a wavy object, a bow, a vessel to hold withal or to drink from, a smooth hard material not brittle, stony, metallic or wooden, something sprouting up, something to thrust or push with, a sign of honour or pride, an instrument of music, etc. (*JP*, 4)

This long note goes on to associate many words in English and other languages with *horn* (the 'original' sense of which Hopkins would no doubt understand to be 'animal's horn'). From its shape, he believes, come *kernel, grain, corn*; from its curve, κορωνίς, *corona*, crown; from its sense of 'spiral' comes *crinis* 'meaning ringlets, locks'. Several other aspects (associations with growing, with the top of the head, and many others) are pointed out, and numerous other associated words are listed, including *crane*, *crow*, *heron*, *corner*, *cornus*, *corns* (of the foot), and even *grin*. As strict etymologies, of course, many of these are wrong, but Hopkins is inspired here as elsewhere by the great fruitfulness of language, which could by association and transference of meaning create such riches from an 'original' simple concept. Similarly, he associates *share*, *shear*, *shire*, *shower* with an original sense of 'cut', and *skill*, Lat. *scindere* and others with the same sense; he also notes that words in *sh* and *sk* are often associated in meaning (*bushy*, *bosky*, *dish*, *discus* and others). This great fruitfulness or inventiveness of language and the creative power of metaphor are major themes of Max Müller's.

The idea that words could be associated in meaning by *metaphor* was of course ancient, but the application of the idea to linguistic change was a nineteenth-century favourite. In 1836 the physical origins of much of our moral and intellectual vocabulary had been expounded – in his own way and for his own purposes – by Emerson.

> Every word which is used to express a moral or intellectual fact, if traced to its root, is found to be borrowed from some material appearance. *Right* originally means *straight*; *wrong* means *twisted*. *Spirit* means primarily *wind*; *transgression*, the crossing of a *line*; *supercilious*, the *raising of an eyebrow*.[19]

Long before Emerson, poets had exploited the 'original' concrete senses of Latin words, for their etymologies were then much better known than those of English words. The great master of the art was Milton:

> while night
> *Invests* (i.e. cloaks) the sea, and wishèd morn delays.
> (*Paradise Lost*, I)

But the idea that words contained their own poetry, that a language was itself far greater than the great works composed in it, was a nineteenth-century view. *Fossil poetry* was Emerson's phrase; it was taken up by Richard Chenevix Trench, and eloquently and persuasively expounded by him:

> Many a single word also is itself a concentrated poem, having stores of poetical thought and imagery laid up in it.[20]

The idea, common to Emerson and Trench, that words may be

themselves morally and spiritually instructive, is not, I think, a major feature of Hopkins's thought, which, early and late, is more a celebration of the 'wonder' of God's creation and of language. Trench's books were so widely read and so frequently reprinted that Hopkins might well have read them; the views he expressed are so much part of the prevailing atmosphere, however, that it is not necessary to assume this. On nearly every page of Trench's work we find the fondness for nature and country lore, for humble and homely words and ideas, which is so much a part of the mid-Victorian interest in English dialect and Anglo-Saxon words.

Max Müller, finding transference of meaning a useful principle in etymology as well as for his work in mythology (which he characterized as 'a disease of language'), forsakes his usual slighting attitude to pre-nineteenth-century views of language, and commends the views of Locke:

> Thus the fact that all words expressive of immaterial conceptions are derived by metaphor from words expressive of sensible ideas was for the first time clearly and definitely put forward by Locke, and is now fully confirmed by the researches of comparative philologists. All roots, i.e. all the material elements of language, are expressive of sensuous impressions, and of sensuous impressions only; and as all words, even the most abstract and sublime, are derived from roots, comparative philology fully endorses the conclusions arrived at by Locke.
>
> (*Lectures*, II, p. 338)

Hopkins was well aware of the idea of roots standing for original 'sensible' ideas transferring their meanings in various ways and often coming to stand for abstract or 'immaterial' conceptions. This is plain in his treatment of the idea of *horn*. Characteristically, this note shows the fine sensuous imagination of an artist – a feeling for shape (spirals, curves, bows, tapers) and for tactile impression, but also for the more abstract associations of strength, honour and pride. But the knowledge that figurative usage was important in semantic change was hardly separable at the time from an interest in the origin of language. There is no doubt that Hopkins knew something about such speculation. As we have seen, he commented in 1863 in a very early etymological note that 'the onomatopoetic theory has not had a fair chance'. The belief that this was so almost certainly came from his reading of Müller.

This speculation had started in ancient times, but in the late eighteenth century, the onomatopoetic theory of language origin had been given a great impetus by Herder's essay on the subject in 1772. Man invented language, he argued, by imitating the sounds of nature. The distinguishing mark of the lamb, for instance, was its bleating, and primitive Man created a name for the creature by imitating that sound. The lamb, therefore, was 'the bleater', and nouns were created from the original verbs. The 'onomatopoetic' or 'imitative' theory received support from able scholars, and in Hopkins's day, from Hensleigh Wedgwood, the introduction to whose etymological dictionary (1859) consists mainly of an exposition of the theory. 'A little examination shows that the principle of imitation has a wider range than we are at first inclined to suppose.' In some words, he shows, the principle is obvious. In others

> although not consciously recognized, it heightens the power of expression, and gives much of that vividness of imagery which we admire in the poetry of Spenser and Gawaine Douglas. In others again, the power of direct representation has wholly gone, and the imitative origin can only be shown by a detailed examination of the mode in which the meaning of the word has developed.

The first class is common amongst bird-names: *cuckoo*, *cockatoo*, Lat. *ulula* (owl) and *peewit*, 'whose melancholy cry gives rise to names in different European dialects, in which we recognize a fundamental identity'. As Hopkins wrote in May 1864, 'they pronounce *peewit* pretty distinctly, sometimes querulously, with a slight metallic tone like a bat's cry'. At this point, Wedgwood draws attention to the consonant variation that Hopkins also observes in his etymological notes – in the relation of *flip-flick*, *flop-flog*, for instance – that it makes 'little difference in the imitation of natural sounds whether we make use of a *p*, *t* or *k* . . . For this reason it may commonly be taken as presumptive evidence of a short descent from an imitative origin, when we find . . . equivalent forms, with . . . interchange . . . as in *clap*, *clack*, or in Sc. *teet*, *keek*, E. *peep*.' Significantly, the word *bell* is also discussed. Wedgwood points out that in the remote Galla language the word for *bell* is *bilbila*, so that it does indeed 'fling out broad its name' (No. 57) in different languages independently.[21]

Wedgwood, however, extends the theory to a wider theory of sound-symbolism that claims something like universal validity. Sounds prolonged with resonance are represented by syllables ending in a 'liquid' (non-fricative continuant): *clang, knell, hum*; words representing motion in the air often have *r, s, sh, z, f* or *w*: *whirr, whizz,* Fr. *siffler.* Modifications in volume are represented by different vowels, sounds of considerable volume being imitated by *a* and *o*, while notes of high pitch have the 'thinner' vowel, *i* (cf. *clank, clink*). This vowel symbolism, he argues, is the origin of the strong verb variation in such series as *sit, sat.* Continuous action is sometimes represented by repetition of the syllables, e.g. in Lat. *turtur, murmur,* a 'more artificial method' of indicating repeated or continued action being to add a syllable in *-r* or *-l.* Thus, *pat, clack* or *clat* give *patter, clatter* and so on. *Stipple* is 'to mark with a succession of dots' (a diminutive of Dutch *stippen*); it is worth pointing out that 'Pied Beauty' is almost an orchestration of these iterative words in *-l*: *dapple, couple, stipple, tackle, fickle, freckled, adazzle,* and this kind of philological discussion could well be the origin of it. There is also a class of words, Wedgwood continues, 'founded on imitation of sounds by which our bodily or mental affections, as those of pain, cold, terror, disgust, etc., are more or less instinctively expressed'. His arguments are considerably strained as the essay progresses, the negative force of the particle *ne,* for example, being attributed to refusal being indicated through clenched teeth. Wedgwood's 'onomatopoetic' theory encompasses much more than the imitation of animal cries.

It is obvious too that the theory of fifty primary roots that Barnes expounds in *Tiw* (1862) has some importance here. Although Barnes makes no specific claims to universality (his roots are Teutonic and therefore language-specific), the initial consonant clusters in BL-, CR-, FL- and so on are given root meanings that associate vast numbers of supposed derivatives. So BL- words, such as *blank, blanket, bleak, black, blatch, blotch, bleach, blow, blue, blowsy, blush, blobs, blebs, blubber* are associated by a root-meaning of light or colour, and FL- words as we have seen come from the 'fluid root'. This comes very close to a claim that within the Germanic languages such initial clusters as BL-, CR-, FL- 'stand for' colour, bending, flying, and so on.

The great opponent of the onomatopoetic theory was Max

Müller. He did not doubt that onomatopoeia might occasionally function in word-coining, but rejected the theory as an explanation of the origin of language. The onomatopoetic theory and the 'interjectional' theory (which also influences Wedgwood) he condemned publicly, in his popular and influential lectures, with the contemptuous appellations *Bow-wow* theory and *Pooh-pooh* theory.

> . . . the onomatopoeic theory goes very smoothly as long as it deals with cackling hens and quacking ducks; but round that poultry-yard there is a high wall, and we soon find that it is behind that wall that language really begins.[22]

Similarly, the idea that language originated in cries of joy, anger, disgust and other emotional states (the 'interjectional' theory, incorporated by Wedgwood into his argument), Müller dismisses as being only 'the outskirts of real language'. If, as seems probable, Hopkins was thinking of Müller when he said that 'the onomatopoetic theory had not had a fair chance', then his comment was reasonable. This theory may be unsatisfactory if taken by itself as an attempted explanation of the origin of all language, but good scholars were much more sophisticated than this. They did not always claim to be explaining the origin of language, but rather to recognize certain universal tendencies in languages that *might* help with such an explanation, and Wedgwood (to take a contemporary example) recognized various kinds of echoism and sound-symbolism far distant from the simple imitation of animal cries. Müller, in separating the onomatopoetic from the interjectional theory and presenting them both as simple-minded, was being rather unfair.

It is odd that he should have gone on to propose a theory that is even less clear and less satisfactory, which those unfamiliar with the subtleties of the argument will find difficult to separate from onomatopoeia. It was later termed the *ding-dong* theory, and dismissed by other scholars. But we must mention it here because it seems quite remarkably relevant to some of Hopkins's views on individuation in natural creation. Here is what Müller says:

> There is a law which runs through nearly the whole of nature, that everything which is struck rings. Each substance has its peculiar ring. We can tell the more or less perfect structure of

metals by their vibrations, by the answer which they give. Gold rings differently from tin, wood rings differently from stone; and different sounds are produced according to the nature of each percussion. It was the same with man, the most highly organized of nature's works. Man, in his primitive and perfect state ... possessed ... the faculty of giving more articulate expression to the rational conceptions of his mind ... So far as language is the product of that instinct, it belongs to the realm of nature. (*Lectures*, II, pp. 370–1)

This curious theory, which seems to be the ultimate in Müller's identification of language and nature, was 'afterwards wisely abandoned',[23] but surely, if Hopkins had read Müller by 1864, this is one of the formative influences in the theory of inscape. Indeed it is hard to resist the conclusion that it is the germ of one of Hopkins's best known sonnets, which I now, appropriately, allow to speak for itself:

As kingfishers catch fire, dragonflies draw flame;
    As tumbled over rim in roundy wells
    Stones ring; like each tucked string tells, each hung bell's
Bow swung finds tongue to fling out broad its name;
Each mortal thing does one thing and the same:
    Deals out that being indoors each one dwells;
    Selves – goes itself; *myself*, it speaks and spells,
Crying *What I do is me: for that I came.*

The 'name' of the bell (and many other things) may be literally onomatopoetic, as Wedgwood believed, but the idea that everything has a characteristic 'ring' is surely also in this poem.

Hopkins's etymologies, as we have seen, recognize a suggestiveness in language that goes well beyond onomatopoeia, and of course he is concerned with suggestiveness in sound as a continuing process – a universal principle constantly repeated and always fresh – part of *current language* and not merely an explanation of origins. His views have found support among linguists of later generations.

Otto Jespersen in 1922 was much more tolerant of the onomatopoetic theory than was Müller, and like Hopkins he interpreted it widely in connection with sound-symbolism or *phonaesthesia*. Jespersen argued that particular sound-combinations are expressive

of movement, state of mind, size, distance and other relations . . .
'a short vowel, suddenly interrupted by a stopped consonant,
serves to express the sound produced by a very rapid striking
movement (*pat, tap, knock,* etc.) . . .' Jespersen's series of *fl-*
words, also thought to be expressive of movement, is like
Hopkins's: '*flow, flag* . . . *flake, flutter, flicker, fling, flit, flurry,
flirt* . . .', and Jespersen finds time to criticize linguists for their
exclusive concern with origins and neglect of the continuing
creativity of language. Far from finding their origin in the very
beginning of language, many of these words expressive of size,
movement and so on appear to be of relatively recent origin, and
etymological dictionaries are sometimes troubled by them.[24]
Hopkins's perception of sound-symbolism as a permanent
principle of language – a perception plainly shown in his etymological notes – accords very well with what is nowadays called 'the
intuition of the native speaker'.[25] We know full well that there is a
sound–sense association in many of Hopkins's series, whether they
are etymologically related or not, and we respond to the exploitation of these associations in his poetry. With their elaborate vowel
or consonant *rhyme* (initial, medial, or final), many of these words
as they are arranged in his poetry *rhyme* not only with one another
but also with the things they stand for.

To emphasize the fact that word associations of a phonaesthetic
kind are taken seriously by modern scholars, we may refer to the
British linguist, the late J. R. Firth,[26] who uses the word *phon-
aestheme* for the associative sequences *sl-, sn-* and others. Firth
claims that the phonetic habits imposed upon us by the language
we speak cause us to associate such series as *slack, slouch, slush,
sludge, slime, slosh, slash, sloppy, slug* . . . *slum, slump, slobber* and
others, all with a pejorative meaning. 'There is nothing inherently
pejorative in the sounds, though it has been suggested that *sl* is
suggestive of salivation.' Firth also mentions words in *sn-* and *sm-*
as pejorative series, and further remarks that other groups of
words 'having common phonetic characteristics are linked by
similar "settings" and have an associated kinaesthetic background'. He suggests that '*stresses* and *strains, strength, straight* or
stretched-out things might be associated in a common motor
background', and he lists: *stripe, stride, strive, struggle, strange,
streak, stream, strike, string,* and others. Although these words have
'no common etymology', Firth remarks that they may nevertheless

'be brought together by alliterative and experiential analogy'. This is what Hopkins does in the *Stroke and a stress that stars and storms deliver* ('Deutschland', st. 6), and may partly explain the sense of physical tension and stress that has been noticed in his poetry. Firth goes on to explain that words may also be associated by end-rhyme, so that *slump* is related by 'phonetic habit' on the one hand to *sl-* words and on the other to *bump, dump, thump* and others. He also goes on to discuss what Hopkins calls *vowelling* (such series as *drip, drop, droop*), but he always insists that phonetic sequences do not directly stand for natural actions, shapes and movements. For him, there is no *inherent* sound-symbolism – the associations that such series undoubtedly have are specific to the language concerned. It is odd that Firth should go on to remark that in English 'the phonetic poet par excellence is Swinburne'. His discussion of these phonaesthetic systems reads almost as if it is a commentary on Hopkins.

The American psychologist, Roger Brown,[27] goes further than Firth in suggesting that phonetic and metaphorical extensions of vocabulary *may* be universal and not necessarily language-specific. He reports on experiments including some by the linguist, anthropologist and critic, Edward Sapir (one of those critics who welcomed Hopkins's poems in 1921). These experiments used nonsense words and asked subjects to classify them in terms of size, brightness and other qualities. There was remarkable agreement. Brown's modest conclusions do little justice to his fascinating account of these experiments, to which I refer the reader. 'With phonetic symbolism', he states, 'the evidence is that speakers of a given language have similar notions of the semantic implications of various phonetic sequences . . . Many, perhaps all, languages make metaphorical extensions of their vocabularies of sensation. It may be that these extensions are founded in the natural correlations of sense qualities. If such correlations exist they could also provide the basis for a universal phonetic symbolism'. These remarks vindicate many of the views of nineteenth-century scholars, together with Hopkins's conscientious attempts to reach a vocabulary as close as possible to the sensations it tried to convey.

The arguments of this chapter may be summed up as follows: Hopkins's etymological notes in his 1863–4 diary have been neglected by critics, but they are rich in clues to his later poetic practice and to the background reading that formed his attitudes to language. Many of the attitudes he expresses are characteristic of mid-century language scholarship. This was the time in which the science of etymology was becoming a mature discipline. Hopkins's notes show an assumption that IE roots were monosyllabic and limited in number, a belief that linguistic change occurred by means of figurative transfers of meaning and a championing of the onomatopoetic theory of language origins and other related theories. These views, together with certain other attitudes, are almost certainly based on Hopkins's reading of Max Müller's *Lectures on the Science of Language*. In Chapter 3, we shall go on to discuss Hopkins's views of dialect and Anglo-Saxon purism in relation to Victorian scholarship.

CHAPTER 3

'The Weeds and the Wilderness': Local Dialect and Germanic Purism

🔯🔯🔯🔯🔯🔯

IT would be difficult to exaggerate the revolution in linguistic interests that took place in England in the middle years of the nineteenth century, or to over-emphasize the progress in knowledge of the history and dialects of English that was made during Hopkins's lifetime. Comparative philology, as we have seen, owed its early development to German scholarship in the early years of the century; side by side with this interest in the ancient origins of languages, there developed a vigorous interest in local dialects and in the folklore and customs of country people. For the first time, the mother-tongue, in all its variety, had become an important focus of interest for the linguist. The centre of attention had shifted from Latin to English, and the eighteenth-century concern with standardizing and codifying vernacular tongues (mainly in their 'literary' forms) had given way to an emphasis on the variety of non-standard and non-literary forms of languages. Not surprisingly, a kind of linguistic nationalism often accompanied this emphasis: some modern language revival movements, for example those in Norway and Ireland, are outgrowths of it.

Already in late eighteenth-century Germany one can detect the signs of this change of attitude. Herder, as we have seen, admired the strength and 'measured pace' of his own mother-tongue. A generation later (1812) we find Jacob Grimm expressing similar views, but with a shift of emphasis. The interest now is in common speech rather than the best literature, in the relics of the medieval past and in popular folklore. Grimm's interests are clearly influenced by the German Romantic movement, by writers such as Tieck (whom Hopkins intended to read in 1864, together with 'German medievalists'). The opposition to the centralized standard and grammatical 'correctness' which is implicit in much mid-century English scholarship – and quite explicitly expounded by some – is already seen in Grimm's preface to his *Deutsche Grammatik* (1819). This wholly rejects previous German grammars. Every German who speaks his language naturally, says Grimm, may call himself his own grammar and leave the schoolmasters' rules alone. We have seen that Hopkins's attitude to the 'schoolmasters' rules', unlike that of some of his critics, is similar to Grimm's; already in his undergraduate years, Hopkins with his observant and inquiring mind knew that the real rules of language lay deeper than those of the schoolmasters. But in Grimm's attitude to language, we also see the same kind of reverence as the Romantic poets often had for wild things in nature. 'Each individuality,' he wrote, 'even in the world of languages, should be respected as sacred; it is desirable that even the smallest and most despised dialect should be left only to itself and to its own nature and in nowise subjected to violence, because it is sure to have some secret advantages over the greatest and most highly valued language.'[1]

In recent years, Hopkins critics have been much concerned with whether he is best described as 'modern', 'Victorian' or 'Romantic'. Clearly there are senses in which he is each one of these, although his 'modernity' has been exaggerated (sometimes, one feels, because a critic thinks that there is something superior about being 'modern', or that all originality is 'modern'). Hopkins is clearly a Victorian in many of his social attitudes, in his sentiments, in his piety; but – despite affinities with Ruskin and his Pre-Raphaelite contemporaries – Hopkins's view of nature has much in it that goes back to early Romanticism, and his attitudes to language partake of the late Romanticism that continued to inspire the philologists well into the 1860s and 1870s. In other words, if we choose to describe his linguistic interests as 'typically Victorian', we must at the same time acknowledge that Victorian language scholarship was largely 'Romantic' in flavour. A study of the linguistic scholarship that forms a background to his early diaries and Journal provides a clear link with the Romantic movement which, in the purely literary sense, he outgrew in his early verse; and it may therefore help to cast light on aspects of Hopkins's mature poetry that still appear to us as Romantic.

Each individuality, even in the world of languages, should be respected as sacred. There is a striking correspondence between Grimm's remark and Hopkins's reverence for the individuality or selfhood of natural objects and scenes. This is celebrated in his poetry, joyfully, as when he speaks of each creature sounding abroad its own name:

> ... *myself* it speaks and spells,
> Crying, *What I do is me; for that I came.* (No. 57)

or, regretfully, lamenting the destruction of *inscapes* in nature that cannot be replaced:

> O if we but knew what we do
> When we delve or hew –
> Hack and rack the growing green! (No. 43)

Much earlier, in his Journal, he had commented:

> (6 December 1868) At night the most violent gale I ever heard. One of our elms snapped in half. Since then (2 February 1870) a grievous gap has come in that place with falling and felling.

And again (8 April 1873):

> The ashtree growing in the corner of the garden was felled. It was lopped first: I heard the sound and looking out and seeing it maimed there came at that moment a great pang and I wished to die and not to see the inscapes of the world destroyed any more.

His careful observation of the 'behaviour' and inscapes of nature is well known. Sometimes he can be observing something as 'un-poetic' as an ink-blot (the comment – 'Spiculation in a dry blot in a smooth inkstand' is accompanied by a drawing – *JP*, 185), or frost-patterns on urinal walls. His descriptions of nature are everywhere in the journal; they are very detailed and very observant:

> The next morning a heavy fall of snow. It tufted and toed the firs and yews and went on to load them till they were taxed beyond their spring. The limes, elms, and Turkey-oaks it crisped beautifully as with young leaf. Looking at the elms from underneath you saw every wave in every twig (become by this the wire-like stem to a finger of snow) and to the hangers and flying sprays it restored, to the eye, the inscapes they had lost. (*JP*, 196)

This is from the journal; in the early diaries the emphasis on natural description is rather less; instead, we encounter, in 1863 –

long before he became interested in Duns Scotus and long before he had actually coined the word *inscape*, an obsession with the inscape of *words*. A few critics have recognized this. Peters comments that 'a word was just as much an individual as any other thing; it had a self as every other object, and consequently just as he strove to catch the inscape of a flower or a tree or a cloud, he similarly did not rest until he knew the word as a self'.[2] E. R. August explains that to Hopkins 'words are like other creatures: they have inscapes beautiful in themselves . . . the numerous philological notes in the journals record word inscapes'. August adds that it is a pity that critics so often overlook the fact that Hopkins 'tries to bring into play the whole self of the words he uses'. Already at the age of nineteen in his note on *horn* Hopkins was concerned with the inscape of the word and the inscape of its relation to the things it stands for; many of his other philological notes further emphasize relations of sound which exist between words of related meanings (as we have noted), and even suggest the 'ring' of the things they stand for. As August remarks: 'Hopkins always suspected that the relation between words and things was not arbitrary'.[3]

The first recorded use of the word *inscape* is in an essay on Parmenides, written early in 1868:

this feeling for instress, for the flush and foredrawn, and for inscape is most striking and from this one can understand Plato's reverence for him as the great father of Realism.

But, as we have seen, he is concerned several years earlier with what is individual and special in words and objects. The earliest appearance of the *idea* of inscape is really in the note on *horn* (1863) in which he tries to catch the individuality of that *word*. Hopkins is clearly concerned with the full semantic suggestiveness of the word, its association with shapes and textures, curves and spirals, and the sensory impressions of touch and sound as well as sight. He is also concerned with its relationships within English and other languages, and he clearly assumes that a relationship of sound may imply relationship in meaning. As we have already seen, Hopkins is aware of the historical perspective and believes that there are certain underlying principles governing linguistic change, notably the principle of figurative change. But we have also noted that the words he discusses in the diaries tend to be monosyllables used in everyday speech, and these monosyllables are usually of Anglo-Saxon (Germanic) origin.

Only very rarely does he interest himself primarily in a long word or a Latinate one. When Hopkins speaks of *current language*, he means the spoken language as opposed to a literary one; but he goes further than most of us would. The essential spoken language is not the educated language of university graduates and the middle classes of large urban centres; it is at its most perfect in the mouths of country people, and, since it is ephemeral and not committed to paper, its interesting features must be jotted down in the diaries just as the inscapes of nature are. Clearly, this *current language* will be largely 'Anglo-Saxon' in vocabulary; and this brings a bonus to the poet, since Anglo-Saxon words are on the whole richer in emotional suggestiveness than is the French or Classical vocabulary of English, and may also have wider networks of structural relationship within the language. We have seen that Hopkins was much influenced by the historical and comparatist interests of his day; in his concern with spoken language in the mouths of the ordinary people he is also part of the strong movement concerned with folk-speech and folk-culture, a movement which can also be said to have had its origins in German scholarship. In Germany and England alike the interest in dialect is at this period difficult to separate from the vigorous linguistic and cultural nationalism that we have already noted.

Throughout the century the tone of English philology was one of reverence for the variety and ancient pedigree of humble speech, together with some hostility to centralization and Latinization of English. The signs of what is to come can already be seen in the work of William Cobbett (*c.* 1818), which displays hostility to the standard classical authorities of grammar. Hazlitt in 1829 is outspoken in his rejection of the classical grammatical tradition, and De Quincey (who is freely referred to in Hopkins's early diaries) calls for more pride in English and its history (1839).[4] In 1864 or 1865 Hopkins thought it worth recording De Quincey's view on Keats: 'Upon this mother-tongue, upon this English language, has Keats trampled as with the hooves of a buffalo' (*JP*, 52). Grimm's influence began to be keenly felt in English academic circles from about 1830. His supporter, J. M. Kemble, indulged in lengthy and acrimonious debates in *The Gentleman's Magazine* with those who resisted this influence. Dean Trench's books on the history of words were widely read, and he was closely involved in the early stages of the *Oxford English Dictionary*. Also in the *Gentleman's Magazine* in the early 1830s there appeared several articles by William Barnes, who was to become the most extreme Germanic purist of the century. Hopkins had read Barnes's dialect poems while still at university, and Norman MacKenzie remarks – understating the matter a little – that the importance of this early influence 'has probably been considerably underestimated'.[5]

MacKenzie is thinking chiefly of Barnes's interest in dialect, but the Germanic purist movement also forms an important background to Hopkins's interests. Its general importance in the period is often underestimated by literary scholars. It can be seen as a reaction against the Latinism of the previous century, and in a relatively mild form it has persisted into the twentieth century. It is discernible in the tenets of the Society for Pure English (founded by Robert Bridges in 1913); it finds its way into language handbooks and the recommendations of composition teachers; and it unquestionably lies behind the views of George Orwell, particularly as he expresses them in his essay 'Politics and the English Language'. 'Never use a foreign phrase . . .' says Orwell, 'if you can think of an everyday English equivalent', and 'Never use a long word when a short one will do'. In his insistence on *in-earnestness*, Hopkins has a great deal in common with Orwell's concern with honesty and decency and his condemnation of those who cover up the truth by using prefabricated phrases. Hopkins's objections to Victorian English have a similar ring and a similar basis in Anglo-Saxonism and simplicity of vocabulary. 'It is true that this Victorian English is a bad business,' he wrote to Bridges in 1888, '. . . They say "it goes without saying" (and I wish it did) and instead of "There is no such thing" they say a thing is "non-existent" and *in* for *at* and *altruistic* and a lot more.' Years before, he had written: 'Disillusion is a bad word; you mean Disenchant-ment. It is as bad as Or-de-al and Preventative and Standpoint and the other barbarisms' (*LB*, 26 October 1880), and then again (5 February 1881), ' "Disillusion" does exist, as typhus exists and the Protestant religion. The same "brutes" say "disillusion" as say "standpoint" and "preventative" and "equally as well" and "to whomsoever shall ask".' It is true that these remarks are not in themselves examples of thoroughgoing Germanic purism, but are more obviously condemnations of pretentiousness, of journalese, of bureaucratic and committee English. As Orwell sought clarity and honesty in prose-writing, so Hopkins had to reject 'prefabricated' language both in poetry and prose. However, in Victorian times, this attitude is in several writers clearly associated with Germanic purism, and Hopkins's delight in local variation of language, which might seem at first sight inconsistent with his rejection of 'this Victorian English', is best understood as an outgrowth of his other linguistic attitudes. These are based on a fondness for dialect and Anglo-Saxon words and are clearly associated with a preference for country as against town, for God's works as against man's works, for what is 'natural' as against what is regulated by man. We shall return to the relation between Hopkins's attitudes to language and attitudes to nature; let us first consider Victorian Germanic purism and its relation to dialect scholarship.

William Barnes was born in 1801 (or 1800 – the date is uncertain), and much of his long life as a country clergyman was devoted to the study of philology, and championship of the cause of Anglo-Saxon purism. His first contribution to the *Gentleman's Magazine* was entitled 'Corruptions of the English Language' – a polemic against borrowing words from other languages. Barnes gave several arguments against borrowing, the chief of which were that borrowing is proof of national inferiority and that it is unnecessary anyway since the English language already has rich resources for the creation of compound words or other derivatives as they are needed. Another article in the *Gentleman's Magazine*, 'Compounds in the English Language', showed in some detail how the resources of English might be used to make new words:

> Lorn, as we have it in lovelorn, is a participle of the old Saxon verb, to lose; as verlohren is in German. Hence we may have,
>> Waylorn, having lost one's way
>> Glorylorn, having lost one's glory
>> Reasonlorn, having lost one's reason . . . etc.
> Fare, is from the old verb to go . . . and means a going, or going: as fare, a going; thoroughfare, a going through; so that landfaring, going by land; airfaring, going in a balloon; are quite as good English as seafaring or wayfaring.[6]

Although Barnes could be scathing about the Latinism of the previous century, and regretful that the Saxon potential of our language was neglected ('I am sorry that we have not a language of our own; but that whenever we happen to conceive a thought above that of a plough-boy, or produce anything beyond a pitch-fork, we are obliged to borrow a word from others before we can utter it, or give it a name . . .'), his purism in these essays was by no means as extreme as it was to become later.

Hopkins, without doubt, was aware of the vast potential for compounding and derivation that lay unused in English, and he was also capable of extending patterns that are in active use. The adverbial *piecemeal* is the model for Hopkins's *leafmeal* (No. 55); *lovescape* ('Deutschland', st. 23), *inscape*, *offscape*, are based on *landscape*; *quickgold* (No. 32) belongs to the same pattern as *quick-silver*; *mealdrift* (No. 38) belongs with *snowdrift*, and suggests it. These simple examples of compounding (and there are many more) closely follow the patterns that Barnes recommended. But Hopkins's poetry is also rich in 'complex' or derivative words that extend patterns already existing in the basic grammatical frame-work of the language. The prefix *a-* (as in *afire, alive, anew*) is extended by Hopkins to *aswarm* (No. 61) and others. The prefix *un-* is extended to nouns like *child, leaf, self, father, Christ* (No. 41) and the resulting forms pressed into service as verbs:

the widow-making unchilding unfathering deeps
('Deutschland', st. 13)
Goldengrove unleaving (No. 55)
Strokes of havoc unselve (No. 43)

Most of these grammatical operations are performed on the Germanic part of the vocabulary. They are basic to Hopkins's art, and a discussion of their grammar follows in Chapter 6.

Hopkins refers to Barnes in a letter to Bridges (26 November 1882):

The Rev. Wm Barnes, good soul, of Dorset-dialect poems . . . has published a 'Speech-craft of English Speech'=English Grammar, written in an unknown tongue, a sort of modern Anglosaxon, beyond all that Furnival in his wildest Forewords ever dreamed. He does not see the utter hopelessness of the thing. It makes one weep to think what English might have been; for in spite of all that Shakespere and Milton have done with the compound I cannot doubt that no beauty in a language

77

can make up for want of purity. In fact I am learning Anglo-Saxon and it is a vastly superior thing to what we have now. But the madness of an almost unknown man trying to do what the three estates of the realm together could never accomplish! He calls degrees of comparison pitches of suchness; we *ought* to call them so, but alas!

Barnes's *Outline of English Speech-Craft* (mis-named by Hopkins) was published in 1878, and its language is remarkable. The technical terms of grammar (*noun, verb, transitive* and so on) are replaced by Germanic words:

'Sundriness of Sex, Kindred, Youngness and Smallness,' says Barnes, are 'marked by sundry names or mark-words or mark-endings'. Grammatical genders become 'the *carl* sex, the *quean* sex . . . *unsexly* things, as a stone'. *Suchnesses*, as we have seen, are adjectives, and may be of *sundry pitches* (different degrees). Transitive verbs are *outreaching time-words*, and intransitive verbs are *unoutreaching*.

However eccentric Barnes may appear, his *Speech-Craft* is merely the most extreme product of a movement which was vigorous at the time, related as we have seen to the growth of the new philology and much more outspoken in condemnation of Latinism or foreign borrowing than we would think reasonable today. Signs of this linguistic nationalism are seen, for example, in contributions to the publications of the *Philological Society* and in the work of dialect scholars and medievalists, culminating (1899) in a rather strong Germanic nationalism in the pronouncements of Henry Sweet, probably the greatest British linguist of the century. Sweet was not at all sure that it was necessary to teach the Classical languages to schoolchildren, but the Classics should in any event come later than German and Anglo-Saxon, which should be taught to every schoolchild.[7] The Balliol scholar, T. Kington Oliphant, in a historical work entitled *The Sources of Standard English* (1873) calls his chapter on French influence 'Inroad of French words into England'. *Inroad into England*, not 'influence on English'. A baleful century it was, he says of the thirteenth century . . .

if we may liken our language to a fine stone building, we shall find that in that wondrous age a seventh part of the good old masonry was thrown down . . . The breach was by slow degrees

made good with bricks, meaner ware borrowed from France . . .
We may put up with the building as it now stands, but we cannot
help sighing when we think what we have lost.

Oliphant is sternly critical of the eighteenth century and the
Latinate prose of Gibbon. He commends the 'many attempts, like
those of Mr Barnes in Dorset, to bring the various dialects of
England before the reading public. How many good old words,
dropped by our literature since 1500, might be recovered from
these sources!' For arousing us from foreign pedantry he gives the
credit to Cobbett, and he commends 'Mr Tennyson' for helping
the revival of pure English. Further strides, however, have been
made by Mr Morris, who has shown us, in his 'Sigurd, how copious,
in skilful hands, an almost purely Teutonic diction may be.'[8]

It is the work of a less gifted writer such as Oliphant that shows
us the true characteristics of this purism – with all its strengths
and weaknesses. The sincere concern with clarity and honesty in
writing is obviously there, and impressed upon us repeatedly. So
too is the conviction that linguistic decline (here identified as
foreign borrowing and use of Latinisms by the middle class) is
somehow bound up with moral or social decline. It is the fault of
shopkeepers, the aspiring middle class, who send their children to
educational establishments instead of schools, and the *penny-a-liners*
who write barbarous English in the newspapers. Oliphant, like
Hopkins, found Victorian English a bad business, and, with
Hopkins, thought Anglo-Saxon vastly superior to 'what we have
now'. It is clear from his own writings that Hopkins showed the
Anglo-Saxonist's tendency to identify the Germanic element and
the 'conservative' rural dialects with what is pure and honest in the
use of language: 'He calls degrees of comparison pitches of suchness; we *ought* to call them so, but alas!'

Hopkins's lifetime coincides with a period of intense activity in
English dialect research and interest in the common speech of
England. In 1847, J. O. Halliwell produced his *Dictionary of
Archaic and Provincial Words*, and this was followed in 1857 by
Thomas Wright's *Dictionary of Obsolete and Provincial English*.
A. J. Ellis, who is often considered the founder of English dialect
research, was active in the 1860s and his *Early English Pronunciation*
appeared in four volumes between 1869 and 1874. The English
Dialect Society was founded in 1873 with W. W. Skeat as its

secretary. Joseph Wright's monumental *English Dialect Dictionary* did not appear until 1898, but the work was in progress in Hopkins's lifetime; amongst the names acknowledged as correspondents and contributors of unprinted collections of dialect words is 'Hopkins, The Rev. G. M.'.

Hopkins's Journal contains many notes on dialect words, expressions and pronunciations; some words that appear to be of dialect origin find their way into his prose, and there are many in his poetry. As we have seen, scholars have considerably underestimated the extent to which dialectal English is woven into Hopkins's writings from the undergraduate years onwards. As Norman MacKenzie points out: 'Even as good a scholar as Professor W. H. Gardner has classified most of them [i.e. dialect words] as effective archaisms . . . But most of the examples which have been quoted by critics as Shakespearian or Spenserian were in fact used by the common people in Victorian England.'[9] Peters also seems to accept that many 'Hopkinsian' words are archaisms:

> Someone might make out a good case against him for employing a language as archaic and as obsolete as that ever used by Dixon or Bridges . . . 'hie' is preferred to 'haste', 'ghost' to 'spirit', 'thew' and 'brawn' to 'muscle', 'lade' to 'load', 'brine' to 'sea' and so on. 'Fettle', 'pash', 'mammock', 'rivel', 'rive', 'reeve', 'wend', 'heft', 'sillion', 'shive', 'barrow', 'bole', 'tuck', 'burl' and 'buck' are all of them good Saxon words, but they can hardly be said to belong any longer to the ordinary modern language of Victorian days.[10]

However, many of these words do appear in contemporary dictionaries, such as Ogilvie or Richardson; others appear in the dialect dictionaries. Peters misses the point. A great many of these words *do* belong to the ordinary modern language; they are not part of the vocabulary of standard literary prose, but are colloquial and dialectal. Others, like *ghost* and *brine*, are certainly part of the standard language, but Hopkins uses them in *senses* that Peters considers to be archaic. The words themselves are plainly not archaic. Inspired by the philologists of his age, Hopkins's notion of *current language* (or 'ordinary modern language') is much broader than that of his critics, embracing the forms of casual speech (as against formal English), country speech and the vocabulary of rural crafts and trades. All of us, without realizing it, are much influenced in our attitudes by the standardization of language. Although critics do not intend it this way, there is actually something slightly presumptuous about dismissing forms as 'archaic' when they do not happen to conform to the usage of standard literary prose or poetry. If they are still labelled 'archaic' or 'obsolete' even when they are known to occur in dialect speech, that is in a sense even worse; there is nothing truly archaic about words and expressions that are part of the everyday usage of fully competent native speakers of English even if they do happen to live a long way from the metropolis. To call such forms archaic is to assign an unwarranted and unscientific superiority to the standard language which is implicitly taken as the norm. It smacks of patronage, and an assumption that 'provincial' language is necessarily quaint, backward, inferior and so on. It is even more unfortunate that those who are not curious about language are thereby enabled to put on their blinkers and to seem justified in so doing. The immense variability of English in the usage of even one person and in the dialects of different areas can with impunity be ignored or underestimated. While Hopkins may often be innovative in the way he uses a dialect word, there is very little in Hopkins's poetry that cannot be directly related to modern speech. Indeed it must be said that Hopkins did not venture into dialect nearly as far as he might have done. There are many dialect forms (seemingly archaic if compared with the standard) that he either did not know or did not wish to use.

The extent of variability in English usage is little appreciated, but the work of dialect scholars and linguists during the past century has made a great deal of the information available, and in recent years students of urban speech have done much to show how variable usage may be even within the same urban community. The *Survey of English Dialects* (1962 *et seq.*) and the archives of the Linguistic Survey of Scotland bulge with information about the sounds, grammar and vocabulary of 'provincial' speech. In Ireland, the background, phonology and vocabulary of Ulster speech have been investigated by such scholars as John Braidwood and G. B. Adams, who have shown in some detail the conservative nature of much local speech. In sound-pattern, for instance, there is no doubt that the 'Elizabethan' distinction between *beat* and *beet*, *peak* and *peek* and so on is very consistently preserved in much Ulster vernacular speech. In syntax, the Middle English *for to* construction (as in 'he came for to see me') is preserved in most Scottish and Ulster vernacular. Even so, it came to me as a surprise to hear a shepherd in a remote part of Donegal referring to his jacket as a *frock* (from frock-coat), and it is commonplace in Donegal to hear small rocky fields referred to as *parks* and one or two cottages in their surrounding wilderness spoken of as *towns* (from townlands).[11]

In Hopkins's day, the great popularizer of English word-lore was Richard Chenevix Trench. *On the Study of Words*, which was first published in 1851, reached its twentieth edition in 1888. In Trench's influential work we find reverence for the treasures of humble speech closely associated with that love of the countryside that is so much a characteristic of Victorian England. Indeed, there is a very close, sometimes an uncanny, resemblance between Trench and Hopkins in their association of language and the countryside.

Poetry, says Trench, is enshrined in the words of a language just as much as in an *Iliad*; indeed a language is itself far greater and richer than the great works composed in it. The poetry inherent in language can be seen in the names of flowers, beasts, birds and fishes: *lady's finger*, *love-in-idleness*, *larkspur*, *rosemary*, *ladybird*, *kingfisher* and many others including, notably, *windhover*:

> Any one who has watched the kestral [*sic*] hanging poised in the air, before it swoops upon its prey, will acknowledge the felicity of the name 'windhover', or sometimes 'windfanner', which it popularly bears.[12]

Trench was by no means an Anglo-Saxon purist, and he calls attention to the fossilized poetry embedded in Latin and Greek borrowings, but it is plain that his richest stores of living metaphor were found in country speech in which the Anglo-Saxon element is, naturally, strong. Significantly, the reference to the windhover occurs in a list of dialect usages: 'in our country dialects there is a wide poetical nomenclature which is well worthy of recognition.' Hopkins thought so too and often noted such usages in his journals: in Lancashire, 'the mossy cankers on rose-bushes' are called '*Virgin's Brier* (they say breer)' (22 August 1872); cormorants, in the Isle of Man, are *Black Divers* (7 August 1872). It is to be expected that Hopkins would prefer the term *windhover* to *kestrel* when he came to write his famous poem: not only is it an Anglo-

Saxon type of compound, it is also a country word obviously expressive of the bird's movement. It is noteworthy too that some of the words that occur in Hopkins's poems and notebooks are those that Trench uses as exemplification: *minion*, for example, is used to show degeneration of meaning. *Shire*, says Trench 'is connected with "shear", "share", and is properly a portion "shered" or "shorn" off.' This is very reminiscent of Hopkins's note on *shear* and other words (1863) in which he too subscribes to the incorrect derivation of *shire* from *shear*.[13] But it is the tone of celebration – of glorying in the associations of words – that is most striking in Trench's book, and this book could well have contributed to the young Hopkins's enthusiasm for language.

Trench is also notable for his clearly expressed preference for what is 'natural' in language and his hostility to prescription, correction and standardization:

There have been found from time to time those who have so little understood what a language is, and what are the laws which it obeys, that they have sought by arbitrary decrees of their own to arrest its growth, have pronounced that it has reached the limits of its growth, and must not henceforth presume to develop itself further . . . But a language has a life, as truly as a man or as a tree . . . As a forest tree, it will defy any feeble bands which should attempt to control its expansion, so long as the principle of growth is in it; as a tree too it will continually, while it casts off some leaves, be putting forth others.[14]

Müller, a few years later, is equally plain in stating that the life of language is in its dialects and that standard languages are artificial:

What we are accustomed to call languages, the literary idioms of Greece, and Rome, and India, of Italy, France, and Spain, must be considered as artificial, rather than as natural forms of speech. The real and natural life of language is in its dialects. (*Lectures*, I, p. 47)

And it is in the dialects that Müller finds the twin principles of 'phonetic decay' and 'dialectal regeneration' that are the pillars of his theory of linguistics as a physical science, to be studied in a manner similar to the study of biology. No longer was it lower class language that was to be 'suffered to perish with other things unworthy of preservation' (Dr Johnson).

The early publications of the Philological Society, which was founded in 1842, demonstrate very clearly the linguistic interests of the period, showing how far they had moved from traditional classical preoccupations. In the volume for 1860–61 there are several articles on English etymologies, observations on plans for the New English Dictionary, collections of obscure English dialect forms, editions of little-known medieval texts in English and Cornish (by Whitley Stokes), articles on exotic languages and language-groups (such as Chinese), proposed emendations of Shakespeare and a rather notable article on 'Metrical Time, or the Rhythm of Verse, ancient and modern' by T. F. Barham, expressing views on rhythm not dissimilar to those of Hopkins. The following quotation from a paper by Ernest Adams, 'On the Names of the Wood-Louse', captures much of the flavour of Victorian word-collecting:

> I am informed, on the authority of a Kentish coastguardman, that the inhabitants of his district uniformly call the creature a *Monkey-Pee*. The explanation of this mysterious word I obtained last summer, on exhibiting a specimen of the animal to an urchin who was tending pigs in a rural part of Kent. He unhesitatingly pronounced it to be a *Molti-pee*, and was supported by a young companion who was invited to give his opinion. This is of course the Kentish form of the Latin *multipes*. I confess I was somewhat surprised at the time, because from that class of English boys, in a thoroughly rural district, I had expected a lawful Saxon word rather than a miserable specimen of corrupt Latin. It was the ghost of Aristotle's πολυπους troubling these shores.[15]

This passage demonstrates the typical attitudes quite plainly. Rural speech, it was felt, was somehow purer, more 'natural', and would preserve older forms unsullied by standardization, bookishness and artificiality. 'Natural' language had an implicit association with the countryside and the soil, and the biological metaphor of growth and decay, which was so commonly used of language, encouraged this association. It went hand in hand with an interest in folklore and country crafts, with Anglo-Saxon purism and with the movement to preserve the countryside from unwanted improvements. In Hopkins's sonnets of 1877–8, the joy and lushness of the countryside is contrasted with the dirt and meanness of towns:

And all is seared with trade; bleared, smeared with toil;
And wears man's smudge and shares man's smell: the soil
Is bare now, nor can foot feel, being shod.

Of the sea and the skylark and the town of Rhyl, he says:

How these two shame this shallow and frail town!
How ring right out our sordid turbid time, being pure!

We have already seen how Hopkins in his notebooks and in his
poems regretted the destruction of the inscapes of nature. His
objection to 'this Victorian language' was an objection to official
and bureaucratic styles that necessarily rise up in urban and
centralized civilizations; it was part of his objection to the mean
and squalid character of industrial cities generally and his corresponding preference for the country. In this last point of view
Hopkins was not unusual among the intellectuals of his day; it was
merely that he extended his views to the sphere of language and,
with typical consistency and dedication, pushed the point as far as
he could. In the country – in the weeds and the wilderness – one
can find not only beautiful words, but also that which is pure and
innocent in speech as well as in natural phenomena:

What is all this juice and all this joy?
    A strain of earth's sweet being in the beginning
In Eden garden. – Have, get, before it cloy. . .
Innocent mind and Mayday in girl and boy,   (No. 33)

These lines, like so many others by Hopkins, can apply to language
as well as to their more obvious topic, and the corruption and
degeneracy of city life and speech are, by implication, condemned.
    Of course it can be argued that Hopkins, together with the
purists and the country-worshippers, went too far. His view of
the country was an idealization and it did not take into account the
harsh and poor conditions in which many country people lived.
He was a townsman, born in what was then the largest city in the
world, and his knowledge of the country was that of a privileged
outsider. But it is all the more striking for that. Few countrymen
would be likely to observe so closely and record their observations
so carefully. The bluebells and the horned violets they would take
for granted, and they would fell the aspens with never a thought,
for it would be part of their daily work. Hopkins comes to the

country scenes with the fresh eye of one who does not take them for granted, and who is moreover gifted with remarkable powers of observation and concentration. His interest in dialect, together with the general movement towards dialect scholarship, can be seen as part of the Victorian town-dweller's flight to the country. The typical interest in flowers, birds and insects, in collection of rock specimens, and in oral folk-tale is all part of this.

It is not merely that Hopkins was *influenced* by this movement; he was part of it. We do not know when his interest in country dialect began, but it was probably in his schooldays. In a letter to Bridges in 1882, Hopkins indicated that he had read Barnes's dialect poetry while he was still an undergraduate. In his early diaries, most of the linguistic notes are on etymology, but there are some entries on regional speech. While some of this information may have come from personal observation, it is likely at this stage that some of it came from reading. It is after September 1864 that the etymological notes really give way to notes on the poet's personal observation of country usage, and there are many such notes in the later Journal. Often it was a dialect word or phrase that took his fancy, but sometimes he was more interested in pronunciation, and occasionally in grammar. If it was a word or phrase that he recorded, it might be its figurative value that interested him (e.g. *Virgin's Brier* and *Black Divers*), or it might be the sound or its etymological associations, or just the fact that it existed. But he was interested too in country folklore (he records stories of ghosts, fairies and mystical experiences) and in the vocabulary of certain trades and professions.

The Journal is best known for its descriptions of natural phenomena, but it is significant that in the midst of this careful description Hopkins should have thought it worth remembering small points of regional usage – often for a few days at a time – to record in his notebooks. On 1 September 1867 several notes on speech are interspersed with description of nature:

One tree – a beech, I think – I saw on which the ground cast up white reflection like glass or water and so far as I could see this could only come from spots of sunlight amidst the shade.

Back to Benediction; then to Bovey by Gappath (which they pronounce Gappa).

When I got to the middle of the common they call Knighton

Heathfields (for heaths they call heathfields here) I saw the wholeness of the sky and the sun like its ace; the colours of Dartmoor were pale but else the common was edged with a frieze of trees of the brightest green and crispest shadow.

Mr Cleave says they call a wooden bridge over the river a *clamp*.

'I am three and twenty' wrote Hopkins, on a warm summer day in the same year. Already, long before he had developed the complex poetic style in which he sought to capture what was special and unique about natural scenes and events, we find him treasuring humble forms of speech alongside the inscapes of nature. As Grimm had urged, Hopkins was holding sacred the individualities of language.

The true language enthusiast is fascinated by the wonder of language, which in its apparently endless variety yet seems to be governed by orderly 'laws'. We have seen this enthusiasm in Müller and Trench, and the implications of the linguists' notions of 'law' in language are as relevant to Hopkins as are the strikingly similar views of Ruskin on the 'laws' of natural beauty, reflected for example in Hopkins's undergraduate essay in which the orderly regularity of leaf patterns is discussed. In 1866, Hopkins defines *law* as 'finding order anywhere' and speaks of the definite *structure* of the wood-lark's song (*JP*, 139, 138). In the same year (*JP*, 144) he remarks that the 'organization' of the oak-tree is 'difficult', and later exclaims (*JP*, 146) that he has now found the 'law' of the oak-leaves.[16] Language in its rich variation is also orderly, not through an artificial order imposed from outside (as in prescriptive rules of grammar), but because of its own inner nature.

This is a simple point, but an important one. Already in the diaries Hopkins's etymological speculations are based on the perception of orderliness in the rich variety of language history. In the Journals, orderly 'laws' of phonology and syntax are assumed to exist in regional speech. After 30 April 1869, he presents what amounts to a phonological analysis of the speech of several of his colleagues. After some remarks about the Latin pronunciation of a Sicilian priest (Hopkins finds this 'instructive'), he goes on to record that 'Fr Goldie gives long *e* like short *e* merely lengthened or even opener (the broad vowel between broad *a* and our closed *a*, the substitute for *e*, *i*, or *u* followed by *r*)'. This appears to mean that Fr Goldie pronounces the Latin long *e* in *Deus* with a vowel similar to the Southern English vowel in *bird*, *hurt*, and not with a diphthong (ei) as in Southern English *gate*, *train*. Hopkins goes on to describe the pronunciation of his superior, Fr Morris (it is plainly North Country) and, as we saw in Chapter 1, he describes lengthening of vowels in certain kinds of open syllables that is still characteristic of Northern English. Hopkins noted these regional features (and examples of 'interference' from other languages) not as mere curiosities or deviations from a more 'correct' standard, but as features which are themselves governed by regularities within the speech concerned.

Indeed, it would be hard to find a poet more acutely conscious than Hopkins of the orderliness and pattern of language. It is implicit in his etymological and philological notes which, as we have seen, assume a certain orderliness in the processes of language change and even an orderliness in the relation of sounds to the things they stand for. The same attitude is implicit in his dialect notes, not only at the level of sound (phonology), but also at the grammatical level.

He is a collector of words that end in the suffix *-le*. In 1869 he notes Br Wells's *grindlestone* for 'grindstone' and in March 1872 he notes that *stickles* are 'Devonshire for the foamy tongues of water below falls'. As early as 1864 we find 'wade: waddle – stride: straddle – swathe: swaddle – ming (mix): mingle'. Hopkins's later notes extended these sound-meaning relationships to dialect words in which the same kind of pattern (*stick*: *stickle*; *grind*: *grindle*) is exhibited, and he is aware of a 'vowel-change' relationship obtaining in some of the pairs. He exploits these *-le* words most obviously in *'Pied Beauty'* (No. 37), where he uses *dappled*, *couple*, *stipple*, *tackle*, *fickle*, *freckled*, *adazzle* (one might also count *original*, the suffix of which has the same pronunciation). In the second line he prefers *brinded* to *brindled*, which must be counted as a deliberate variation in the sound-pattern of the poem; it also reminds one of the *grind–grindle* relation of Hopkins's note on Br Wells.

It is clear that Hopkins sees the characteristics of dialectal *syntax* as regular meaningful alternations rather than random and degenerate deviations from a more 'correct' norm. This is illustrated by his remarks on what he takes to be the omission of the definite article in Northern English: 'The omission of *the* is I think an extension of the way in which we say "Father", "government", etc: they use it when there is a relative in order to define.' Hopkins appears to mean that the North-country usage extends the 'standard' omission of the article with proper nouns, mass nouns (*milk*, *water*, etc.) and abstracts, but for once his basic observation is wrong. The definite article is seldom actually omitted in Northern speech, but is usually present in reduced form (often a 'glottal stop'). Later, in 1872, Hopkins describes a Lancashire youth who 'called felly/*felk* and *nave* short like *have*. *Wind* he pronounced with the *i* long. When he began to speak quickly or descriptively he dropped or slurred the article.' Whatever Hopkins thought, it is clear that he recognized that dialectal syntax has its own rules or 'laws'. Indeed, there seems to be a connection with Hopkins's observations on the article and his practice in some of the poetry (my italics):

> ... and *thrush*
> Through echoing timber does so rinse and wring
> The ear ...   (No. 33)

> It dates from *day*
> Of his going in Galilee   ('Deutschland', st. 7)

> ... sheer plod makes *plough* down sillion
> Shine ...   (No. 36)

> Pining, pining, till *time* when reason rambled in it ...
>   (No. 53)

The reasons for this, and the effects it has, are more complex and variable than has been recognized. But it is clear that in the last example Hopkins, in a poem about a Lancashire farrier, is trying to suggest North Country language, just as he does in *all road* (*road*='way') later in the same poem. Even if this is not always his purpose, the speculations in the Journal provide an important guide to his later practice.

It is a compliment to Hopkins's observation of syntax that in current work by the American linguist William Labov and his associates on the use and understanding of variable syntax, an allusion made to Wright's *EDD* turns out to refer to Hopkins's contribution. It is the sole clear example of 'positive *anymore*'

('anymore' used in a positive rather than in a negative sentence or in a question): 'n. Ir. A servant being instructed how to act will answer "I will do it any more" (G.M.H.)'. Hopkins was certainly right. Positive *anymore* is common in colloquial use in many American states ('There's a good movie at the Regal *anymore*'), but in the British Isles it is restricted to Northern and Western parts. It is elusive and not generally known. As Hopkins observed, it occurs in the Northern part of Ireland. In my own work I have noted it only in Co. Donegal: 'I'll be getting six or seven days' holiday *anymore*'; 'The nights will be turning [getting longer or shorter] *anymore*'. It can also occur with present rather than future reference: 'Anymore [i.e. nowadays], you have to do it this way.'[17]

Most of the dialect entries in the Journal are concerned with vocabulary or pronunciation rather than syntax, and items of vocabulary are often recorded because they suggest to Hopkins a figure of speech or an analogy, or some underlying rule of language, or sound-symbolism.

In February 1869 he records the dialectal *whisket* for 'basket', and in June of the same year he comments that 'Br Sidgreaves has heard the high ridges of a field called *folds* and the hollow between the *drip*.' These words appeal to Hopkins because they are figurative: *whisket* suggests something that is *whisked* alongside the carrier and is much more suggestive of action than *basket*. It is a 'better' word than *basket* in the same way that *windhover* is better than *kestrel*. *Fold* is one of Hopkins's favourite words – both as noun and verb, in prose and poetry – and is often applied to landscape:

> Aug 6 – Unusually bright. From Jeffrey Hill on the Longridge fell in the ridge opposite with Parlock Pike the folds and gullies with shadow in them were as sharp as the pleats in a new napkin ... (1871)

> Landscape plotted and pieced – fold, fallow and plough
> (No. 37)

> Of a fresh and following folded rank   (No. 43)

Indeed, Hopkins is particularly fond of words that seem to him descriptive of ridges and the gullies between: *fold, drip, comb* (possibly) *drift, cleave* ('Devon cleave', No. 159, and in the prose) are but a few of them. Figurative interest is further exemplified in

Br Wells's remark that the gathering of stones from the meadow was not to be done at random but *in braids* (22 February 1869) and in the earlier note on Devonshire *clamp* for a wooden bridge over a river. *'Braids'* for ordered rows suggests braids of hair, and *clamp* for bridge suggests the firm action of holding together the two banks of a river. It is noticeable too that many of the words we have discussed – and other favourite words that are not especially dialectal – are monosyllabic and ambiguously noun and verb. The basic principles discernible in Hopkins's etymological notes are also discernible here. These simple monosyllables have a rich syntactic as well as figurative potential, and they are often suggestive of clear, firm and decisive *actions*. They are plainly useful to a poet.

Otherwise, Hopkins's dialectal notes are rather varied. In January 1868 he notes that Shropshire people use *nesh* for 'unwell, ailing' and records some observations of child language. Later in the same year he notes *'shrimpled up'* (of corn in dry weather) and *wants* for 'moles' in Devonshire. Surely *shrimple* appeals to him because it seems to be a *portmanteau* (blend) of *shrink* and *crumple*. In 1869 he has a series of notes on vocabulary, grammar and pronunciation (including Br Wells's *grindlestone* and Fr Morris's pronunciation of Latin). He notes the Northern use of *lead* for 'carry' (a field of hay, etc.), *geet* as the Northern preterite of *get*, and the expressions *top* and *lop* and *Dead Creepers* for white bryony 'because it kills what it entwines'. In 1870 he records a list of idiomatic expressions used by Irish priests ('I wouldn't put it past you' and so on) and describes the pronunciation of Br Gordon. In 1871 he records the Lancashire dialect of Br Wells and the vocabulary of haymaking. In March 1872 he notes the Devonshire *stickles, th'hoo road* for 'the high road' and *steel* for 'stile'. In August 1872 he comments on the Manx language, the expression *Black Divers* for cormorants, *Virgin's brier* for cankers on rose bushes, and the Lancashire vocabulary of spinning and weaving. On 17 July 1873 he records Mr Vaughan's imitation of 'Cornelius the philosopher's servant':

'– bullockin', ay and a-bullyraggin' teoo', that is bullying, using abusive words; also (as I heard afterwards) how the Queen told the Shah when he wanted one of his courtier's heads struck off for bad horsemanship at Windsor that he had better not coon ahn, that road.

This looks like a forerunner of *all road* in 'Felix Randal'.

Some of the most interesting entries are those which emphasize Hopkins's untiring curiosity about agricultural and industrial processes and crafts, and the language appropriate to them. He comments on the language of weaving (August 1872) and ploughing (September 1873), and in some detail on haymaking (24 July 1873):

> Robert says the first grass from the scythe is the *swathe*, then comes the *strow* (tedding), then *rowing*, then the footcocks, then breaking, then the *hubrows*, which are gathered into *hubs*, then sometimes another break and *turning*, then *rickles*, the biggest of all the cocks, which are run together into *placks*, the shapeless heaps from which the hay is carted.

The eighteenth century had devoted its efforts to establishing and codifying the huge Latinate vocabulary that English had acquired, and had largely ignored the words of the 'laborious and mercantile part of the people'. Hopkins, in his delight in country crafts and customs, and the underlying assumption that each activity must have its own special vocabulary with its own rich associations, shows a true nineteenth-century attitude and owes much (directly or indirectly) to the gentleman scholars who trod the country seeking out the names of the wood-louse and so on. He also owes much to the example of men like Trench, Barnes, Max Müller and Jacob Grimm. The vocabulary of the various branches of farming and its associated trades is indeed rich. There are, for instance, words for animals of different ages and sexes, for all the different parts of a plough (or any other tool) and all things associated with the activity of ploughing (or any other activity). Often these industries preserve the literal senses of words which in Standard English are used only figuratively (their 'original' senses being forgotten). This is true, for example, of words like *clue* (clew) and *clinch*, which were part of the vocabulary of rope, and are used today in thatching and stack-building. To fail to use the 'proper' term is the sign of the outsider, and may cause a raising of eyebrows: the use of the 'correct' word in the 'correct' circumstances is prescribed. Again, Hopkins the middle-class townsman, might well have been incited to this interest by reading Trench or Müller. Not only are there living dialects of regions, says Müller, but also dialects 'of shepherds, of sportsmen, of soldiers or farmers', and he adds:

I suppose there are few persons here present who could tell the exact meaning of a horse's poll, crest, withers, dock, hamstring, pastern, coronet, arm, jowl, and muzzle.　　(*Lectures*, I, p. 60)

Müller goes on to quote Grimm:

'The idiom of nomads', as Grimm says, 'contains an abundant wealth of manifold expressions for sword and weapons, and for the different stages in the life of their cattle. In a more highly cultivated language these expressions become burthensome and superfluous. But in a peasant's mouth, the bearing, calving, falling and killing of almost every animal has its own peculiar term . . . The eye of these shepherds, who live in the free air, sees further, their ear hears more sharply, – why should their speech not have gained that living truth and variety?'

(*Lectures*, I, pp. 60–1)

There are two major points to be made about this. First, just as there is an uncanny resemblance between Hopkins's *inscape* and Grimm's individuality of dialects, so too there is a great deal implicit in this quotation that relates closely to Hopkins's notions of *in-earnestness* in the use of language. The speech of peasants, according to Grimm, has 'living truth and variety'. Its usage is more *true* and more sincere than the generalized terms of standard speech because it is particularized and accurate. In its natural context, it leaves no room for doubt or vagueness about its meaning. The words used by the blacksmith, the farmer, or the sailor have about them the smell and feel and flavour of their crafts. They cannot lie. Hopkins is interested in these words for their own sake, but also because he feels that, if he can use them aptly, they will help him to capture accurately the inscapes of the world. The second point is that these specialized and dialect usages can be seen as helping to build up a new poetic vocabulary to replace the diction of the standard model that Hopkins rejected. Words like *pash, fettle, mammock* and *sillion* help to give Hopkins's poetry its special flavour: that which marks it out as different from all other poetry. His poetry is *arch-especial* in this sense, as the music of Purcell seemed to be to him. In his language-*inscape* he seems to owe more to nineteenth-century linguistic scholarship that to any other single source.

We are mainly concerned in this book with the diction of Hopkins's mature poetry and the current language that he believed to be its basis. However, while we are discussing the poet's interest in dialect and his concern with using language appropriate to the subject in hand, it is necessary to consider the special style that he developed up to 1875 in the descriptive prose of his Journal. This highly developed prose, carefully adapted to the purpose of detailed description of natural events and phenomena, and clearly intended to communicate feeling, movement, texture, colour, tactile and visual impression, is an important forerunner of the mature poetry. Just as there is a vocabulary appropriate to the crafts of the farmer, the weaver or the blacksmith, so there has to be a vocabulary in which natural phenomena can be described in a way appropriate to one who professes the craft of language, that is, a writer of poetry. This appropriate vocabulary cannot be taken over in full from any established discipline. The terminology of the natural sciences and linguistics will be too abstract, too generalized; it will not communicate the uniqueness of particular events and insights. The vocabulary of literary and art criticism may be slightly more suitable, but it will also be defective in some respects, particularly in the value-judgements that tend to be incorporated in the meanings of many of its terms, which must be inappropriate for pure description. For the enormously difficult art of descriptive prose, Hopkins requires a language that is simple and unaffected and at the same time precise and unambiguous. In a little-known essay written in 1959, Angus McIntosh[18] argued that the English grammatical tradition gave Hopkins considerable problems in his poetry. The idea that words mean 'things or relations of things' (*JP*, 125) and the necessity to think of subject and action as distinct, make the notion of *inscape* difficult for us to grasp and for Hopkins to explain. There is no doubt that *inscape* is at least as much concerned with processes as it is with things, and it becomes necessary for Hopkins to develop a very careful and characteristic way of talking in prose about processes. In the very early note on *horn* (1864) he is already beginning to concern himself with movements and processes as properties of the 'thing' he is talking about:

> it may be regarded as a projection, a climax, a badge of strength, power or vigour, a tapering body, a spiral ... something sprouting up, something to thrust or push with ...

But it is particularly clear that the prose of the later Journal is developed largely for the description of processes, and in the following quotation we can see some of the vocabulary that Hopkins had found it necessary to adapt or invent:

> A beautiful instance of inscape sided on the slide, that is a successive sidings of one inscape is seen in the behaviour of the flag flower from the shut bud to the full blowing: each term you can distinguish is beautiful in itself and of course if the whole 'behaviour' were gathered up and so stalled it would have a beauty of all the higher degree.

Hopkins has here devised for himself an 'enabling' vocabulary. Without the terms *inscape, siding, behaviour, stalled,* he could not describe this process and effect nearly so precisely. To dispense with the special vocabulary would mean that he would either have to start with the flower itself ('the flag flower is beautiful at every stage of its development . . .') or use more conventional general terms ('stage' for *siding*; 'process' for *behaviour* and so on). If he chose the first alternative, it would be more difficult for him to generalize in the latter part of the passage, and the description would be more verbose and less precise. If he chose the second alternative, his vocabulary would not be *in-earnest*, it would mis-lead; 'if the whole *process* were gathered up and so *fixed*' would be wrong because Hopkins is not thinking of an abstract process that imposes itself on the flower, but of the flower itself as being and *behaving*. It is not a 'process', nor is the behaviour gathered up and 'fixed'. I can think of no word but *stalled* that will say what Hopkins means to say without suggesting further meanings that he does not intend.

Hopkins's eye for fine detail is remarkable, and the descriptions in his Journal are careful and precise. The key words are always *inscape* and *instress*; he is concerned not with static objects alone, but with relationships, processes and metamorphoses. One of his interests is the formation of vapour from liquids, and there is a remarkable passage (1871) in which he associates the forming of clouds with the bubbling of molten chocolate:

> I have been watching clouds this spring and evaporation, for instance over our Lenten chocolate . . . The throes can be perceived/like the thrills of a candle in the socket: this is precisely to *reech*, whence *reek*. They may by a breath of air be laid again and then shew like grey wisps on the surface . . . They

seem to be drawn off the chocolate as you might take up a napkin between your fingers that covered something, not so much from here or there as from the whole surface at one reech . . . The film seems to rise not quite simultaneously but to peel off as if you were tearing cloth; then giving an end forward like the corner of a handkerchief and beginning to coil it makes a long wavy hose you may sometimes look down, as a ribbon or a carpenter's shaving may be made to do. Higher running into frets and silvering in the sun with the endless coiling, the soft bound of the general motion and yet the side lurches sliding into some particular pitch it makes a baffling and charming sight. – Clouds however solid they may look far off are I think wholly made of film in the sheet or in the tuft. The bright woolpacks that pelt before a gale in a clear sky are in the tuft and you can see the wind unravelling them and rending them finer than any sponge till within one easy reach overhead they are morselled to nothing and consumed – it depends of course on their size. Possibly each tuft in forepitch or in origin is quained and a crystal. Rarer and wilder packs have sometimes film in the sheet, which may be caught as it turns on the edge of the cloud like an outlying eyebrow. The one in which I saw this was in a north-east wind, solid but not crisp, white like the white of egg, and bloated-looking.   (*JP*, 203–4)

Like many of Hopkins's descriptions, this passage is difficult to follow, not least because of the vocabulary. Norman MacKenzie suggests that one reason for this kind of difficulty is that so many of Hopkins's descriptive terms are borrowed from dialect. This is certainly true of *reech*, although Hopkins seems to use it in a sense rather different from the dialectal one of 'smoke'; and suggestive of the phonetically similar *retch* (the chocolate is *heaving*). Some of the other usages, however, are not especially 'dialectal'. They are merely words from the current language that Hopkins has pressed into service and used in rather special senses that deviate from everyday usage. Words like *throes* and *thrills* are used in a literal (rather than the usual metaphorical) sense; *coil, fret, pitch, forepitch, quained* are characteristic Hopkinsian words, some of them used in the poetry as well as the prose; *caught* is used as it is in the first line of 'The Windhover' (how much weaker the prose would be if 'perceived' were used); *in the sheet* and *in the tuft* are Hopkins's expressions for two types of cloud formations, and they are strongly suggestive of the kind of terms that might be used in some craft or industry to refer to metal (or some such thing) in its different states. Certainly, this is prose that could have been written by no one except Hopkins.

Professor MacKenzie[19] has cited many other examples in the Journal in which dialectal influence seems likely, for example, the use of *lodged* and *shock* in the following:

> The bluebells in your hand baffle you with their inscape, made to every sense: if you draw your fingers through them they are lodged and struggle with a shock of wet heads.

It is possible, as MacKenzie suggests, that *lodged* is from the dialectal *lodge* (to lie flat, of corn or grass; to be beaten down by wind or rain: Wright) and *shock* from the Southern and West Country word for a *stook* of corn. But *lodged* may simply mean 'stuck fast' and although Hopkins uses *shocks* for 'stooks' in his poetry (No. 32) a 'shock of hair' is also a familiar expression. MacKenzie also points out the use of *tretted* (from *treat* or *trete*: 'the second quality of bran') in 'tretted mossy clouds' (*JP*, 142) and 'tretted like open sponge or light bread-crumb' (*JP*, 177); and he discusses the remarkable phrase: 'a *pash* of soap-sud-coloured gummy *bim-beams*' (*JP*, 233). Here, MacKenzie suggests that *pash* is the dialectal word for a medley, or collection of crushed or broken fragments, and connects *bim-beams* with the Somerset *bimboms* ('originally referring to church bells, but applied to anything dangling down, such as tassels, drops of rain hanging from a rail, or icicles').

It is indeed probable that many of these usages originate in country dialect, but it is also important to note that when Hopkins uses them, or variants of them, he does not necessarily use them as they are used in their original dialect. In prose and poetry alike, his overwhelming desire is to select the word that most perfectly captures the present inscape. Country words will obviously be valuable for this, but Hopkins is always influenced by the belief that sound and sense are related. *Pash* and *bim-beams* are suggestive of sound, colour and texture, and are associated in phonetic pattern with other words in the language (*splash, pom-pom*). Therefore, even when we cannot trace a dialectal origin for such words, we can sense what they mean in context from their sound. In his prose, as in his poetry, Hopkins aims at earnestness, sincerity, honesty. When the prose is purely descriptive, this means in effect using language which is accurate and which correctly and memorably communicates the inscape of the sight or event that gave rise to it. Hopkins's descriptive prose is a special language devised by him for the special purpose of recording precise impressions and, like the poetry, it is largely Anglo-Saxon in character.

'CURRENT LANGUAGE
HEIGHTENED'

CHAPTER 4

'Inscape Must Be Dwelt On': The Heightening of Current Language

𝔊𝔊𝔊𝔊𝔊𝔊

IN 1879 (*LB*, 89) Hopkins wrote that 'the poetical language of an age should be current language heightened, to any degree heightened and unlike itself, but not (I mean normally: passing freaks and graces are another thing) an obsolete one.' We have discussed the breadth and variety of Hopkins's notion of *current language*, and we have established certain points. Some of them are negative points – stating what current language is *not*. First, it is not the standard model of nineteenth-century poetic diction; second, it is not the standard *prose* language – the written language of narrative or argument; third, it is not necessarily the language usually associated with logical statement. Much of current language has nothing to do with logic or objective statement, and it is dangerous to believe that to be 'grammatical' an utterance must necessarily be logical in all respects. We have also suggested some of the positive characteristics of current language as Hopkins – to judge from his papers and letters – appears to have understood it. Above all, current language has that 'living truth and variety' of which Grimm spoke. It is 'ordinary modern speech' in the mouths of speakers – emphatically *speech* and not writing. In that ordinary speech one can discern underlying pattern and regularity just as one can speak of 'laws' in natural creation – in the shapes and *behaviour* of clouds, leaf-sprays, bluebells. This current language has a rhythm of its own, and it has sounds that suggest natural sounds, feeling and textures. It is incomparably richer and more various than the written language or what Hopkins considered to be the degraded jargon of urban civilization. Clarity, precision and truth are possible in this language, and Hopkins aims at these things in the descriptions in his Journal (1866–75). It is also an appropriate language for the description of *inscape* (and, by the same token, relatively unsuitable for generalized, intellectualized, abstract purposes).

Hopkins does not explain in the 1879 letter what he means by 'heightening' current language. His notes on 'Poetry and Verse' (*JP*, 289) associate the language of poetry with the notion of *inscape*:

Poetry is in fact speech only employed to carry the inscape of speech for the inscape's sake – and therefore the inscape must be dwelt on.

We may thus suggest that *heightening* is related to inscape in so far as heightening consists of linguistic devices which may be used to bring about inscape (word-inscape as well as thing-inscape). Thus, if we ignore for the moment Hopkins's concern with the inscapes of *things*, we may now consider the relation of his methods of *heightening* language to those of poets in general, assuming that all poetry consists of heightened language in some sense, and attempts to call attention to language for its own sake. Hopkins's poetic theories (*JP*, 289) show that he was much concerned with the word-inscapes of poetry. In some circumstances,

. . . *oftening, over-and-overing, aftering* of the inscape must take place in order to detach it to the mind and in this light poetry is speech which afters and oftens its inscape, speech couched in a repeating figure . . .

Hopkins's theories have some resemblance to those of the Prague School literary structuralists of the 1920s and 30s who were much concerned with the relation of poetic language to the language as a whole.

Paul Garvin summarizes their basic approach thus:

Every object or action, language included, can be assigned a practical function – utilitarian for tools, communicative for language, and so on. If, however, an object or action becomes the focus of attention for its own sake and not for the sake of the practical function it serves, it is said to have an esthetic function; that is, it is responded to for what it is, and not for what it is *for*. Thus, the esthetic function as such is not limited to works of art and literature but can appear in connection with any object or action. It comes about by virtue of what I have translated as *foregrounding*, as opposed to *automatization*.[1]

Foregrounding may come about on any plane: in ordinary speech when for humorous or aesthetic purposes a distortion of the norm is brought about, or in ordinary experience as when a particular effect of sunlight through the leaves is observed. But in ordinary experience, foregrounding seems to be random and unpredictable.[2] In art and literature, on the other hand, foregrounding is consistent and systematic, and tends in a given work to move in a stable direction giving an internal consistency to the work in question. *Automatized* language, of course, is conventional language, seen at its most extreme in the formulae of conventional greetings, bureaucratic language and so on.

We need not subscribe in detail to every tenet of Prague School theory (and of course scholars differed amongst themselves on some points) to see that some of their perceptions may assist us in talking about the poetic theory of such a language-centred poet as Hopkins. Indeed it may be that Hopkins's poetics and practice afford a testing ground for Prague School theory itself. Clearly, Hopkins was interested in objects and events for their own sakes (rather than for their utilitarian functions); hence his view was *aesthetic* (in Prague School terms) and his method *foregrounding*. His views on poetic language were, like Prague School theory, based on an assumption that this rose out of ordinary language; 'this Victorian English' that used such 'barbarisms' as *standpoint* and *Or-de-al* and *equally as well* (LB, 121) was part of automatized language, in which the basic motive for using the 'barbarisms' was conformity. Another kind of *automatized* language was the standard model of poetic diction.

Prague School theorists allowed that a poetic tradition which had originally consisted of aesthetically effective *foregrounding* and distortion of 'the norm of the standard', might through imitation become *automatized* – a cliché.

> It is possible in some cases for a component which is fore-grounded in terms of the norms of the standard, not to be foregrounded in a certain work because it is in accord with the automatized poetic canon. Every work of poetry is perceived against the background of a certain tradition, that is, of some automatized canon with regard to which it constitutes a distortion.[3]

The language of a poem, in other words, may be distinctive and different if it is viewed only in relation to what we have called the literary prose standard, but may at the same time be cliché in terms of poetic language.

The following rather mediocre stanza of Tennyson (which is probably not without *some* merit) may be used to demonstrate the point:

> Then stole I up, and trancedly
> Gazed on the Persian girl alone,
> Serene with argent-lidded eyes
> Amorous, and lashes like to rays
> Of darkness, and a brow of pearl
> Tressed with redolent ebony,
> In many a dark delicious curl,
> Flowing beneath her rose-hued zone;
> The sweetest lady of the time,
> Well worthy of the golden prime
> Of good Haroun Alraschid.
>
> ('Recollections of the Arabian Nights')

This language differs from the norm of the standard in a number of ways. The vocabulary is exotic and far from that of prose: *serene, argent-lidded, tressed, rose-hued, zone*: there are inversions and other kinds of archaism: *Then stole I up, like to rays, eyes amorous*; the adverb *trancedly* is typical of the kind of coining one finds in nineteenth-century verse, serving to compress the language and having almost a dual function. Its effect is different from 'in a trance' which, besides being longer, would refer only to the subject *I* and not have the second function of describing the manner of the gaze. While it differs from the standard, it is obviously very close to the 'automatized canon' of Victorian poetry. In terms of this, it is conventional and does not attract attention to itself. Clearly it is possible to write with some ease in this style and to produce many long discursive poems (as Tennyson in fact did). As Mukarovsky adds:

> The outward manifestation of this automatization is the ease with which creation is possible in terms of this canon, the proliferation of epigones, the liking for obsolescent poetry in circles not close to literature. Proof of the intensity with which a new trend in poetry is perceived as a distortion of the traditional

canon is the negative attitude of conservative criticism which considers deliberate deviations from the canon errors against the very essence of poetry.[4]

Hopkins's rejection of archaism was, as we have seen, a rejection of 'poetic' archaism, and his attempt to infuse new life into poetic diction was indeed seen by conservative critics as an offence 'against the very essence of poetry'. As Bridges said:

> For these blemishes in the poet's style are of such quality and magnitude as to deny him even a hearing from those who love a continuous literary decorum and are grown to be intolerant of its absence. *(Poems, 239)*

Indeed, many of the attempts to read into Hopkins echoes of Shakespeare, Donne and others can be seen as attempts to make him respectable, to incorporate him into the canon, to find in him some evidence, however slight, of respect for *continuous literary decorum*, and this is so whether the supposed echoes are actually there or not.

Plainly, Hopkins's poetry should not be read as if it were in essence merely a variant of the traditional poetic language, or, in Prague School terms, a distortion of the traditional canon. Whatever his techniques of *heightening* consist of, they are not mainly those of traditional poetic diction.

Does his language then achieve its effect by being a *distortion of the norm of the standard*, as Tennysonian diction may be said to be? This, I think, is obviously true of Wordsworth, who deliberately reverts from the eighteenth-century poetic canon to the prose standard as his model, and 'heightens' that by metrical, rhythmic and figurative devices. But it is true of Hopkins only if we violate the usual meaning of *norm* or *standard* and allow that Hopkins has to some extent constructed his own standard. It is as if Hopkins had set about reforming poetic diction from the bottom up, creating for himself a new *standard* and on top of that a *canon* which is also new – admittedly incorporating at both levels some elements (stanza-form and strict rhyme-schemes, for example) that can be regarded as traditional.

We must pause at this point to insist that the terms that are being used to help us to understand Hopkins's method (*foregrounding, heightening* and so on), some of which are Hopkins's own terms, are not emotionally loaded or evaluative. We are not implying that Hopkins's innovations in language, or his heightening of current language, are necessarily more successful *in their effects* than the methods of other poets. Allowing that his methods of heightening are frequently successful in some way, we are merely attempting to understand what these methods are and how the poet puts them into practice. In order to do this, we must attempt to be like Hopkins himself as he expressed his views on poetic diction and theory. His mind was a careful, analytic one and, unlike some of his critics, he was able to distinguish between methods of composition and the final poetic 'effect'; although well able to evaluate, he was also obsessively interested in how things worked. His diaries and Journal are full of accounts of *behaviour* (mainly of nature, language and country industries), and he is much concerned with using a vocabulary that describes objectively and precisely. To understand such a poet and his work, we too must carefully separate descriptive or analytic terms from evaluative terms and attitudes. We are unlikely to succeed fully, but we must try.

A particularly loaded term that has recently been used of Hopkins is the word *game*, which to most people suggests frivolity or lack of seriousness. In certain respects, it has been suggested, Hopkins in his poetry was playing a language-game, and had much in common in this respect with his contemporaries, the nonsense poets Edward Lear and Lewis Carroll. John Wain[5] has suggested that Hopkins has more in common with Lear and Carroll than with his other contemporaries, and even suggests that these three were the most truly serious poets of the age. Paradoxically, their language-games involve an ultimate seriousness. The same paradox is involved in the title of David Sonstroem's fine essay 'Making Earnest of Game: G. M. Hopkins and Nonsense Poetry' (*MLQ*, 1967), in which the game-like nature of much of Hopkins's language is pointed out. Hopkins, the most earnest of poets and the most scrupulous of men, is seen as playing a game with language.

Many of the devices of heightening that we discuss in later chapters fall into this category of *game*. Sonstroem mentions the unconventional end-rhymes that were condemned by Bridges, and the complex phonetic play (involving alliteration, vowelling-off, *skothending*, assonance and internal rhyme) that we shall later discuss. In four lines of the 'lush-kept sloe' stanza ('Deutschland', st. 8), Sonstroem estimates that there are twenty-eight phonetic 'echoes'. Similarly, the long linked series (often of a kind that we later call *gradiences*) of such a poem as 'The Leaden Echo' are seen as game-like:

> How to keep – is there any any, is there none such, nowhere
>   known some, bow or brooch or braid or brace, lace,
>   latch or catch or key to keep
> Back beauty, keep it, beauty, beauty, beauty . . . from vanish-
>   ing away?

At the same time, no one can doubt the seriousness of the poet's intention: to capture as precisely as possible in his language-game the effect of the echoes that are the subject of his poem. Whether Hopkins is fully successful or whether such a topic is an apt one for serious poetry are quite other matters.

Sonstroem suggests that Hopkins's *game* has 'much in common with the old word-game whose object is to progress from one word to another . . . through a series of words formed by changing only one letter of the previous word', and notes that in such series he frequently moves from pessimism to optimism, from black to white. The movement from one to another is a 'phonetic drama', as in (my italics):

> Be beginning to despair, to despair,
> Despair, despair, despair, *despair*.
>
> Spare!
> There is one, yes I have one . . .

(No. 59)

And in other poems, where the word-game is less overt, the play on the form of a word ('accidental' homonymy) may still occur, with a similar reversal of mood:

> I cannot, and out of sight is out of *mind*.
> Christ *minds* . . .

(No. 34)

It is only recently that the idea of literary composition as an earnest language game has been taken seriously. Many critics would still resist the idea, and would insist on a relatively low evaluation of poetry in which this game-like element is obvious. This could involve them in some difficulties with Joyce, Shakespeare and the Metaphysicals, as well as with Hopkins. However, we must point out that in other disciplines the analogy between games and 'serious' thought or behaviour has been of great theoretical importance for many years. In Wittgenstein's linguistic philosophy, the structure of games is compared generally to rule-governed behaviour and particularly to language. Games theory has been taken seriously in political and social studies. The roots of modern linguistic theory lie in De Saussure's comparison of the rules of language to the game of chess.[6] In such disciplines it is possible and useful to strip the word *game* of its associations with childishness and lack of seriousness, and to use the analogy of the game as an insight into laws or rules of human language and behaviour. This involves the perception that all language-behaviour in so far as it is rule-governed is like a game, and that the composition of poetry, being language-behaviour, necessarily incorporates game-like elements. Like a game, language and poetic language would be meaningless without rules. In this sense, we can claim that all poetry or verse, not only that of Hopkins, involves a language-game. In order to distinguish writers like Joyce and Hopkins from those who follow the rules of the game more slavishly, it is convenient to distinguish two levels of game-like activity, which amount to two stages of poetic 'heightening'. These in turn can be interpreted in terms of the Prague School categories that we have discussed.

In his lecture-notes on 'Rhythm and the Other Structural Parts of Rhetoric, Verse' (*JP*, 267–88) and 'Poetry and Verse' (*JP*, 289–90) Hopkins states clearly and in detail that there are rules, generally of a phonetic kind, for the composition of *verse*. His own poetry follows such general rules, and is verse. However he may further manipulate the language, all the finished poems of Hopkins's mature period are based on underlying rules of rhyme-scheme, metre and stanza-form, which differentiate verse from speech and prose alike and constitute what we distinguish as a first stage of heightening. But, as we have noted, to follow the basic rules unimaginatively will produce verse of a kind; the good poet like the good chess-player will take the rules of the game for granted and, while observing them, will interpret them with flair and originality. Although some believe that Hopkins *broke* the rules, it is difficult to read his lecture-notes and still accept that such a man would have thought it proper to break rules. We gain a better understanding of his practice if we accept that the basic rules of verse (a first stage of heightening) were observed, but that in the second stage of heightening Hopkins exploited the very great freedoms that were still available to him just as a talented player in any game can excel without breaking its rules.

In order to clarify the points we are making about heightening, it is useful to discuss the chronological development of Hopkins's own poetry, distinguishing the early poems (1860–c. 1873) from the mature poems (1875–89). In this we shall bear in mind some of the categories distinguished by the Prague School critics.

Hopkins's attitude is very similar to that of the Prague School in so far as their notion of *aesthetic function* is the same as his (my italics):

Poetry is speech framed for the contemplation of the mind by the way of hearing or speech framed to be heard *for its own sake* and interest over and above its interest of meaning. Some matter and meaning is essential to it but only as an element necessary to support and employ the shape which is contemplated *for its own sake.* (*JP*, 289)

Inevitably, Hopkins then introduces the notion of *inscape*. Poetry carries the inscape of speech for inscape's sake, and it is this speech-inscape that 'must be dwelt on'. We need hardly emphasize that Hopkins's attitude to the inscape of things is also fundamentally similar to the Prague School insistence that the *aesthetic function* can apply to *anything* that is contemplated for its own sake.

Hopkins's earliest poems are frankly imitative. They lack inscape in the fullest sense, and they are clearly not derived from or based on *current language*, but on what we have loosely called the 'standard model' of poetic diction. Their language is lush and archaic. If anything, they are further away from 'ordinary modern speech' than is the language of Keats, their main model.

Here, in 1860, is the grand style:

> There is a massy pile above the waste
> Amongst Castilian barrens mountain-bound;
> A sombre length of grey; four towers placed
> At corners flank the stretching compass round;
>
> (No. 1)

More sensuously Spenserian, if less grand, is 'A Vision of the Mermaids' (1862):

Careless of me they sported: some would plash
The languent smooth with dimpling drops, and flash
Their filmy tails adown whose length there show'd
An azure ridge; or clouds of violet glow'd
On prankèd scale; or threads of carmine, shot
Thro' silver, gloom'd to a blood-vivid clot.
Some, diving merrily, downward drove, and gleam'd
With arm and fin; the argent bubbles stream'd
Airwards, disturb'd; and the scarce troubled sea
Gurgled, where they had sunk, melodiously.

In these lines, and in the poem as a whole, there are many lexical and syntactic features which *foreground* it against the 'norm of the standard' and in the direction of 'the poetic canon'. We find archaisms, or quasi-archaisms, like *bronzen, withouten, cleped* ('called'), *had gotten him, antique chaunt*; adjectives used as nouns ('the languent *smooth*') adjectives as adverbs ('then saw I *sudden*', '*scarce* troubled') and compound or derivative coinings of a clearly Keatsian type: 'the *stirless* bay', *satin-purfled, rosy-lipp'd*. As contrasted with the mature Hopkins there is also a considerable emphasis on colour, characteristic of the poets that he later described as 'medievalist': *azure, violet, carmine, silver, argent*. The syntax is characterized by relatively little inversion, but by a very heavy use of premodifying adjectives – not long lists of them as in his later poetry, but most of the nouns are preceded by one: *dimpling drops, filmy tail, azure ridge* and so on.

In these very early poems, therefore, the language game is being played within rules which apply, not to the language as a whole, or to verse as a whole, but to the grammar and lexicon of the poetic canon. Their language is heightened, just as much as Hopkins's later language, but it is not based on *current language*. It is in his later poetry that Hopkins brings together his idea of current language as a basis of heightening, and his search for inscape. It is doubtful whether we would be able to say without benefit of hindsight that the early verse we have quoted is by Hopkins. There is nothing in it that carries the unique stamp and individuality of Hopkins (*his* inscape). These poems could have been written by any very talented youngster.

This is not the case with all his early poems. In some of these there are substantial indications of his mature style. His diaries began (effectively) in 1863 and his Journal in 1866. His concern with the inscape of words and things is first evident in the diaries, and the diaries and Journal together chart the progress of his views on poetic language as they record and describe the inscapes of words and the inscapes of things. As these views develop, they are in part put into practice in his poems.

Two of the best of these are 'Heaven-Haven' and 'The Habit of Perfection'. The first appeared in an early draft in the 1864 diary and went through a number of changes; it is an experiment in syntactic variation as well as in rhythm and variable length of line. 'The Habit of Perfection' has clear signs of the later Hopkinsian word-choice. Neither poem uses language that is strongly imitative or wholly and obviously based on the standard model, and they are of interest here because they show Hopkins moving some distance towards finding his language in current speech, purging it of the elaborate traditional diction, and giving careful attention to how the language is to be 'heightened' in his own way. 'Heaven-Haven' (the title is itself a minor language-game) is probably the best known of Hopkins's early poems, and its apparent artlessness conceals the skill and originality that went into its making.[7] A nun, taking the veil, seeks peace and silence, and the place where she desires to go is defined for the most part by negations or near-negations 'where springs not fail', 'no sharp or sided hail', 'where no storms come', 'out of the swing of the sea'. The only semi-positive statement in the poem is 'and a few lilies blow'. The line 'where the green swell is in the havens dumb', which is gram-matically positive, suggests absence, or even negation, of sound. The two stanzas are parallel in syntax and rhythm, and those variations that do occur draw clear attention to themselves. 'I have desired to go' parallels, with slight rhythmic and syntactic variation, 'And I have asked to be'. The second line in each stanza is the easily remembered one. Like the first lines, the second lines contain three metrical feet, but in each the last two feet can be read as 'sprung' in that they contain juxtaposed stressed syllables: *where springs nót fáil, where nó stórms cóme*. The superficial similarity to 'La Belle Dame Sans Merci' should not mislead us. Despite the fact that one stanza is a syntactic reflection of the other (a practice completely rejected by the mature Hopkins), the poet has moved some distance towards his later diction. In particular, the last lines of each stanza have different numbers of syllables. *And a few lilies blow* has six syllables and can be read as a 'counterpointed' iambic line with three feet. The last line: *And out of the swing of the sea,* has *eight* syllables, but similarly appears to have three feet with stresses on *out*, *swing* and *sea*. It matters very little whether we label this 'sprung rhythm' or metrically irregular. It comes to the same thing. Hopkins is already seeking the freedom in syllable-counting that sprung rhythm will give him. The measure of his success in this poem is the ease and naturalness with which it can be read aloud. The rhythm asserts itself without any effort being made by the reader to 'impose' a metre: it 'reads' itself.

In this excellent poem, the young Hopkins has begun to break away from the poetic canon and is beginning to seek the basis of his heightening in the rhythms of current language. The very complex artifices that he uses in his later poems for heightening that language are foreshadowed in 'The Habit of Perfection'. Thematically, this poem resembles 'Heaven-Haven' to the extent that it speaks of silence, negation, darkness, privation. But it is not an experiment in rhythm and metre; its similarities to the later poetry lie in its syntax, vocabulary and phonetic devices. These are exemplified in the following lines:

Shape nothing, lips: be lovely-dumb:

This ruck and reel which you remark
Coils, keeps and teases simple sight.

Palate, the hutch of tasty lust,

O feel-of-primrose hands . . .

And lily-coloured clothes provide
Your spouse not laboured-at nor spun.

Lovely-dumb and *feel-of-primrose* follow conventions of compounding characteristic of the later Hopkins (consider *lovely-felicitous Providence*, 'Deutschland', st. 31; and *drop-of blood-and-foam-dapple*, No. 42). Apart from the witty allusion to the Biblical lilies of the field, the last two lines anticipate the elliptical and unconventional grammar of the 'Deutschland'. They mean: 'provide lily-coloured clothes that your spouse did not labour at or spin'. The ellipsis of the relative pronoun, together with the unconventional use of the negative and the rather daring prepositional verb *laboured-at* (such as would send a shudder down the spine of the schoolbook grammarian), give it a compressed, abbreviated quality, and make it difficult to comprehend at first reading. Most 'Hopkinsian' are the various types of vowel and consonant rhyme in the second and third quotations. 'Ruck and reel' alliterate, but the final *k* of *ruck* is also rhymed by the final *k* of *remark*. Apart from the fact that *coils* (like *ruck*) is a favourite word in the Journal and occurs in the later poetry, 'coils, keeps and teases' also has alliteration and assonance. 'Palate, the hutch of tasty lust' has end-consonant rhyme (skothending) on the syllable-final consonants, but also near-rhyme (*t* matches up with the *tch* of *hutch* and the *st* of *tasty* and *lust*) and vowel-rhyme. This line is a forerunner of the famous *plush-capped sloe* stanza of the 'Deutschland', the mouth-watering sensuousness of which it clearly anticipates. The sounds of the words seem to be necessarily connected with the actions and sense-impressions they describe.

In a book on a poet's language which seeks to 'explain' his linguistic usage in general, it is easy to forget that this special language had a chronological development. Hopkins's mature views on current language and his methods of heightening did not suddenly spring full-grown, as it were, from his head. Our discussion of these early poems has been in part an attempt to correct the natural tendency of our analytic approach to see the poems as simultaneous on the page and forget that they were not simultaneous in reality. But we have had another purpose, to which we now return.

All poetry, whether it is like Hopkins's early 'conventional' poems or his later 'original' ones, is composed according to rules of some kind, just as the playing of a game conforms to rules. In Hopkins's case these were in the early poems the rules of the standard model, or the canon, in metre, rhyme-scheme, syntax and choice of vocabulary. These characteristics, conventional as they are, are *foregrounded* sharply against ordinary language (the norm), and Hopkins agrees with all other poets that poetic language must be foregrounded in some way so that the object (a linguistic one in this case) may be contemplated *for its own sake* (in Prague School terms, its 'function' is *aesthetic*). Even this conventional foregrounding is brought about by heightening of a kind, and we may distinguish a first stage of heightening which is used in all competent verse no matter how lamentably dull it may be. It is that level which Hopkins in his own writings recognizes as necessary to verse: rules of metre and rhyme-scheme particularly. As Hopkins's views on language matured (largely through the careful observation of language and nature recorded in his diaries and Journal), he rejected the unnecessary features of the canon (features like archaism and 'poetic' inversion), which he believed detracted from the close and intimate relation that could be achieved between words and the things they describe. 'It destroys earnest: we do not speak that way.' This meant that even the standard prose language was an insufficient basis for poetry. As we shall later see, any language has deficiencies, which a poet intensely concerned with precision and *in-earnestness* must somehow make good. Hopkins therefore uses as his basis rhythms, syntax and vocabulary which are not necessarily found in the standard literary language, and develops very intensely a *second* stage of poetic heightening which foregrounds his language much further than was possible in the more predictable conventions of standard verse. Devices such as alliteration, compounding, word-blending (Lewis Carroll's *portmanteaus*) and syntactic premodification are not original to Hopkins. It is the extent to which he uses such devices and the ways in which he applies them that are uniquely his; and the intensity and richness of his mature poetic diction result from them. In our next three chapters, therefore, we examine Hopkins's heightening at three levels: the phonetic, the lexical and the syntactic. This division is normally made by linguists, but we must recognize that the divisions are not clear-cut. In practice, Hopkins often exploits all three levels in the same figure.

CHAPTER 5

'Read with the Ear': Patterns of Sound

ⓢⓢⓢⓢⓢⓢ

HOPKINS repeatedly insisted that his poems were written to be heard, and there are many poems, stanzas or lines in which the sound-effects are particularly foregrounded:

> The ear in milk, lush the sash,
> And crush-silk poppies aflash,
> The blood-gush blade-gash
> Flame-rash rudred
> Bud shelling or broad-shed
> Tatter-tangled and dingle-a-danglèd
> Dandy-hung dainty head. (No. 138)

The statement made in this poem ('The Woodlark'), as in 'The Leaden Echo and the Golden Echo', is largely a statement about sounds, and it is not inappropriate that sound should be emphasized. But it is worth noticing that the effect of the sound of the words is to transfer from sound to other sense-impressions. The poppy-field is bright and rich with colour, and there is even an appeal (in the *-sh* words) to the sensations of taste evoked by the *plush-capped sloe* of the 'Deutschland'. Thus, it is possible for a Hopkins poem, or part of it, to use sound-pattern as its main artifice, and to appeal primarily to hearing and other senses.

Generally speaking, however, poems (or sections of them) that are notable for their sound-patterns are also notable for other devices, syntactic or lexical, and the effect of such lines is really a unified effect of phonetic, syntactic and lexical structure. We separate these levels only in order to be able to talk about them clearly from a linguistic point of view, and the reader will notice that we sometimes return to the same examples in successive chapters, to examine in turn their sound-patterns, their vocabulary and their syntax. If such an approach should seem too analytic, it should be remembered that our subject, Gerard Manley Hopkins, had himself a notably careful and analytic mind. We are unlikely to achieve the same high quality of analytical thought that Hopkins bestowed on every event and perception, and on the language he used.

In our necessarily analytic approach we bear in mind that the effect of a poem is, or should be, unified. The import of a poem, as Susanne Langer has said:[1]

> is not the literal assertion made in the words, *but the way the assertion is made*, and this involves the sound, the tempo, the aura of associations of the words, the long or short sequence of the ideas, the wealth or poverty of transient imagery that contains them . . . and the unifying, all-embracing artifice of rhythm . . . the poem as a whole is the bearer of artistic import . . .

While the poem as a whole has a unified 'import', it should be possible to explain at least some of the linguistic devices through which that 'import' is brought about. We begin by considering the 'all-embracing artifice of rhythm', and we base our approach to Hopkins's sound-patterns on the poet's own statements about sounds.

SPEECH RHYTHMS

Not all of Hopkins's poems are in sprung rhythm, but, whether or not we believe Hopkins to have succeeded in carrying out its principles, sprung rhythm is plainly a key to his poetic art. It has been thought to lie at the basis of many of his innovations in diction, and many of his phonological and grammatical peculiarities are said to be conditioned by his espousal of sprung rhythm. W. H. Gardner comments (*Poems*, xxlx):

> Since Hopkins tends to subordinate grammatical and logical form to the melody or strongly marked pattern of his poetry, he sometimes matches his counterpointed and Sprung Rhythms with a kind of 'sprung' syntax. This licence accounts for most of the 'faults' condemned by Bridges in his original *Preface to Notes*.

Gardner is probably thinking of the well-known lines in which Hopkins omits a subject relative pronoun: 'O hero savest' (No.

41), 'Squander the hell-rook ranks sally to molest him' (No. 48). In addition, many 'sprung' lines can be quoted in which some of the metric feet have only one strongly stressed syllable. The following instances carry the poet's own stress-marks (No. 55):

Áh! ás the heart grows older

. . .

Sórrow's springs áre the same.

And in the same poem, it is clear that the last two feet in the following line are single-syllabled:

What heart heard of, ghost guessed:

While it is not unusual for such lines to give an impression of grammatical compression, and while Hopkins's fondness for single-syllable feet may *sometimes* account for his syntactic schemes, there is nothing non-standard about the *grammar* of these lines from 'Spring and Fall'. Moreover, if the relative pronouns were supplied in the lines quoted from 41 and 48, they could *still* be regarded as sprung or counterpointed lines. In short, the principle of sprung rhythm does not in itself control or condition Hopkins's grammar or account for his 'liberties'. On the contrary, it gives him great freedom, since he recognizes that the feet in sprung rhythm can contain a large number of unstressed syllables. Rather than requiring him to resort to grammatical liberties in order to observe its rules, sprung rhythm allowed Hopkins to escape from the restraints of traditional syllable-counting rhythms and metres, which forced poets to resort to syntactic inversions and grammatical and lexical archaisms which are *not* 'current language'.

The grammatical and lexical devices of such a poet as Keats, which foreground his language in the direction of the *poetic canon* and away from the *norm of the standard*, are clearly linked to the requirements of his dominant iambic metre:

And silent was the flock in woolly fold.

Given the inversion, Keats cannot write 'in *its* woolly fold'. Given sprung rhythm, Hopkins could if he wished. Many thousands of examples from the history of English poerty could surely be quoted to suggest that the requirements of traditional metre are so strong that they force poets to depart considerably from the syntax and vocabulary of ordinary speech or prose – to such an extent that at times it has been thought necessary to write in a special 'poet's grammar' in order to be accepted as a poet at all. Sprung rhythm, I suggest, tends to free Hopkins from these grammatical shackles, and does not in itself enforce syntactic liberties.

One of the principal arguments of Walter Ong's fine essay on sprung rhythm is that Hopkins *found* this rhythm in the language as it was spoken around him: he did not *invent* it, nor yet did he *derive* it from the literary tradition. The examples that Hopkins gave in his Preface from older verse, and his references to Old English and the rhythm of nursery rhymes and weather saws, were not intended to suggest that he derived sprung rhythm from these sources. These examples merely demonstrate the sporadic or consistent use of sprung rhythm elsewhere in the language: in other words Hopkins was suggesting that the rhythm is so insistent in the language that it is bound to appear in unselfconscious verse and sporadically in verse constructed with more learned schemes in mind. It is easy to find it, and it is even possible to describe some lines in such a poem as 'La Belle Dame Sans Merci' as 'sprung rhythm':

> The sedge is withered from the lake
> And nó bírds síng.

Hopkins's own explanations of sprung rhythm are made somewhat obscure by their rather learned presentation, and it is not surprising that it has been regarded as a stumbling-block. But the significant statements, when they are unravelled from his arguments about *counterpoint*, music, traditional metres and 'other structural parts' of poetry, leave little doubt that he meant the natural rhythm inherent in ordinary English speech. 'In the winter of '75 . . . I had long had haunting my ear the echo of a new rhythm which I now realized on paper. To speak shortly, it consists in scanning by accents or stresses alone' (*CD*, 14). This of course is the natural scansion of English speech, and it had been 'haunting' his ear because he heard it all around him. In the Author's Preface (*Poems*, 46-8), Hopkins makes it clear that he regards sprung rhythm as *simple*, whereas counterpointed rhythms ('the superinducing or *mounting* of a new rhythm upon the old') are *complex*. Milton, he says, is the great master of counterpoint, as in /Hóme to his móther's hóuse *private* retúrned/ (*Paradise Regained*, iv, 639) where two of the expected iambics are reversed; but, he adds, the choruses of *Samson Agonistes* have the 'disadvantage' that if they are intended to be counterpointed, Milton does not let us know what the 'ground-rhythm' is, so that 'what is written is one rhythm only and probably Sprung Rhythm'. 'Sprung Rhythm differs from Running Rhythm in having or being only one nominal rhythm ... strict Sprung Rhythm cannot be counterpointed.' Hopkins's arguments about the counterpointing of running rhythm are based on traditional metrics (the mixing of different metres), and he does not explain precisely why sprung rhythm cannot be counterpointed. But it is clear that the argument is best understood on the basis that sprung rhythm is the rhythm of speech and as such has in Hopkins's view no alternative 'dominant' rhythm against which to measure it (as trochaic feet have in an iambic line). For, as Hopkins goes on to argue in a typically purist way, sprung rhythm is 'the most natural of things' – the rhythm of common speech and prose and the rhythm of 'all but the most monotonously regular music'.

Hopkins was entirely right to perceive that ordinary English speech has a strongly marked rhythm – as we saw in the first chapter. Although phoneticians argue about the nature of stress and different degrees of stress within English sentences, there is general agreement that English, together with Celtic languages and other Germanic languages, is timed by feet which are subjectively perceived as equal in length with a varying number of syllables in each foot. Thus, such a sentence as 'Her Májesty the Quéen visited Sándringham todáy' consists of four feet with stresses on the syllables marked and a possible secondary or additional primary stress on 'visited'. If you listen to English speech some distance away, perhaps on a radio in the next room, you will notice the rhythmic character even if you cannot hear exactly what is being said. Certain words or syllables have greater prominence, and it happens that these are usually the words which carry the main information in the sentence as against those with a mainly grammatical function. Nouns, adjectives, verbs and most adverbs tend to be inherently stressed; articles (determiners), prepositions, conjunctions and most pronouns tend to be unstressed. There is no difference in principle between the rules of English sentence stress and Hopkins's idea of *strict* sprung rhythm. It is a property of the current language upon which Hopkins

claimed to base his poetry, and as such it is not in itself 'heightening'. Strict sprung rhythm in Hopkins's view is not supposed to be
foregrounded against the rhythms of speech.

Despite this, it is essential to understand the function of sprung
rhythm in Hopkins's art, since many of the effects that are uniquely
Hopkinsian are wholly or partly explained by his espousal and use
of this principle. Although the principle is simple in itself, the use
of sprung rhythm greatly complicates the rhythms of his poetry in
so far as he mixes it with more traditional rhythms, uses many other
kinds of special linguistic device to bring about his effects, and in
later poems develops it into a kind of chanting rhythm, far removed
from speech.[2] It is not surprising that some critics have insisted
that Hopkins was deluding himself and that much of his poetry
can, with a little forcing, be scanned perfectly well in a traditional
way.[3] Of course, it very often can, and Hopkins himself knew that
all but monosyllabic feet in sprung rhythm could be labelled
iambs, *paeons*, *anapaests* and so on. But the plain fact is that if we
insist on seeing it this way, we can never understand what Hopkins
was trying to do. We may also miss an important opportunity of
explaining how he achieves his special effects.

'The Wreck of the Deutschland' is like no other ode in the
language, and its difference from other odes is partly explained by
the fact that, although many kinds of poetic artifice are used to
heighten the language, the poet manages to maintain *an illusion of
ordinary speech*. It is not, of course, the effect of speech in one simple
colloquial variety. There are many registers or styles of speech:
formal, ritual or incantatory speech; narrative, conversation,
declamation; emotionally charged speech, 'objective' explanatory
speech, casual speech. Hopkins, while he maintains an emotionally
heightened tone throughout the poem, is able to suggest a much
greater variety of speech style than would be possible in the
regular 'running rhythms' of Swinburne or Tennyson. Sprung
rhythm does not *explain* everything, but it makes everything
possible.

Above all, it is flexible. Here is the Deutschland leaving Bremen:

> Into the snow she sweeps
> Hurling the haven behind
> The Deutschland, on Sunday . . .   (st. 13)

The smooth alliterative rhythm of the first two lines changes abruptly as the poet adds two important pieces of information that, according to prescriptive rules of composition, he should have incorporated into the early part of the sentence. The grammatical figure, as we noted in Chapter 1, is common in speech, and the illusion of speech is partly due to this. But it would be difficult to accomplish without the rhythmical flexibility that Hopkins allows himself. The lines that follow in the same stanza demonstrate well enough the freedom that sprung rhythm gives the poet:

> ... and so the sky kéeps,
> For the ínfinite áir is unkínd,
> And the séa flint-flake, bláck-backed in the régular blów,
> Sítting Eástnortheast, in cúrsed quárter, the wínd;

Few poets would find room in their metrical scheme for an expression such as 'Sitting Eastnortheast'; the most accurate account of the wreck described the wind as 'Eastnortheast', and Hopkins was not the man to falsify for the sake of a smooth metre. This is precisely the kind of rhythmic feature that typifies Hopkins. If you have in mind the metronomic regularity of running rhythm, you find it abrupt and arresting.

It has often been noticed that sprung rhythm enables Hopkins to use juxtaposed full stresses. This is not the case in *flint-flake* and *black-backed* in the above quotation (which are required by the five-foot line to carry only one primary stress each), but it is commonly used and is one of the most striking features of Hopkins's poetry. It allows him to give a measured emphasis to his language when he wants to. To use the analogy of music (a favourite of Hopkins), it enables him to use the long breves of organ music rather than the crotchets and quavers of delicate airs. It also has the effect of seeming to alter the timing very suddenly and very obviously (my italics):

> ... the hurl and gliding
> Rebuffed the *big wind* ...   (No. 36)

> I did say yes
> O at lightning and *lashed rod*;
>   ('Deutschland', st. 2)

In a letter to Bridges (*LB*, 46), Hopkins explained that sprung rhythm gave him the freedom to write such lines as the last one quoted, which, in traditional metre, would have to be *lashed birch-rod* or something of the kind. When the two stresses fall together like this, it is quite plain that something is gained. The syllables are emphasized, the timing is slowed, and in the last example, the lashing of the rod is to that extent sharper and more violent than it would be in iambic metre.

To examine in some detail the effects of varying such strong syllables with the polysyllabic feet, we return to the 'Deutschland', starting with the first stanza (and allowing secondary stresses on certain words):

> Thóu màstering mé
> Gòd! gíver of bréath and bréad;
> Wórld's stŕand, swáy of the séa;
> Lórd of líving and déad;   (st. 1)

Several feet here can be taken as single-syllable stresses, and none of the feet have many syllables in them. These lines contrast with the longer lines later in the stanza, and their incantatory tone is achieved largely by the device of heavy stressing. The timing is slow and deliberate. Conversely, the longer lines of the remainder of the stanza give a strong impression of personal emotional involvement. Except for the last line they have a higher proportion of unstressed syllables, and in this respect they suggest animated conversation or monologue:

> Thou hast bound bones and veins in me, fastened me flesh,
> And after it almost unmade, what with dread,
>   Thy doing: and dost thou touch me afresh?
> Over again I feel thy finger and find thee.

The effect of emotional agitation, distress or anxiety, that appears so often in the 'Deutschland', is not due to these effects alone; they are blended with elements of conversational grammar and various other phonetic effects. But the variability of the rhythm, ranging from rather regular rhythms in many of the short lines to irregular ones in the longer lines, and from numerous heavy stresses in some lines to numerous light stresses in others, is responsible for the basic impression of speech variability that the poem gives, and lays the groundwork in current language upon which the 'heightened' effects can be based. Here, for example, is a six-stress line with *twenty-three* syllables:

> Startle the poor sheep back! is the shipwrack then a harvest,
>> does tempest carry the grain for thee?   (st. 31)

Other six-stress lines may have as few as *nine* syllables:

> The sour scythe cringe, and the blear share come.   (st. 11)

Sometimes the tone is that of resignation:

>> Well, she has thee for the pain, for the
> Patience; but pity of the rest of them!   (st. 31)

It could be spoken language. Sometimes it is the poet's comment – his summing-up:

>> Ah! there was a heart right!
>> There was single eye!   (st. 29)

Despite the ludicrously different subject-matter, this is not far from the kind of comment a speaker might make on the effects of a football match, a regatta, a pageant, or give his opinion of a village worthy: 'Yes, there was a fine man – there was a good heart!' It is from rhetorical *speech*, 'heightened' conversation. Sometimes, when the rhythm is more regular, the effect is nearer to that of standard diction:

>> Hope had grown grey hairs,
>> Hope had mourning on,
>> Trenched with tears, carved with cares,
>> Hope was twelve hours gone;   (st. 15)

But most significant, because most original, are those passages where the syntax, together with the rhythm, is 'broken' in order to suggest great emotional agitation:

>> But how shall I . . . make me room there:
>> Reach me a . . . Fancy, come faster –
>> Strike you the sight of it? look at it loom there,
>> Thing that she . . . There then! the Master,
> *Ipse*, the only one, Christ, King, Head: (st. 28)

These lines can be compared in their rhythm with the famous speech in *Macbeth*, I. vii, 1: 'If 'twere done when 'tis done, then 'twere well 'twere done quickly', but Hopkins, since he is not writing blank-verse dialogue, is under no obligation to *return* to the syllable-counting regularity of that metre. Thus, he is able to resolve the agitated effect in his own original way by returning to the single-syllable stresses of emphasis and incantation, with their marked alteration in timing:

> Ípse, the ónly one, Chríst, Kíng, Héad:

An impression of 'thinking aloud' and abrupt change of mind is also characteristic of the 'Deutschland', as it is of speech; and it is accompanied by abrupt changes of rhythm and timing:

> Heart, go and bleed at a bitterer vein for the
> Comfortless unconfessed of them –
> *No not uncomforted*: lovely-felicitous Providence
> Finger of a tender of, O of a feathery delicacy, the breast of the
> Maiden could obey so, be a bell to, ring of it, and
> Startle the poor sheep back! . . . (st. 31 – my italics)

The poet reflects that the fate of those outside the Church will be much crueller than that of the nun. Suddenly – thinking aloud – he changes his mind, remembering that they had the example of her faith and courage to 'startle' them back to the fold. He blurts out: 'lovely-felicitous Providence', and the next two lines have the effect of the speaker searching around for the right way to express what he wants to say, until he finally alights on the appropriate image of the startled sheep. Clearly, Hopkins exploits the syntactic uncertainties of speech which, in *performance*, as Chomsky has pointed out, frequently departs from the strict syntactic regularities that underlie it in the *competence* of speakers.[4] The false starts, the incomplete and straggling phrases and sentences, are all suggested in Hopkins's lines, and they are made possible chiefly by his adoption of the principle of sprung rhythm.

Alas, we have no further space to discuss the rhythmic architecture of this great poem, and the reader is invited to consider its ever-changing rhythms in greater detail. Sprung rhythm is the key to Hopkins's art, even though it does not in itself account for everything. It forms the link between 'current language' and the heightened diction of the poetry. While it is in principle the same thing as speech rhythm, it cannot *in practice* or *in function* be precisely the same. The rhythms of speech are far more variable than those of sprung rhythm; a poet could not reproduce them in all their diversity and still maintain a sense of rhythmic unity in his poem. In 'The Deutschland' Hopkins abstracts from, and exploits, the rhythms of speech, and fits them into a metrical framework, which for him is a necessary part of *verse*-structure (as against prose, or speech).

Typically, Hopkins takes the principle of speech rhythm very seriously, and there are passages where odd or eccentric usages that seem at first sight dissimilar to speech, are in fact conditioned by this principle. In connected speech, disyllables are often reduced to one syllable, and monosyllables to a single sound, as when *there is*, for example, becomes *there's*. Hopkins makes full use of such colloquial reductions, but goes much further than most. Here is Harry Ploughman:

> In him all quail to the wallowing o' the plough: 's cheek
> crimsons:

His is reduced to *'s*, as it commonly is in speech, but not in conventional poetry. And many of Hopkins's daring rhymes are explained by his awareness of 'reduced' forms in natural speech. The conjunction *and* is normally pronounced with a reduced vowel, and without the *d*. Hence he can rhyme 'Provi*dence*' in 'The Deutschland' (st. 31) in the following way:

> . . . be a bell to, ring of *it, and*
> *S*tartle the poor sheep back . . .

The last syllable of *providence* does have a reduced vowel like *and* (since it is the unstressed syllable); *-t-* and *-S* forms a perfect rhyme to it. Similarly, in 'The Loss of the Eurydice', *all un-* (st. 1) is a perfect rhyme on *fallen*; *portholes* (l. 39) in some Victorian pronunciations probably rhymed perfectly with *mortals*; *wrecked her he* /*c*-ame (ll. 23-4) when reduced to *wrecked'r e* /*c*-ame rhymes with *electric*. There are many such examples in the 'Eurydice' and elsewhere, and it is clear that Hopkins was fully aware of English phonological rules for unstressed syllables. Broadly speaking, these rules allow loss of syllables in many naturally unstressed words, reduction of 'full' vowels, and loss of certain consonants, particularly [h]. Few other poets have taken such advantage of these facts, because they were more obedient to the rules of standard poetic diction.

Thus, while *sprung rhythm* looks in one direction backwards to the spoken language which is its basis, it also faces in the other direction towards poetic heightening. 'The Deutschland' mixes various effects of the rhythm. In other, shorter poems, the freedom that sprung rhythm allows is exploited 'in a stable direction'. That is to say, the rhythmic potentialities of English are used to give one dominant impression, and Hopkins attempts to suggest the subject-matter by the rhythm. His greatest success is 'The Windhover', where the rhythm is an essential part of the description of the bird's inscape. The first line, in which the poet 'catches' the windhover, is iambic; but many of the following lines, which describe the bird's movements, are considerably lengthened in the number of syllables, and the swoop and gliding of the windhover is suggested by the rhythm as much as by the words:

> . . . in his riding
> Of the rolling level underneath him steady air, and striding
> High there, how he rung upon the rein of a wimpling wing
> In his ecstasy! then off, off forth on swing,
> As a skate's heel sweeps smooth on a bow-bend: the hurl and
> gliding
> Rebuffed the big wind . . .

As the falcon hovers, the stresses come on the words that emphasize the buoyancy of the air he hovers on – rolling, level, steady. As he circles 'upon the rein of a wimpling wing' the feet continue to be polysyllabic, suggesting the continued hesitation in the bird's movement. Then, as he hurls himself 'off, off, forth on swing', the line is shortened, the stresses are heavy and decisive, the movement is sudden and swift. The next line is longer as the long curve of the descent is emphasized, and finally the effect of the wind on his flight is described in heavy stresses – 'rebuffed the big wind'. The kestrel is perhaps beginning to rise against the wind. At this point the *wheel* or swoop of the bird (and the rhythm of the poem) is *buckled* (see Chapter 6 and Commentary, p. 234, s.v. *buck*).

We have noticed that Hopkins's espousal of *sprung rhythm*, together with his blending of this stress-timed metre with syllable-timed metres, allowed him a number of 'freedoms' that were denied to other Victorian poets. We must now emphasize that these freedoms were only *relative* freedoms. He was relatively free from what he regarded as artificial constraints imposed from above by prescribed rule, but in keeping with mid-century views on the 'laws' of language, he was *not* free from those regularities that were inherent in the language. As Norman MacKenzie comments, Bridges at first concluded that there was 'no conceivable licence' which Hopkins would not be prepared to justify within the system of sprung rhythm. But Hopkins was highly critical of 'licence' in verse, as in morality, and insisted that 'all English verse, except Milton's, almost, offends me as "licentious".' His own apparent 'licences' he describes as 'laws'. 'With all my licences, or rather laws, I am stricter than you and I might say than anybody I know' (LB, 44–5). These views are not special pleading or an attempt to justify his practice after the event, but are entirely consistent with the attitudes to language (and nature) that we examined in Chapters 2 and 3 and with his rejection of the obsolete language required by 'continuous literary decorum'. Language, like nature, is governed by 'laws' which are not imposed by man, but are God-given and therefore inherent in the phenomena – to be 'discovered' and revealed rather than suppressed, controlled or distorted by rules imposed from outside. The long and flowing lines of the octave of 'The Windhover' are appropriate to the 'behaviour' of the bird: other subjects have other inscapes, and their rhythm is different.

In order to examine Hopkins's rhythmic practices in detail and compare them with those of his contemporaries, we must of course discuss much more than the principles and practice of sprung rhythm. For Hopkins was willing to use almost any phonological device that would help him to capture 'inscape' – to make his language sound and feel like the things he described, to 'tell' of them, to 'fling out broad' their *names*. Some of the devices – alliteration, assonance, internal rhyme, end-consonant rhyme, echoism, onomatopoeia – are not *regularly* and *thickly* used in the poetic tradition; others, such as stanza-form and end-rhyme and some kinds of regular metrical requirement, are conventional in verse and not part of 'current language'. This latter type, which can be regarded as *imposed* on current language rather than simply extended out of it, constitutes one kind of *heightening*. In Hopkins, it constitutes a first stage of *heightening*. All poetry, including that of Hopkins, uses these devices in order to separate itself from speech and prose, and Hopkins believed that metrical regularity was a necessary part of 'verse'. Poetry without metre would merely be poetic prose.

In 'The Wreck of the Deutschland' (one of the relatively few poems by Hopkins that are written in stanzas) each stanza has the same number of lines, and each conforms to the same basic metrical principles. As Hopkins wrote in manuscript A (known to us in Bridges's transcript):

> Be pleased, reader, since the rhythm in which the following poem is written is new, strongly to mark the beats of the measure, according to the number belonging to each of the eight lines of the stanza, as the identation guides the eye, namely *two and three and four and three and five and five and four and six*: not disguising the rhythm and rhyme, as some readers do . . . but laying on the beats too much stress rather than too little; nor caring whether one, two, three or more syllables go to a beat
>
> (quoted from *Poems*, 255–6; my italics)

No matter how long or short a line may seem when the syllables are counted, it has only two beats if it is the first line and six if it is the last. 'Well she has thee for the pain, for the' is a nine-syllabled first line with *two* stresses; 'The sour scythe cringe, and the blear share come' is a nine-syllabled *last* line with *six* stresses. The requirements of the stanza-form thus impose a certain pre-dictability on the rhythms derived from speech, which are the basis of the diction, and which enable the poet to capture an impression of great diversity within these constraints. If the strict stanza form were allied to syllable-timed metre, the variabi-lity would be less and the 'artificiality' of the language might be greater. In a long poem there would also be a greater risk of monotony (a phenomenon discussed very seriously by Hopkins in his 1873–4 Lecture Notes). Even in such a poem as 'Inversnaid', where the rhythm is much less complex and variable than 'The Deutschland', the stanza-form and the rhythm combine to produce something very different from the usual Victorian river-poem.

Tennyson, according to Hopkins, was a master of *Parnassian* – that form of poetic language which, although good, stood some-where below 'the language of inspiration' – the highest. Tennyson's song in 'The Brook' has many of these qualities that Hopkins sought to avoid. First, the metre is a syllable-counting one, so that each stanza is an almost perfect metrical and rhythmic echo of the next (I quote the first three stanzas):

> I come from haunts of coot and hern,
> I make a sudden sally

> And sparkle out among the fern,
> To bicker down a valley.
>
> By thirty hills I hurry down,
> Or slip between the ridges,
> By twenty thorps, a little town,
> And half a hundred bridges.
>
> Till last by Philip's farm I flow
> To join the brimming river,
> For men may come and men may go,
> But I go on for ever.

Without denying that this famous poem is charming and effective in its own special way, we must point out that the effects that Hopkins seeks to achieve are much more subtle and complex. His stanzas are not rhythmic images of one another, and he does not in anything but 'occasional' poetry use the regularly recurrent *refrain*, such as:

> For men may come and men may go,
> But I go on for ever.

In 'Inversnaid', the rhyme-scheme is just as regular as in 'The Brook', and each stanza has four four-stressed lines. But the 'darksome burn' does not behave like Tennyson's brook. It is in spate: the froth blown by the wind moves with a different rhythm from the dark whirlpool beneath it, and this again is different from the rushing torrent in its headlong course. Tennyson captures the quiet rippling of the brook as it flows on 'for ever' with the same rhythm; Hopkins captures the inscape of a river as it strikes his imagination all at once, in one particular state. It is a complex state with many facets (its counterpart in prose is the description of Hodder Roughs, *JP*, 233), and variable timing is required to suggest the 'behaviour' of the river, just as a special prose language is needed in the journals for the accurate description of the inscapes of nature (I quote the first two stanzas, marking the stress):

> This dárksome búrn, hórseback brówn,
> His róllrock híghroad róaring dówn,
> In cóop and in cómb the fléece of his fóam
> Flútes and lów to the láke falls hóme.

A windpuff bónnet of fáwn-fróth
Túrns and twíndles óver the bróth
Of a póol so pítchblack, féll frówning,
It róunds and róunds Despaír to drówning.

Despite the strong regularity of rhythm in its four-stress lines, this poem has great variability in the timing of each phrase, and the number of syllables to a line varies between seven and twelve. Unlike 'The Brook', it has no hint of *refrain*. Indeed, *refrain* as such is confined, as I have said, to Hopkins's occasional pieces, and pieces such as 'Margaret Clitheroe', which is unfinished and not among Hopkins's best.

Despite his apparent 'freedoms', Hopkins imposed upon himself rigid conventions of stanza-form, metre and rhyme-scheme. Paradoxical as this may seem, it is wholly in tune with the character of this earnest and scrupulous man. His sonnets are strict 'Italian' sonnets, usually with the demanding ABBA ABBA CCD CCD (or CDC CDC) rhyme-scheme. This insistence can be seen as part of his purism, in no way contradicting the other kind of purism that directs him back to 'ordinary modern speech'. Many English poets (including Shakespeare) had avoided this difficult rhyme-scheme, which was of course the 'original' one. In so far as all poetry involves *artifice*, it would be wrong to suppose that the demanding *artifice* of this rhyme-scheme in some way detracts from Hopkins's claim that his diction was 'current language heightened'. There is no such contradiction. Indeed, the semantic range of the term 'heightening' must include 'artifice'. Hopkins's end-rhyme-schemes and stanza forms are a first stage of *heightening* – one which he has in common with other poets, and required by his own definition of verse.

Hopkins's 1873-4 lecture notes on 'Rhythm and the Other Structural Parts of Rhetoric – Verse' and 'Poetry and Verse' (*JP*, 267-90) show us very plainly how interested Hopkins was in poetic theory and how observant he was of time, rhythm and 'other structural parts' in verse and in language generally. These notes are impressive for their wide learning (he quotes examples of different rhythms, metres, stress; pitch and length-patterns from a variety of languages and refers to such exotic tongues as Tamil and Magyar), evidence of an acute ear for speech and an excellent analytic mind that always seems to be cutting through the superficial facts and trying to explain the principles that lie behind. Verse, Hopkins begins, is 'the various shapes of *speech* called verse' [my italics], and verse is defined as 'speech having a marked figure, order of sounds independent of meaning and such as can be shifted from one word or words to others without changing. It is *a figure of spoken sound*'. After some mention of *figures of grammar* (grammatical parallelism, as in 'Foxes have holes and birds of the air have nests but the Son of Man has not where to lay his head'), which he seems to regard as secondary, he goes on to specify 'the kinds of resemblance possible between syllables'. These are five in number: musical *pitch*, length or time or *quantity*, *stress* or emphatic accent, 'likeness or sameness of letters and this some or all and these vowels or consonants and initial or final. This may be called the *lettering* of syllables', and *holding*, 'to which belong break and circumflexion, slurs, glides, slides etc.'. Obviously fully aware a century ago of the now fashionable linguist's distinctions between *langue* and *parole*, *competence* and *performance*, or in this case *principles* and *practice*, Hopkins goes on to mention some inessential features – voice quality, regional accent, loudness and so on – which he seems to consider *performance* features relevant in particular readings or recitations of a poem. After a detailed discussion of quantity, stress and pitch in different languages, with particular reference to stress accent in English and the existence of secondary accent (stress) in such words as *incomprehensible, underneath* (a point clearly relevant in the reading of sprung rhythms), Hopkins goes on to list in full the different syllabic feet recognized in Greek – *pyrrhic* ⌣ ⌣, *spondee* - -, *iamb* ⌣ -, *trochee* - ⌣, and so on, including the *paeonic* feet (as in 'The Windhover': 'falling paeonic rhythm, sprung and outriding'). This means in effect that 'The Windhover' has many four-syllable feet with one of the syllables long and the other three short (paeons), but the rhythm is complicated by being 'sprung'. That is to say that *stress* rather than length of syllable is the key to the rhythm, and that considerable variation is allowed, so that some feet have fewer than four stresses. An *outride* is an extra foot standing outside the dominant scansion pattern as in:

> As a skate's heel sweeps smooth on a bow-bend . . .

Hopkins marks *heel* as an outride, because in his view it must be given heavy stress in any natural reading of the poem, but that is not allowed for in his metre (which here requires five, and not six, feet to the line). He is, as usual, perfectly consistent within the system he sets up, and his reasoning is analogous to that of linguistic scholars, who attempt to set up rules to account for the behaviour of language and then have to account for exceptions to those rules by devising further rules to explain the exceptions. It does not of course follow that Hopkins's own way of describing his practice is necessarily the best way of so doing. It seems to me possible to describe the rhythm of "The Windhover" without recourse to the notion of *outrides*, although it does become important in scanning his later poems, in which whole phrases may lie outside the dominant metrical rules. But it is necessary to understand what Hopkins thought he was doing, and that is why his early notes on *Rhythm and the Other Structural Parts* are so important.

He is absolutely clear on the distinction between *rhythm* and *metre*:

> The repetition of feet, the same or mixed, without regard to how long, is *rhythm*. *Metre* is the grouping of *a certain number* of feet. There is no metre in prose though there may be rhythm.

We shall do well to bear this in mind. Hopkins's poems are written in lines which are regular to the extent that they have a prescribed number of feet (except for outrides), and he would regard this as required in verse. In other words, random variation in the number of feet to a line would produce rhythmic *prose*, and not verse. One of the reasons why James Joyce (who so clearly resembles Hopkins in his treatment of language)[5] can write so freely and so exuberantly is that, being a prose writer, he does not impose upon himself rigid requirements of metric regularity and rhyme-scheme.

We conclude our discussion of Hopkins's rhythm and metre by referring briefly to their development in his later poems. It is obvious that 'Spelt from Sibyl's Leaves' and others have departed a long way from everyday language, and it seems that the stresses required in these poems (unlike those of 'The Deutschland') are not always clearly based on speech. He is insistent (*LB*, 245-6) that 'Sibyl's Leaves' is made for *performance*, reading aloud 'with long rests, long dwells on the rhyme and other marked syllables'. His own directions for stressing clearly show that we must depart from natural stress in such series as *part, pen, pack*, where only the first and last are marked by Hopkins as stressed. Similarly, his stress-marks on pronouns (*Óur tale, O óur oracle*; *wind/ Off hér once skéined*) often seem counter to natural stress. To describe these later poems as artificial (particularly 'The Leaden Echo and the Golden Echo', 'Sibyl's Leaves', 'Harry Ploughman' and 'Tom's Garland') is not to condemn them as bad. It is quite clear that 'Sibyl's Leaves' is to be chanted, almost as if it were music, and it is Hopkins's attempt to bring poetry as close as possible to the purity of music (hence his elaborate notation to indicate which syllables are to be hurried over, etc.) that makes these poems seem so far from current language. In them Hopkins has achieved the limit of his own art and artifice. Of 'Tom's Garland' he wrote (*LB*, 274): 'And I think it is a very pregnant sonnet and in point of execution very highly wrought. Too much so, I am afraid . . .'. Of 'Harry Ploughman', which is 'very highly wrought', he admits that it may strike Bridges as 'intolerably violent and artificial'.

'LETTERING OF SYLLABLES'

Hopkins's poetry is distinguished by its rhythmic subtleties, but many heightened effects of sound are brought about within that general structure by various figures that involve rhyming or chiming of vowels and consonants. End-rhyme is part of the general metrical structure that we have been discussing. Measured in terms of the metre rather than number of syllables, Hopkins's end-rhymes occur at regular intervals, and are part of the necessary properties of verse as he understands it. This is why the end-rhymes frequently do not call attention to themselves whereas alliteration, internal rhymes, echoic effects and so on may stand out very clearly (they are *foregrounded*), as in this example (consonant-rhyme italicized):

> Is out with it! Oh
> We *lash* with the be*st* or wor*st*
> Word *last*! How a *lush-kept* plu*sh-capped* sloe
> Will, mouthed to *flesh*-bur*st*,
> Gu*sh*! – *flush* the man, the being with it, sour or sweet,
> Brim, in a *flash* full! . . .   ('Deutschland', st. 8)

Here Hopkins follows the required metre and rhyme scheme of the poem, but we hardly notice that *Oh* rhymes with *sloe* and *worst* with *burst*. Our attention is drawn much more insistently to the remarkable effects of vowel and consonant rhyme, alliteration and assonance that occur within the lines and throughout the stanza. It is possible to read a Hopkins poem many times and fail to notice particular instances of end-rhyme. It is easy to overlook, for example, a remarkable end-rhyme in this extract:

> But vastness blurs and time' beats level. Enough! the Resur-
> rection,
> A heart's clarion! Away grief's gasping, 'joyless days, de-
> jection.
> Across my foundering *deck shone*
> A beacon, an eternal beam.   (No. 72)

But this is as it should be, for Hopkins did not intend his end-rhymes to call special attention to themselves (they are part of the skeleton of the verse), and the fact that we often miss his unconventional rhymes is a measure of his success. Bridges's strictures on Hopkins's rhymes in the original Preface (reprinted in *Poems* 242–3) merely show that Bridges did not really know how to read the poems (*with the ear*):

> The rhyme to *communion* in 'The Bugler' is hideous, and the suspicion that the poet thought it ingenious is appalling; *eternal*, in 'The Eurydice', does not correspond with *burn all*, and in 'Felix Randal' *and some* and *handsome* is as truly an eye-rhyme as the *love* and *prove* which he despised and abjured.

Bridges's ear surely betrayed him in the last instance (*and some/ handsome*): the rhyme is perfectly good. 'Some of my rhymes I regret' wrote Hopkins in 1883 (*LB*, 180), and in 1885 he wrote to his brother Everard (quoted in *Poems*, 243) that his run-over rhymes were 'experimental, perhaps a mistake', but he tried to justify (rightly, in my opinion) the rhyme on *electric* in 'The Eurydice': 'it must be read "startlingly and rash". It is "an effect".'

There are a few end-rhymes in Hopkins's pre-1880 poems (particularly in 'The Eurydice') which call too much attention to themselves and do seem forced or comic. Bridges cites *boon he on/ communion* (No. 48), and we may add *fully on/bullion* (No. 41), which involves the same kind of affectation in reading if it is to be a perfect rhyme. There may be others ('grubs in amber') in 'The

Eurydice', as Hopkins says, but the last two lines of that poem have always seemed to me excellent:

> . . . till doomfire burn all,
> Prayer shall fetch pity eternal.

The rhyme on *burn all* forces us to read the last word of the poem with that slow emphasis that the poet wants. The effect is hymn-like.

But it is wrong to suggest, as Bridges does, that Hopkins chiefly laboured to find *ingenious* end-rhymes. Some of them *are* ingenious, but this is not the point. The *and some/handsome* rhyme in 'Felix Randal' is, as we shall see, only a small part of the larger phonetic patterning of that poem and is not to be dwelt on for its own sake. Much the same can be said for the unconventional rhymes in this stanza of 'The Deutschland' (in one line the rhyme is 'run-over'):

> She drove in the dark to *leeward*
> She struck – not a reef or a rock
> But the combs of a smother of sand: night *drew her*
> *D*ead to the Kentish Knock;
> And she beat the bank down with her bows and the ride of her
>   keel;
> The breakers rolled on her beam with ruinous shock;
> And canvas and compass, the whorl and the wheel
> Idle for ever to waft her or wind her with, these she *endured*.
>
> (st. 14)

It is only if we read with the eye that the rhymes *leeward/drew her d-/ endured* stand out as odd. If we read with the ear and allow the logic of the rhythm and metre to carry us along, we hardly notice them even though they are perfect rhymes. It is probable that *leeward* was widely pronounced in the old-fashioned nautical way in Hopkins's day (like *bo'sun* and *fo'c'sle*), but even if it was a restricted usage, then this is merely another instance of the poet's purist insistence on using the right word in the right way – as it is used in the trade concerned. It is not archaism.

Although Hopkins sometimes allowed that an end-rhyme might be 'an effect', contrived like a stage-effect for some artistic end, his end-rhyme is often much less obtrusive than his other phonetic effects. It is therefore best seen as forming part of the necessary skeleton of his verse. Without stanza-form, sonnet-form, metre and end-rhyme, Hopkins's poetry would not in his opinion be verse at all. From our point of view, therefore, end-rhyme belongs (apart from some exceptional cases) to the first stage of heightening. It is an imposed structural principle of a kind common to most English poetry, and it is therefore less remarkable than these phonetic features that Hopkins exploits *within* the lines of his verse. These artifices, which also involve the principle of rhyme, are characteristically Hopkinsian. We regard them as belonging to the second stage of heightening. They are referred to in his Lecture Notes as *lettering of syllables*.

Under this heading Hopkins discusses all the features that we find so thickly used in 'The Deutschland' and later poems, some years before he wrote them.

> To this belong rhyme, alliteration, assonance. They are all a sameness or likeness of some or all of the elementary sounds, the letters, of which syllables are made. Syllables so agreeing or resembling may be said to *chime* or widely *rhyme* but we keep rhyme for a more special or narrower sense.

Alliteration, says Hopkins is 'the beginning with the same sound'. A consonant normally alliterates with the same consonant (*m* with *m*, *s* with *s*, and so on), but a vowel can alliterate with any vowel:

> Therefore the line – 'And apt alliteration's artful aid' – alliterates but not for the reason the writer thought, for in the six alliterated syllables there are at least three vowels (reading *and* and *alliteration* without slur), not one only – the hard or dry short *a*; the long shut English *a*; the Italian long *e*; and the long broad *a*.

Hopkins allows that there might be a 'very soft' alliteration between 'a consonant and its belonging aspirate' (i.e. plosive and fricative) – '*p* and *f*, *b* and *v*, etc.' But 'the belonging pairs of sharps and flats, as *p* and *b*, *t* and *d*, *th* in *th*ick and *th* (*dh*) in *th*ere, do not and offend the ear if represented as doing so, just because of their nearness'. Although Hopkins speaks of lettering of syllables, he plainly means sounds (sound segments belonging to phonemic classes) and not letters. He is unusual amongst English poets for his very explicit understanding of the principles of the phonetics of English speech.[6]

He is also unusual for his interest in end-consonant 'rhyme' and his perception that this is a kind of alliteration.

In Icelandic verse an opposite kind of alliteration (skothending) is made use of, namely ending with the same consonant but after a different vowel, as *bad led*, *find band*, *sin run* (from Marsh, who calls it *half-rhyme*). This is also a grace but less marked.

Hopkins's discussion of assonance ('sameness of vowel in syllables' as in *meet/sleep*; *meeting/evil*) is brief, and he is more interested in what he calls *vowelling-off*. Assonance is *vowelling-on*; *vowelling-off* is 'changing of vowel down some scale or strain or keeping'. This *vowelling-off* is not necessarily accompanied by *skothending*, since in vowelling the end-consonants are not necessarily 'rhymed': thus 'On that *lone shore loud moans* the sea' is quoted as an instance of *vowelling-off*, although *lone* and *moans* are actually full rhymes if one ignores the final *s* on *moans*.

Rhyme (what we shall call *full rhyme*) is then defined by Hopkins as a likeness of vowel plus end-consonant in a strong syllable, with a necessary difference of initial consonant. Thus, *no/know* is not a rhyme. Even full rhyme involves variation, and it is important to remember that rhyme in general is not exact reproduction of the same form, but involves both variety and parallelism. 'Commonly the rhymes end the line, sometimes a half-line but in any case mark off certain bars or clauses'. He clearly recognizes the principle of full rhyme (together with other kinds of 'lettering or syllables') as an artifice valid within the line as well as at the end. He then discusses various kinds of imperfect rhyme (*balance/talons/gallants*), eye-rhyme (*love/prove*) unlawful rhyme (e.g. rhyming -*m* and -*n*) and 'licences in rhyme'.

In these lecture notes, Hopkins recognizes many kinds of artifice which are all reducible to the principle of *rhyme*, and he uses these 'verse figures' thickly in the poetry he wrote after that date. Before we go on to consider his use of these figures, however, we must remark on two things.

First, the figures that he discusses in the lecture-notes are to some extent foreshadowed in the etymological notes that we discussed in Chapter 2, particularly in such series as *flick*, *fleck*, *flake*, where he remarks on the different *tones* of the vowels. *Vowelling-off* and *skothending* are clearly suggested in such series; onomatopoeia and echoism, which he remarked on in the etymological notes, are as we shall see not irrelevant to his actual use of the figures. For twelve years before 'The Deutschland', Hopkins had been considering very carefully the principle of rhyme. The second thing that we must notice is that Hopkins was by 1873 aware of the high development of these various figures in *Germanic* poetry. Although he mentions Italian and Greek examples of *vowelling*, he quotes at length only from Old Norse (his example is from G. P. Marsh, *Lectures on the English Language* 1st series, 4th edn., 1863, p. 556):

> It will be seen that all these verse figures . . . are reducible to the principle of rhyme, to rhyme or partial rhyme. Alliteration is initial half-rhyme, 'shothending' [*sic*] is final half-rhyme, assonance is vowel-rhyme. There is a beautifully rich combination of them in Norse poetry, especially of initial and final consonant rhyme leaving out the vowel, the effect of which is not that the vowels go for nothing but that they seem to be sided or intentionally changed, vowelled off. Here is one instance:

> > Hilmir hjalma skurir
> > herðir sverði roðnu,
> > hrjota hvitir askar,
> > hrynja brynja spangir;
> > hnykkja Hlakkar eldar
> > harða svarðar landi,
> > remma rimmu gloðir
> > randa grand of jarli.

This skaldic verse, which was already highly developed by the tenth century, had incredibly complex rules of metre and rhyme. It was court poetry, *heightened* in Hopkins's sense, to such a degree that it was 'unlike itself' – far removed we presume from the 'current language' of the average Norseman. The rules were actually more complex than Hopkins implies. The metre of this stanza is a variant of *drottkvætt*; it had to consist of eight three-stress lines in each of which the last word had to have the stress-pattern: $'\smile$. In this variant of *drottkvætt* all the feet are of this form, with a required stressed long syllable followed by a short unstressed one. Internal rhyme was required – in this case alliteration and *skothending* in the odd lines and full syllable rhyme in the even lines.

Furthermore, this metre also required that the alliteration on the first two feet of the odd lines should carry over to the first foot of the even lines. Most of the other skaldic metres were equally complex, and in all of them various combinations of full rhyme (including end-rhyme) and partial rhyme were required principles of composition.[7]

Surviving examples of Old and Middle English poetry are much less complex than this. In 1882 Hopkins wrote to Bridges (*LB*, 156):

> So far as I know – I am inquiring and presently I shall be able to speak more decidedly – it [sprung rhythm] existed in full force in Anglosaxon verse and in great beauty; in a degraded and doggrel [*sic*] shape in *Piers Ploughman* . . .

Old English verse was indeed scanned by stresses, although there were strict limits on the number of unstressed syllables allowed, but it was required that one or both stresses in the first half-line should alliterate with the first stress of the second half-line. Alliteration was a required principle of composition, and was analogous in this respect to end-rhyme in later poetry. Contrary to the general belief, end-rhyme and near-rhyme or assonance also occurred in Old English and Middle English alliterative verse, but they were not fundamental; they did not enter into the rules of composition. Here are some examples from the twelfth-century alliterative poem, Layamon's *Brut* (MS Caligula), but rhyme also occurs in the tenth-century poetry of Cynewulf (my italics):[8]

> Ah of eou ich wulle *iwiten*   þurh soðen eouwer wurð *scipen*,
> whæt cnihten ȝe *seon*   and whænnenen ȝe icumen *beon*,
> and whar ȝe wullen beon *treowe*   alde and æc *neowe*.
> Þa andswerede þe *oðer*   þat wes þe aldeste *broðer*:
> lust me nu lauerd king   and ich þe wullen cuðen
> what cnihtes we *beoð*   and whanene we icumen *seoð*.

Here, it will be observed, rhyme and near-rhyme are used freely within the general structure, which is a relatively free version of the alliterative stress metre ('degraded and doggrel' if you like). The rhythm is very like sprung rhythm, except that there are probably few monosyllabic feet in the *Brut*.

Hopkins had read very little early English or Germanic verse by 1873, but he had already learnt a good deal about it from his reading; he was aware of the complex metrical requirements of skaldic verse and understood the alliterative principles of Early English verse. The point to note is that, whereas Germanic verse used one or more of the various kinds of half-rhyme as strict, structural requirements in composition, Hopkins used these figures as additional but very important forms of heightening and not as requirements in versification.

One of his most successful exploitations of consonant rhyme is 'Felix Randal' (alliterating consonants italicized):

> Felix Randal the *f*arrier, O is he *d*ead then? my *d*uty all
>   ended,
> Who have watched his *m*ould of *m*an, *b*ig-*b*oned and *h*ardy-
>   *h*andsome
> Pining, *p*ining, till time when *r*eason *r*ambled in it and some
> Fatal *f*our disorders, *f*leshed there, all contended?

It is obvious that alliteration on different sounds is used in the different phrases sometimes linking two breath-groups (*four disorders, fleshed there*), but sometimes the 'rhyming' consonants come on syllables with secondary or light stress. In such cases, the alliteration is, as it were, a background effect and, although we are conscious of it, it is not prominent. Occasionally it links a whole line:

> My *t*ongue had *t*aught thee comfort, *t*ouch had quenched thy
>   *t*ears,

And in the last two lines, alliterative phrases are deliberately raised to prominence:

> When thou at the random grim forge, *powerful amidst peers,*
> Didst fettle for the great grey drayhorse his *bright and battering*
>   sandal!

Internal rhyme is also used, and the most noticeable instance is:

> . . . Impatient he *cursed* at *first* . . .

It may be that this is too prominent, and the effect of *great grey drayhorse* more successful. Assonance (vowelling) is also seen in this example and elsewhere.

But the most important phonetic heightening in this poem is brought about by a combination of syllable-rhyme and *skothending*, which operates throughout the poem, and includes the rhyming words *ended, contended, mended, offended, Randal, sandal*. The primary effect is on disyllabic words with stressed syllables ending in *-nd*, but there are related effects on *-ld*, *-n*, *-mb*, *-nt*, and *-d*.

Felix *Randal* the farrier, O is he *dead* then? my *duty* all *ended*,
Who have watched his *mould* of man, big-*boned* and hardy-
    handsome
Pining, pining, till time when reason *rambled* in it *and some*
Fatal four *disorders*, fleshed there, all *contended*?

Sickness broke him. Impatient he cursed at first, but *mended*
Being *anointed* and all; though a heavenlier heart *began some*
Months earlier, since I had our sweet reprieve and *ransom*
Tendered to him. Ah well, *God* rest him all *road* ever he *offended*!

This seeing the sick *endears* them to us, us too it *endears*.
My tongue had taught thee comfort, touch had quenched thy
    tears,
Thy tears that touched my heart, *child* Felix, poor Felix *Randal*.

How far from then forethought of, all thy more boisterous
    years,
When thou at the *random* grim forge, powerful amidst peers,
Didst fettle for the great grey *drayhorse* his bright and battering
    sandal!

No poem could be a clearer vindication of 'current language heightened'. The heavily consonantal structure of English speech is here exploited as no one before or after Hopkins has ever exploited it. The *skothending* and syllable-rhyme extend from the blacksmith's name in the first line to *sandal* in the last and pick out particularly the words *tendered* and *random* within the lines. Hopkins's metaphor of the horseshoe as *sandal* is daring and far-fetched, and reminds one of the Old Norse or Old English *kenning* in which apparently irrelevant associations may be yoked together by violence.[9] Hopkins ought to be implying that the drayhorse walked on sand, but he is not. The metaphor ought therefore to be unsuccessful, but for some reason it works. Almost certainly, we accept it because of the insistent rhyme and *skothending* on *-nd*, which dominates the sound-structure of the poem.

Hopkins indicates in his lecture-notes that a 'soft' alliteration is possible between related stops and fricatives (*p* and *f*, for instance), but objects to full rhymes on *n* and *m* because 'though they are like enough roughly to satisfy the ear they offend the mind by the essential difference between a labial and a dental'. He is too scrupulous to use a full end-rhyme such as *stain/same*, although other poets have been less scrupulous. But he has no objection to assonance and other kinds of partial rhyme within the lines: *rambled* in the third line has so much in common with *Randal*, *random*, *handsome* in its sound-structure that the variation on *-nd*, *-mb* is pleasing. The same can be said of of *anointed* in the sixth line, which chimes or partially rhymes with other trisyllabic words in the poem: *disorders, contended, offended*. Common to all of these is the dental (alveolar) sound at the end of the stressed syllable. Even the choice of the dialectal *road* for 'way' is partly conditioned by the consonantal structure of the poem: *all road* is less idiomatic in Northern dialect than 'any road', and *all road ever* is not idiomatic at all (see Commentary). The 'current language' in the poet's mind would be something like: 'Ah well, God rest him and forgive him for his sins'. This is 'translated' or heightened in accordance with the requirements of the dominant sound-structure of the poem and at the same time *suggests* local dialect. As John Wain remarks, it communicates something of the demotic flavour of the smith. But it is not itself dialect.

In the first half of the sestet, the emphasis on voiced alveolars and related sounds is reduced, and the dominant chiming is on voiceless sounds, particularly *t*. In the word *endears, -nd* occurs at a syllable boundary rather than at the end of a stressed syllable, and is not so prominent. The second line alliterates on *t*, but nearly all the consonants in this, and in the first breath-group in the third line, are *voiceless*. The voiced consonants that occur tend to be in unstressed words, or in positions where voicing is normally reduced owing to the proximity of voiceless sounds: *mf, nch*, for instance (note that the final sound of *quenched* and *touched*, despite the spelling, is *t*):

> My tóngue had táught thee cómfort, tóuch had quénched thy
> téars
> Thy téars that tóuched my héart . . .

This passage is signalled by the prominent *tendered* in line 8, with its initial *t* and convenient ambiguity in meaning. The emphasis has switched from the strength of the farrier and his rebelliousness in his last illness, to a passage of quiet tenderness. In *whispering*, only voiceless consonants can occur, and their use in these lines emphasizes the contrast between quietness and the noisy turbulence of the first and last sections of the poem. In English, voiceless stop consonants, especially initial ones, are aspirated; that is to say that, after the tongue makes contact with the lips, teeth, the teeth-ridge, or the soft palate, there is a sudden release of air, like an *h*. Clearly, this fact of English phonology is used by the poet to emphasize the effect of whispering. Nor is it wholly accidental that the consonants used by Hopkins are those in which the tip and blade of the *tongue* come most into play; nor indeed would Hopkins regard it as coincidental that the word *tongue* itself should begin with a tongue-tip consonant. Characteristically, the physical facts of speech are exploited to suggest the sense of *touch*, for in such words as these the speaker is most conscious of the tongue lightly *touching* the teeth and teeth-ridge.

'Felix Randal' is a successful example of Hopkins's striving to suggest or reinforce aspects of *meaning* by careful manipulation and arrangement of *sounds*. By his own standards as set out explicitly or implicitly in his diaries, Journal and letters, it seems to be one of his best poems. The sound-sense relationships of the undergraduate etymologies, the various principles of rhyme set out in the lecture-notes, and the injunction to 'read with the ear' are all clearly relevant here. It is not too far-fetched to suggest that the *heightening* consists of a careful manipulation of the sounds of English to reinforce meaning by suggesting the violence, agitation and the rhythmic noise of the blacksmith's trade in the octave and final lines, and contrasting this with quietness and tenderness in the first three lines of the sestet.

We must now, more generally, consider alliteration, *skothending*, internal rhyme, assonance and vowelling-off as devices for heightening current language. Very seldom can we say that in a particular section, one, and only one, of these devices is used, although some poems use them much less thickly than others. It is characteristic of Hopkins to extend a subsidiary phonetic feature of a particular phrase to immediately succeeding ones (we shall label this *gradience* and discuss it later), and it is essential to understand that the phonetic effects of particular phrases and word-groups tend to be woven into the structure of whole poems, in a complex way. Furthermore, the devices of 'rhyme' that Hopkins distinguishes are not all of the same order. Clearly, vowelling-off (*gradation*) can be seen as an *effect* of keeping the consonant-structure constant (as in, for example, *drink, drank, drunk*), through alliteration and *skothending*. One is a *result* or *effect* of the others. Vowel alliteration (in which any vowel can alliterate with any other) is clearly one aspect of vowelling, and a series like *earnest, earthless, equal* can be seen either as vowel alliteration or as vowelling-off. Usually, but not always, it appears that Hopkins used initial and final consonant rhyme as his primary devices, and that these devices (mixed to some extent with play on the vowels) result in bringing about widespread *effects* of *vowelling-off*. There are good reasons for regarding consonantal devices as primary. English is rich in consonants divided into various series (according to place and manner of articulation and whether voiced or voiceless) and in consonant clusters (*sk-, skr-, skl, st-, str-* and many others). Hopkins, as we have seen, thought that semi-alliteration between related series could be allowed only between plosives and fricatives: *p* and *f* perhaps, or *b* and *v*. Thus, *thou hast bound bones and veins in me* has semi-alliteration of *b* with *v*. Otherwise, however, it was not permissible, and Hopkins did not allow himself complete freedom to alliterate on other related pairs. Consonantal devices, therefore, must be relatively restricted, whereas vowels, for Hopkins, could be *freely* varied. As it happens, English is also very rich in vowel-distinctions, and one of Hopkins's great contributions to English verse is to exploit this particular wealth of English within relatively ordered frameworks of mainly consonant 'rhyme'. Phoneticians distinguish twenty or more distinct vowel phonemes in the 'received pronunciation' of Southern British English, as against the five or six of Italian or Spanish.[10] Clearly, full rhyme is easy to find in these latter languages. English, however, is relatively poor in full rhyme, but ideally suited to Hopkins's vowelling (gradation), or 'changing of vowel down some scale or strain or keeping' as he so memorably puts it.

Alliteration is everywhere in Hopkins's poetry. Commonly, it is used to 'bind' two or three words in a phrase or half-line, and within the line as a whole there may be two or more separate alliterating series. Here are some examples:

It *gathers* to a *greatness* / like the *ooze* of *oil*   (No. 31)

The *bright boroughs* / the *circle citadels* there! (No. 32)

Re*buffed* the *big* wind. / My *heart* in *hiding* (No. 36)

And *thicket* and *thorp* are merry
With *silver-surfed* cherry (No. 42)

Not *mood* in him nor *meaning* / proud *fire* or sacred *fear*
(No. 45)

In *coop* and *comb* / the *fleece* of his *foam* (No. 56)

Man, how *fast* his *firedint*, / his *mark* on *mind*, is gone
(No. 72)

Often, it will be noticed, the second half of such lines contains a phrase which is in apposition to the first half: the *bright boroughs* and *circle citadels* are variant phrases referring to the same thing. Similar devices are commonplace in Old English verse. Hopkins, even more than Old English poets, extends these parallel phrases into series so that they may become lists of *items*, all in apposition to, or co-ordinate with, the head-phrase. We shall discuss this further in the following chapters.

Sometimes, but more rarely, alliteration is the main phonetic principle used to bind a whole line. This is more obviously so in the earlier mature poems (Nos. 28–42), the phonetic organization of many of the later ones being much more complex. Again, Hopkins's practice is similar to, though not identical with, Old English, in which two half-lines are obligatorily linked by alliteration. I quote some examples:

Over again I *feel* thy *finger* and *find* thee.

('Deutschland', st. 1)

And wears man's *smudge* and share's man's *smell*: the *soil*
(No. 31)

And all *trades*, their gear and *tackle* and *trim*. (No. 37)

It may also carry over from one line to another:

. . . why wouldst thou *rude* on me
Thy *wring*-world *right* foot *rock*? . . . (No. 64)

We are not accustomed to notice *skothending* (end-consonant rhyme) when it occurs in English. Hopkins uses it very liberally.

Often, it combines with another device; thus when it is used together with vowel-rhyme (assonance) it results in full rhyme: 'the *goal* was a *shoal*; . . . he *cursed* at *first*; . . . and in *comb* the fleece of his *foam*; . . . dough, *crust, dust*; . . . scooped *flank, lank/* Rope-over thigh; . . . *skeined, stained, veined* variety'. These full internal rhymes are not always entirely pleasing in their effect. They seem to me to be most acceptable under four conditions: first, when the rhyming items are also semantic 'rhymes' or closely grammatically, or referentially, linked (thus 'the goal was a shoal' seems good to me); second, when they are justified by the dominant rhythm and metre (as in 'in coop and in *comb* the fleece of his *foam*); third, when they are at some distance from one another (*treadmire* in No. 72, l. 9, rhymes with *bonfire* in line 10); fourth, when they are only part of a more complex phonetic series in which other devices are involved (*skeined, stained, veined* in No. 61 also relates to *wind* in the previous line). Note that *he cursed at first* in 'Felix Randal' is not justified by these conditions, and therefore appears to be more contrived. In combination, however, with other rhymes and other devices, such rhyming can be very effective indeed:

> Stones *ring*; like each tucked *string* tells, each *hung* bell's
> Bow *swung* finds *tongue* to *fling* out broad its name;
> Each mortal *thing* does one *thing* and the same: (No. 57)

Skothending also occurs in combination with alliteration. In syllables which have a simple CVC structure, the effect of this is to keep constant the consonantal framework of the syllables while the vowel varies. When the syllable-structure is a little more complex, the effect is, if anything, better. In most of the following quotations, the consonant structure is constant but in at least one it is slightly varied:

> I am *soft sift*
> In an hourglass . . .   ('Deutschland', st. 4)

> And *canvas* and *compass*, the *whorl* and the *wheel*   (st. 14)

> . . . *heeds* but *hides, bodes* but *abides*;   (st. 32)

> Generations have *trod*, have *trod*, have *trod*;
> And all is seared with *trade*; . . .   (No. 31)

> Whatever is *fickle, freckled* (who knows how?)   (No. 37)

... as a *stal*lion *stal*wart ...   (No. 38)

On meadow and river and *wind-wand*ering *weed-wind*ing bank.
                                                     (No. 43)

... *wrink*les, *rank*ed *wrink*les deep   (No. 59)

... Let life, *wan*ed,
  ah let life *wind*   (No. 61)

... This to *hoard* un*heard*,
Heard un*heed*ed, leaves me a lonely began.   (No. 66)

This *Jack, joke* ...   (No. 72)

Simple *skothending* is itself an important device in Hopkins's poetry. We have noticed it in 'Felix Randal', where it was largely associated with nasal consonants and clusters consisting of nasals (*n*, *m*, *ng*) and another consonant. Many of Hopkins's *skothendings* are nasal consonants or combinations consisting of *l* plus *d*.

                     ... has wi*ld*er, wilful-wavier
Mea*l-d*rift mou*ld*ed ever and melted across skies? (No. 38)

Ma*n*'s mou*n*ting spirit in his bo*n*e-house, mea*n* house,
  dwells   (No. 39)

Left-ha*nd*, off la*nd*, I hear the lark asce*nd*,
  His rash-fresh re-wi*nd*ed, new-skeined score   (No. 35)

                     O why are we so
haggard at the heart ... so fa*gg*ed, so fashed, so co*gg*ed, so cumbered
                                                     (No. 59)

                     womb-of-all, *home*-of all,
hearse-of-all night   (No. 61)

But plainly, the simple devices of alliteration and *skothending* tend to be mixed with others in a complex way. If alliteration and *skothending* are used together, the effect is strict vowelling-off or *gradation*. If only alliteration is used and the final consonant varies, then there may be a looser kind of vowelling-off. This is a frequent effect in Hopkins's poetry:

When weeds, in wheels, shoot *long* and *lovely* and *lush* (No. 33)

Shivelights and in shadowtackle in *long lashes lace*, *lance*, and pair
                                                     (No. 72)

Over again I *feel* thy *finger* and *find* thee. ('Deutschland', st. 1)

Sometimes, in such cases, we encounter vowel-rhyme (*assonance*) either alone or in combination. *Great grey drayhorse* is a case of assonance with consonant variation. When *skothending* is used, on the other hand, additional vowel-rhyme will result in full rhyme (as we have seen), whereas *skothending* without vowel-rhyme will produce the looser kind of vowelling off that we have distinguished.

Vowelling-off (gradation) is one of the greater glories of Hopkins's poetry. Some may judge it more effective when it is not too obviously accompanied by insistent and repeated consonantal devices. The effectiveness of the *skate's heel* image of 'The Windhover' owes much to the 'scale or strain of keeping' down which Hopkins varies the vowels. Nine different vowels can be distinguished in the eleven words which carry natural sentence-stress; the two repetitions occur only consecutively where extra emphasis is wanted; no vowel is repeated at a later stage:

As a skate's heel sweeps smooth on a bow-bend: the hurl and
    gliding
Rebuffed the big wind.

The order is long *e* →long *i* (repeated) →long *u* →long *o* (*bow*) → short *e* (*bend*) →long central vowel (*hurl*) →diphthong *ai* →short *u* →short *i* (repeated). Consonant devices are also present, but it can be argued here that they are not too insistent and are subsidiary in their effect to the elaborate vowel figure.

It is chiefly in his later poetry that Hopkins uses the most complex combination of these devices with the most complex sound-effects. 'The Leaden Echo and the Golden Echo' (No. 59) is a poem in which sound effect is very important (its theme would lead us to expect this), and the poet's own directions for reading 'Spelt from Sibyl's Leaves' ('The sonnet shd. be almost sung: it is most carefully timed in *tempo rubato*': LB, 245–6) suggest the same conclusion. Frequently, and especially in such poems, we cannot say that any one phonetic device necessarily dominates; they are used in a very complex way, often giving rise to the strange 'mirror' effect noticeable in line 3 of the following:

Earnest, earthless, equal, attuneable, vaulty, voluminous,
    . . . stupendous

Evening strains to be time's vast, womb-of-all, home-of-all,
    hearse-of-all night.
Her *fond yellow hornlight wound* to the *west*, her *wild*
    hollow hoarlight hung to the *height*
Waste . . .   (No. 61)

The full phonetic orchestration of these lines (and of the remainder
of this poem) is not easy to describe, and it is also mixed with
grammatical, semantic and etymological play of various kinds
(which complicate the matter still further). The vowel alliteration
of the first three words is taken up by *evening* in the second line;
attuneable, voluminous, stupendous have a vowel echo; *vast, west* and
waste are carefully distributed so as to point to a connection in
form and suggest a connection in meaning. Successive stages of
the pattern are not necessarily linked phonetically to stages
immediately preceding.

Such a passage is difficult to explain in terms of a single dominant phonetic device, or to reduce to any hierarchical ordering of
the devices used, with one dominant and the others subsidiary.
However, it is possible to describe one at least of Hopkins's most
characteristic complex devices in a consistent way. This is what we
shall label *gradience*; it is a kind of extended 'rhyming'.

It is noticeable that Hopkins's lines are often organized in *steps*,
in which a phonetic characteristic (say, alliteration), present but
not necessarily dominant in the first step, is taken up by the
second, which at the same time usually abandons the dominant
principle of the first; the third then takes up a subsidiary phonetic
effect of the second, again abandoning the dominant, and so on.
We may demonstrate *gradience* first by a simple example (in what
follows the *steps* are marked off by vertical lines):

The down-dugged / ground-hugged / grey
                                    ('Deutschland', st. 26)

The first step is unified by alliteration on *d*; the second abandons
this, but links itself to the first by vowel (and consonant) rhyme (in
this case so nearly completely that step 2 is an 'echo' of step 1).
Finally, the third step abandons rhyme and is linked to the second
by alliteration on *gr*.

Hopkins's fondness for lists of synonyms or near-synonyms, or
of items grammatically in apposition to one another, allows him
considerable scope for phonetic gradience. We may best demon-

strate it in a table, in which bracketed figures label devices which
link with the *previous* step. Often, it will be seen, a particular step
may itself have a dominant device which characterizes it alone.

TABLE I

1	2	3	4
flint-flake	b*l*ack-ba*ck*ed	in the regular	
	(1) (1)	*bl*ow	
		(2)	
wiry	and white-*fiery*	and *wh*irlwind-	*s*now
	(1)	(2)	(3)
		swivellèd	
Stanching,	o*c*ean	of a *motion*able	*m*ind
quenching	(1)	(2)	(3)
in all that toil	that *coil*	since (seems) I	
	(1)	*k*issed the rod	
		(2)	
cloud puffball	torn t*uf*ts	*t*ossed pillows	fla*un*t forth
	(1)	(2)	(3)? or (2)?
poor potsherd	*p*atch	ma*tch*wood	im*m*ortal diamond
	(1)	(2)	(3)

The paradigmatic example of a *gradience* is the first line of 'The
Leaden Echo'. This starts by stating the end-point of the gradience
(the word *keep*), then moves away and slowly returns through a
linked string of devices to the word *keep* at the end of the line:

TABLE 2

How to keep –

or *k*ey to *k*eep	*k*	8
*l*atch or catch	*l*	7
la*c*e	*acc*	6
or *br*aid or *br*ace	*br*	5
b*o*w or broo*ch*	*o*	4
*n*owhere *kn*own *s*ome	*n, s*	3
is there *n*o*n*e such	*n*	2
is there a*n*y, a*n*y		1

There are eight stages in this concatenation. The first is not
connected with *How to keep*, since its head-word, *any*, has neither
vowel nor consonant in common with *keep*. The second step
(ignoring the *semantic* relation between *any* and *none*, which is also

important) 'rhymes' on *n*, particularly syllable-final *n*. The third step takes up two features of the second. The primary feature is initial alliteration on *n*. This comes on the strong stresses: *nowhere*, *known*. The link between *such* and *some* (which differ only in their final consonant) is secondary. The fourth step is linked by the vowel *o*: *bow* and *brooch* 'rhyme' with *no-*, *known*. The fifth step alliterates with the fourth on *b* or *br*. The sixth takes up the rhyme on *brace* changing the initial consonant; the seventh alliterates *latch* with *lace* (in the sixth), and the eighth alliterates *key* and *keep* with *catch* (of the seventh). In addition, most steps are internally linked by some phonetic scheme. Thus, in the second, *none* and *such* have vowel-rhyme between themselves at the same time as their initial consonants provide the linking device to the third step; *braid* and *brace* are linked by their initial consonants to the previous step, but have vowel-rhyme themselves; *latch* and *catch* are full rhymes (semantically as well, since they are, or can be, synonyms), with the initial *l* reaching back to the previous step, and initial *k* pointing forward to the next. The vowels are not repeated in the gradience, except in adjacent steps when vowel-rhyme is itself the link (long *o* in 3–4 and long *e* as in *lace*, in 5–6). The series is: (1) short *e* (*any*) →(2) short *u* (*none*) →(3, 4) long *o* (*known, bow*) →(5, 6) long *e* (*brace, lace*) →(7) short *a* (*latch*) →(8) long *i* (*key*).

There is, as always, an additional subtlety in Hopkins, and we have already remarked on it. Not only are the steps in this series phonetically linked, they are also linked semantically. The words in Hopkins's list are not full synonyms (except possibly *latch* and *catch* when the latter 'means' a *door-latch*), but they all refer to items that are used, or can be used, to restrain, or hold back, or close something in. They belong roughly to the same semantic *field*, and this tendency of Hopkins to give lists of items that are closely related semantically can be seen as an extension of his principle of rhyme (or partial rhyme) to the sphere of meaning as well as sound. Plainly this is foreshadowed in the undergraduate etymological lists, where sound and sense are obviously considered to be related, and we shall further consider the point. *Earliest stars / earlstars / stars principal* is a semantic-etymological gradience. Grammatical *gradiences* are in themselves hardly possible, but sometimes a phonetic gradience shows additionally a marked grammatical parallelism of the steps, as in '*womb-of-all / home-of-all / hearse-of-all* night'.

It is characteristic of a simple gradience not to repeat a particular
principle of organization in steps which are not consecutive; two-
step figures (although sometimes complex) are necessarily consecutive and are not sufficiently extended to be called gradiences.
The following examples have the makings of gradience but fail to
follow out the concatenative principle:

> ... that *country* and *town* | did
> Once *encounter* in ... (No. 44)

> Let life, *waned|* ah let life *wind|*
> Off her once *skeined* ... (No. 61)

In the first example, the phonetic characteristics of the first step are
conflated in the second, and the figure is therefore completed; in
the second, the third step reverts to the first and a new series is
developed on *skeined/stained/veined* variety. If we take the series
waned/wind as belonging to the longer series we have to recognize
that, although gradience occurs, the dominant principle involved
in the set is full rhyme; on this principle, and not on concatenation,
the series is built up.

Sometimes a gradience can be interrupted by the introduction of
a new principle, only to be recapitulated in a further step. In the
following, the interrupting step is bracketed:

> Delightfully/ the *bright* wind/ *b*oisterous/(ropes, wrestles,)/*b*eats
> earth *b*are (No. 72)

The possibility of such interruption leads in complex cases to the
further development of the *interrupting* (secondary) figure and even
the conflation of the primary with the secondary series. In the
following quotation the *steps* of the primary figure are capitalised:

> O why are we so
> HAGGard at the heart/ so care-coiled/ care-killed/ so FAGGed/
> so fashed/ so COGGed/ so cumbered (No. 59)

The second step (*care-coiled*) does not follow from the first, and the
fourth refers back to the first, ignoring the intervening steps. The
sixth step (*cogged*) does not follow from the fifth, but is related to
the main series (*Haggard, fagged*) by *skothending* and also to the
secondary series (*care-coiled, care-killed*) by alliteration. It conflates
the two series, and the series continues to completion in a seventh

alliterating step (*cumbered*). The following diagram demonstrates the organization:

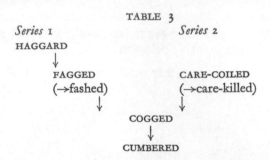

TABLE 3

Series 1	*Series* 2
HAGGARD	
↓	
FAGGED	CARE-COILED
(→fashed)	(→care-killed)
↓	↓
COGGED	
↓	
CUMBERED	

While it is true that many of Hopkins's lines are organized on a concatenative principle, the phonetic organization of some of his later poems is often so complex that we have to recognize that it cannot be described as based mainly on consecutive series. Commonly there is a dominant principle (*skothending*, as above or in 'Felix Randal', or alliteration) to which the poet returns at intervals, and development of subsidiary figures which are not necessarily linked with one another. We may conclude this discussion by considering the following lines from 'Heraclitean Fire' (words relevant to the dominant figure are italicized):

> *Squandering* ooze to *squeezed* dough, crust, dust; *stanches*,
>   starches
> *Squadroned* masks and manmarks treadmire toil there
> Footfretted in it. Million-fueled, nature's bonfire burns on.
> But *quench* her bonniest, dearest to her . . .

Squandering is the head-word of the figure. Its initial consonants are taken up in *squeezed* (which conflates the *squ* and the *z* of *ooze*, with vowelling-off); its vowel (+*n*) is taken up in *stanches*; *squadroned* in the next line recalls *squandering*, but the principle is not developed in this line or the next; in the fourth line *quench* conflates characteristics of *squandering* and *stanch*. It most clearly recalls *stanch*; arguably, it belongs to the same semantic field, and it is used here as a phonetic link between the description of the first three lines and the analogy with Man to be developed later. Otherwise, there is a number of alliterative and rhyming figures in the lines, and some of these show development within themselves.

We may now return to Hopkins's claim that poetry should be 'the current language heightened', and summarize our conclusions. Hopkins's phonetic link with the current language is the principle of sprung rhythm, which is fundamentally the sentence rhythm of speech. His partial rejection of a syllable-counting metre enables him to exploit the variety of speech-rhythm, most memorably in 'The Deutschland'. But at the same time Hopkins imposes on himself strict metrical and stanzaic rules (the first stage of heightening, which is common to all, or most, poetry), and the tension between this and the variety of sprung rhythm creates a language which is heightened speech. To this he adds various devices grouped under the principle of *rhyme*, which have the effect of extreme heightening and are used in a subtle and complex way. These devices apply to poems which are in standard rhythm and to those in sprung or mixed rhythm. We have noticed that in certain late poems the heightening through phonetic devices of rhythm and 'rhyme' is so elaborate that these poems depart considerably from current language, but in Hopkins's own unique way and according to his own principles. The inscape of the words is 'dwelt on' (*JP*, 289). In these, his attempts to inscape *sound* have reached their most extreme form, and are partly influenced by his concern with the analogy between linguistic sound and musical sound.

CHAPTER 6

Wordscape: Hopkins's Vocabulary

꧁꧁꧁꧁꧁꧁

I T is relatively easy to describe in a general way the main characteristics of Hopkins's lexicon, to note its differences from the usage of other poets, to point to the origin of much of it in dialect, trade usage and colloquial English, and even to show the development of this special 'enabling' language in his diaries and Journal. In our discussion of the formative influences on Hopkins's concept of 'current language', we gave considerable attention to the nature and sources of this vocabulary. Hopkins favours monosyllabic words of early English origin (usually Anglo-Saxon, Scandinavian or early Norman French), which are currently or potentially used in two or more parts-of-speech classes (*catch, coil, comb, ruck*). Many have phonaesthetic or etymological associations within connected series (*st-, sk-, fl-, gr-* series and others are listed in the diaries; *trod* and *trade* are etymologically connected; *dew: degged* is an etymological doublet). In their form, some of these words are not standard English (*pash, mammock, slogger*), but more often words which are standard in form are used in senses which are not the normal standard ones. Sometimes a dialectal sense must be invoked (*road*, No. 53), and this is often difficult to separate from the usage of traditional crafts and trades (*random* in No. 53 is a localized usage, but it is also specific to masonry). Yet others (*pitch, sake, -scape*) have developed specific Hopkinsian usages, usually in the prose of the Journal. Like the others, these tend also to be words of early English origin, and they are part of the linguistic purism and *in-earnestness* that we discussed in Chapter 3. Sometimes Hopkins explains the meaning of these key terms in his prose writings, and other general terms developed for the craft of description (*siding, stall* and the like) are frequent in the Journal. Hopkins's exploitation of etymology (even though it sometimes becomes a language-game) is also part of his purism and *in-earnestness*. It is not undertaken for the sake of resuscitating obsolete meanings (any more than his dialectal uses are motivated by a desire to 'preserve' dialect), but because it enables him to exploit and draw attention to patterns and relationships that actually do exist in the language and to return to literal rather than metaphorical senses of many words (thus, *trade* implies the act of treading as well as the derived sense: 'commerce'). The rich semantic texture and suggestiveness of Hopkins's poetry are largely due to his exploitation of these various lexical and semantic patterns. As Norman MacKenzie has noted, many of these words and usages have been wrongly ascribed to the influence of English literary classics (*gear* for example has been ascribed to Spenser). Overwhelmingly, the sources of Hopkins's lexicon lie, not in the classics, but in his observation of the patterns of current language, aided by knowledge derived from dictionaries and language scholarship.

But the relation of Hopkins's poetic uses of this vocabulary to its sources in the language is complex and difficult to explain. Every reader of Hopkins experiences difficulty in knowing the precise meaning of a word in a given context. Some ordinary words, like *buckle* in 'The Windhover', are notorious cruxes, but many others which have been less often discussed, are equally troublesome. What precisely does the poet mean by *pied and peelèd May* or *belled fire* or *disseveral*? If we do not fully understand them, our understanding of his poetry is limited to that extent. When the word is not a normal standard word at all (*brandle*, *sloggering*), we may think we have found the answer by tracing a dialectal or historical origin, only to discover that the dialectal or 'original' meaning does not quite fit the use in context. There is also a set of favourite Hopkinsian words, which constitute his basic vocabulary for describing inscape (*skelned*, *rope*, *comb*, *ruck*, *bow* and others). These stand out because they often depart from expected norms and, although we usually understand them in an obvious sense, we do not fully grasp or 'catch' them unless we are aware of a complex set of semantic associations which they usually carry. Their inscape 'must be dwelt on'.

We do not *explain* the special effect of this rich language by merely stating that individual words are of provincial or early English origin. We must also ask why he uses these words and not others, and consider them in relation to his methods of heightening language in context in the poetry. The word *doom* occurs three times in his completed mature poems (*doomfire* and *doomsday* once each); *comb(s)* four times; *coil* once (also *care-coiled*); *rack* five times. They stand out because they occur where we might expect a different word, and their choice is conditioned by Hopkins's ideas about language in general and the phonetic, grammatical or semantic effects he wants to achieve in given contexts. The kinds of example we must bear in mind as we discuss his lexical usage are these: why does the poet prefer *braids of thew* to, for example, 'cords of muscle'; or *of a fourth the doom to be drowned* to 'of a quarter the fate to be drowned'? It is less relevant to suggest that Hopkins might be conditioned by metre and rhythm than it would be to suggest it of other poets: sprung rhythm gives freedom. Other phonetic devices such as alliteration and vowelling may be more important, but they are only part of an explanation (*fate* is indeed a puny word beside *doom*), since semantic associations are relevant too. The obvious preference in these passages for Anglo-Saxon words (*braids, thew, fourth, doom*) is hardly more of an explanation, since we must further ask *why* Anglo-Saxon words should be preferable. The answer to this is broadly a semantic one. As we noted in Chapter 2, native English words contract much more complex, subtle and far-reaching networks of relationship within the language than do Classical borrowings, and that is so whether the relationships are grammatical, semantic or phonaesthetic. Such words can be said to have more 'meaning' in the sense that they have more associations, and one word from the set (e.g. *stalwart*, from the *stand, stall, stallion, stead, steady* set) suggests the 'meaning' of one or more of the others and partakes of some of their 'meanings' by association. *Doom* is a more sublime and magnificent word than *fate* partly because it belongs to a set that includes *doomsday*. Similarly, as some semanticists argue, a word commonly used in everyday speech (therefore usually Anglo-Saxon) may pick up associations from the collocations in which it is frequently used; thus, in a sense *dark* is part of the 'meaning' of *night* and *night* part of the 'meaning' of *dark*.[1] Again, since they are more frequently used, it is Anglo-Saxon and other early English words that we are most likely to 'know' in this way by the company they keep.

WORD-SYSTEMS

In this chapter it is our task to explore how Hopkins employs and selects from the vocabulary of current language to heighten his language, to make us savour words for their own sake as he savours them, to give them richer meaning and association than they have in ordinary speech, and make them 'ring' or echo their whole beings. In this we must remember two things. Hopkins believed that sound could echo sense, and he also believed that language, like nature, conformed to natural laws in that it was organized and structured in consistent and systematic ways. We shall discuss these two points in order.

First, as we have seen, modern linguistic scholars take perfectly seriously the idea of *phonaesthesia*, not to the extent of believing that there is necessarily universal phonetic symbolism and that languages are based on strict onomatopoeia, but they do agree that, within particular languages, certain phonetic structures may carry sense associations of various kinds. Hopkins's 'etymological' series are based on associations that are psychologically real for speakers of the language. It is a pity that literary critics in speaking of spiralling vowels and thundering consonants have so often descended to gibberish through a failure to read with the ear and through confusion of spelling with sound.[2] The experiments described by Roger Brown establish that people do tend to associate back vowels and open front vowels (e.g. *u* as in *doom*, *o* as in *road*, *a* as in *dance*, *bad*) with magnitude, and the other front vowels with smallness. Thus a *roll* is 'large', and a *reel* relatively 'small' (Hopkins exploits this; see Commentary), *doom* is a 'large' word, *fate* a 'small' one. Similarly, consonants can be arranged along a scale of relative 'brightness'; voiceless consonants are 'brighter' than voiced, and of the voiced consonants dental-alveolars (*d*) are 'darkest', labials less 'dark' and palatal-velars (*g* as in *get*) least 'dark'. Plainly, on this scale *doom* is a 'dark' word whereas *fate* is 'bright'. These considerations, even if they are probably more language-specific than Hopkins thought, are plainly of the utmost relevance to his poetry, especially since he seems to have held these views himself.

They are most obviously relevant when Hopkins in his Journal or poems is trying to suggest the sound of something by the words he uses, for example the backdraught of the tide that *shrugged* the stones and *clocked* them together (*JP*, 223). *Click* is a 'small' sound; *clock* a 'large' one. And if Hopkins had coined *sliggering* rather than *sloggering* (of the *brine* in 'The Deutschland'), the sound suggested would be less heavy and sharper. Most would accept that, in our general vocabulary of action, movement and sensation, such words as *thud*, *thump*, *bump* are heavier, larger, darker words than *hit*, *flip*, *kick* and so on. *Flint-flake* waves on a *black-backed* sea are light and sharp, *flecks* on a relatively dark, heavy, rolling background. It is clear that Hopkins is aware of such phonetic suggestiveness, and he often exploits it.

Important as it is to understand that Hopkins believed that many words 'rhyme' with the texture, shape and sense-impressions of the things they stand for, it is probably more important (because it is less obvious) to understand Hopkins's exploitation of structural patterns specific to and inherent in the English language. He was well aware that a language was organized in phonology and grammar and that there were systematic relationships through derivation or phonetic similarity. We have noticed his use of *-le* words in 'Pied Beauty', but from his poetry in general many more may be added, including *brandle*, *buckle*, *cobble*, *dimple*, *nursle*, *throstle* (a thrush), *truckle*, *twindle*, *wimple*. For Hopkins this derivational sub-system was supremely productive. In his diary and Journal he can be seen collecting such provincial uses as *rickles*, *stickles* ('foamy tongues', i.e. the small 'sticks' of water in waterfalls, *JP*, 219), and *grindlestone* for 'grindstone' (*JP*, 191). But he also finds these *-le* words useful in the descriptive prose of the Journal. Clouds are frequently *curdled*; in colour they may be *ruddled* (*ruddle* is related to *red* and is ochre for marking sheep). Carnations are 'powdered with *spankled* red glister', mountains are 'shaped and *nippled*'. Water *wimples*, and the wavy markings in glaciers are *wimplings*. A tree is described 'rubbing and *ruffling* with the water', and other trees *dapple* their 'boles' with shadow. The wind also *dapples*, foam is *cobbled*, and waves are *scuppled*. Hopkins observes a *brindled* heaven, and the lightning streaks in veins of '*riddling* liquid white'.[3] Some of these words are complex coinings (*scuppled*, *spankled* and others will be discussed later), but others can clearly be associated with root forms: *dapple* with *dab*, *brindled* with *brinded* and so on. In one case, Hopkins is kind enough to indicate his derivation by its context: *ruffle* is a derivative of *rub*, phonaesthetically if not etymologically (Onions: 'of unkn. origin'), and its further association with *rough* (and cf. *shuffle*) merely strengthens its meaning. The consonant changes (*b* – *p*, *b* – *f*) in these pairs would not trouble Hopkins at all; they are frequent historical changes, and, as he recognized in his lecture-notes, these consonants are closely related phonetically (in this case they belong to the *labial* series). [4] Similarly, the *b* of *rub* is 'darker' and 'heavier' than the *f* of *ruffle*. In his poetry also, Hopkins frequently helps us to understand a word by placing it in a context where meaning can be 'carried over' from one neighbouring word to another, as with *rubbing* and *ruffling*.

Hopkins was acutely conscious of the interrelationship of pairs like *curd*: *curdle*, *brand*: *brandle* (cf. also *honeysuck* in No. 159), and it is prudent to remember this when we consider *buckle* in 'The Windhover'. He may have believed it to be in some way related to *buck* (which he applies to the leaping, rolling waves in 'The Deutschland'), and we suggest in the Commentary that those critics who believe *buckle* to mean 'collapse' are probably nearly correct. Since Hopkins was fond of semantic blends as well as phonetic ones, we may suggest here that, taking into account his liking for imagery of violent motion and fluid substances, *buckle* may carry with it a suggestion of leaping, thrusting or quick movement (like the *buck* of the waves) together with the idea of *bending* (from a false etymology, OE *bugan*: bend) and collapsing (as the waves of 'The Deutschland' collapse in a flood over the deck). But, however we may view this suggestion, it is undoubtedly important to bear in mind that Hopkins was keenly aware of derivational systems of this kind.

This kind of system is strictly part of the grammar of a language, but since it is relevant to word formation, and does involve meaning, we treat it here as part of our discussion of semantic structure in general. Hopkins uses the normal grammatical resources of the language to derive words from one other by affixation and by compounding. In this way he can create new words not normally recognized as part of the language. Thus, *overvault* (No. 41), *overbend* (No. 61), *under be* (No. 51), are modelled on *overthrow*, *underlie* and the like. They are always potential in the language, and their precise meaning is suggested by their membership of a derivational class. They differ in meaning from *bend over*, *be under* because they are systematically related to words which have a stative (almost permanent state) meaning, as *lie under* (temporarily) differs from *underlie* (with duration, even permanency and rest, implied).[5] The -*le* and -*er* suffixes have a number of possible meanings. Apart from the agent-noun use of -*er* (*bake*: *baker*), they seem very often to have diminutive or frequentative force. Just as he favours prefixed or suffixed derivatives, so Hopkins is capable of back-formations: *encumbered* becomes *cumbered*, *overwhelms* becomes *whelms* (in 'Sibyl's Leaves'); in 'Pied Beauty' the 'normal' word *brindled* becomes *brinded*. Harry Ploughman's muscles, that 'onewhere *curded*, onewhere sucked or sank' are not only like stringy curds, but also *curdled*. Thus, even when such pairs or sets exist in standard usage with standard meanings, Hopkins is capable of using the words in new ways and suggesting new meanings and associations by exploiting the internal relationships in sub-systems which he has perceived in the language. At the level of morphology, this is analogous to the principle of rhyming that he exploits phonetically. Series which alliterate or partly rhyme phonetically are like these derivational series; to a certain extent the derivatives rhyme and have the same 'meaning' as the root forms; to a certain extent they differ. The language enthusiast derives pleasure from such controlled variation in the vocabulary.

The effects of Hopkins's exploitation of these grammatical-semantic relations are various. Words like *disremember* ('Sibyl's Leaves'), *disseveral* ('Heraclitean Fire'), *unchild*, *unfather* ('Deutschland'), *onewhere* ('Harry Ploughman'), *leafmeal* ('Spring and Fall'), *after-comers* ('Binsey Poplars') belong to derivational series. Most of these words require the context in which they occur for the full interpretation of their meaning (or better, *inscape*); but all are at least partly interpretable from their relationships within the language. The prefixes *un-* and *dis-* have various uses, of which Hopkins prefers the *privative* or *reversative* ones. God (in the 'Deutschland') has made him and then almost *unmade* him; in 'Carrion Comfort' he will not *untwist* 'these last strands of man'. To *disremember* is similarly reversative. Something *remembered* can quite logically be *disremembered* (*forgetting* is not necessarily a reversal of remembering, but rather its absence), and the word's exclusion from the general English lexicon is accidental. The meaning of *unchild* and *unfather*[6] is privative – to deprive of children and fathers, or to do away with children and fathers, but the prefixes could potentially have different force; the verbal uses of *to child* (to give birth) and *to father* (to be, or act as, a father) are not parallel. Clearly, to *unfather* could mean 'to cause not to be a father'; to *unchild* someone could similarly mean 'to cause not to be a child'. That Hopkins does not intend these meanings is made obvious largely by the context: 'the widow-making, unchilding, unfathering deeps'. *Disremembering* and *disseveral* belong to contexts in the poems where etymological and phonetic association is important, and our understanding of them depends partly on this. Hopkins suggests relationships of meaning and grammar by using words in consecutive series in which the words concerned seem to have similar reference and by the device of *variation*. The contextual clues in 'Manshape that shone *sheer off, disseveral*, a star' suggest that Hopkins is alluding to the creation of Man in God's image and Christ in Man's shape. *Sheer off* and *disseveral* seem to refer to the *star*, which is Man. The star is distant (*sheer off*); *disseveral*, however, is difficult to interpret. It looks like an adjective formed from *dissever* ('to cut, separate': in this case *dis-* is an intensive, not a reversative, prefix), which would give the meaning *cut off* (and therefore at a distance), and this is reinforced by the pun on *sheer off* (also 'cut off'). But *disseveral* is also interpretable as *dis+several*, with *dis-* acting this time as a negative prefix. In this case, the meaning is 'not several', therefore only *one*, 'unique'. On the semantic level, we can discern here the beginnings of a concatenation of the kind that we have called *gradience* on the phonetic level, in which the terms are linked by common properties: *sheer off* ('pure, clear, shining', and also 'cut off'); *disseveral* ('cut off', and also 'unique'); if a third term had been added, we may speculate that it would have maintained the notion of singularity and added something new. We may also see such a series as an instance of semantic 'rhyme', and note that each word in a series may also carry two or more clear meanings. They are semantic blends, of complex meaning.

The interpretation of Hopkins's coinings or special uses of words depends, therefore, on the relationships contracted by the words in two different dimensions of language: on the one hand, the underlying systems to which the words are made to belong, and on the other, the order in which Hopkins actually employs them – their contexts in the poems. Linguists distinguish these two kinds of relationships as *paradigmatic* (systematic relations within the language by which forms belonging to the same class or system can be substituted for one another in like environments) and *syntagmatic* (sequential relations).[7] Thus, in a phrase such as *the big man*, the sequential relation of the items to one another is syntagmatic, whereas the relation of *big* to the class of adjectives that may be substituted for it is paradigmatic. In this way, word-classes (parts of speech) within the grammar of a language may be defined or delimited; if we further require that substitutable words belong to particular semantic sets (colour-words, adjectives of size, verbs of motion) we are defining particular *semantic fields*. In some of Hopkins's derivatives (*overbend, onewhere*), the paradigmatic relations of the words are alone sufficient to account for their meanings; in others the contexts are necessary, and sequential relations in the text must be invoked. Indeed, it may even be suggested that Hopkins *defines* many such words by his actual use of them in particular contexts, and even that it is one of his purposes to *define* words by *foregrounding* such relationships. As we shall see, the disposition of words in their contexts can sometimes be a more decisive clue to the meaning of the less familiar words than their origins in dialect or elsewhere.

We have seen that systems of derivation (by prefixes and suffixes) play an important part in the sources of Hopkins's vocabulary. As we have indicated in passing, there are also other systematic kinds of relationship in meaning which are not necessarily shown in the surface form (morphology) of the words concerned. Words can be classed as belonging to particular 'semantic fields'[8] (colour words, words for animals, kinship words, various abstract fields), often with superordinate terms of more general reference subsuming more particular terms (*brown*: beige, cocoa; *livestock*: cattle, sheep: cow, ewe). Notoriously, such fields commonly have gaps in them. Common English manages well enough with the word *dog* as a superordinate for 'canine domestic animal', but there is no commonly accepted non-collective term to subsume *cow*, *bull* and *calf*. English has no single word to cover all members of the 'nuclear' family unit, to refer to brothers and sisters all together, or to distinguish between maternal and paternal relatives. Scientists and social scientists have had to invent suitable terms (*canine, sibling*) and we have all, no doubt, sometimes felt the lack of some of these in everyday use. The existence of *lexical gaps* is at least part of the reason for many of Hopkins's coinings; he is not content with a phrase or circumlocution since he is usually anxious to compress and intensify, to inscape words and things together, and to avoid words with relatively slight semantic content (conjunctions and prepositions). Thus, when a single word does not exist for a concept he wants to express, he resorts to derivational systems (*overbend, onewhere*), to telescoping and portmanteau words (*throughther* for 'through one another, mixed up together', *twindles* for 'twitches and dwindles'), to systems of phonetically related words of the kind that his diaries record and which he clearly felt to be semantically related and often *echoic*, to compounding, and to metaphor. It is relevant to observe that all users of language may use such devices (*coolth* has frequently been 'invented' as the opposite of *warmth*; yesterday my young son used *tunch* as a portmanteau – *tea+lunch* – for a late lunch), but in describing, say a pencil (if we have to), we are more likely to say 'that rounded bit of the pencil between the point and the stem, that is left by the pencil-sharpener' than make use of a broadly metaphorical term like '*cone* of the pencil'. Hopkins, unlike the general user of language, was impatient of circumlocution or vagueness. This struggle for clarity, precision and truth is observed first in the notes in his undergraduate diaries and later in much greater detail in the Journal. It is here that we can best observe the development of his poetic vocabulary, the assumptions that underlie it and its systematic nature.

VOCABULARY OF INSCAPE IN THE JOURNAL

Hopkins's Journal is devoted largely to the inscapes of nature. The main topic is cloudscape, but many of his descriptions of sea, rivers, mountains, trees, flowers and field-landscapes are also well known and relevant to his poetry. Many of the topics of his poems are foreshadowed, (e.g. the 'couple-colours' of 'Pied Beauty'), but more precisely his imagery and the word series used in it. Apart from the fact that it is not in rhythm and metre and lacks some of his heightening devices of poetry, the language of the Journal is much the same as that of his poetry, both in the words or imagery used and in the methods of deriving words from the linguistic system. The Journal is the verbal storehouse for Hopkins's mature poetry. (In what follows we italicize words quoted that are significant for his poetry.)

Certain passages are suggestive in a general way of the poetry. In 1870 (*JP*, 200–1), he describes an aurora and sunset suggestive of 'Sibyl's Leaves'. It was 'taken as a sign of God's anger'. The aurora was 'a knot or crown . . . of dull blood-coloured *horns* and dropped long red beams down the sky on every side, each impaling its lot of stars'. In the sunset 'all was big and there was a world of swollen cloud holding the *yellow-rose light* like a lamp . . .' In 1874 (*JP*, 252) he notices a hawk 'hanging on the hover'. 'Chestnuts as bright as coals or spots of vermilion' (*JP*, 189) is the germ of *fresh-firecoal chestnut-falls* and the embers that 'gash gold-vermilion'.

Amongst the actual words favoured in the poetry, we find the following and others in the Journal: *beak, beam, burl, coil, comb, crisp, curd* (of clouds), *dapple, flint* (of waves), *flix, horn, lade, lash, meal, mess, pash, pied, quain, race, rack, ramp, rope* (verb), *ruck, shire, skein, thew, wimpling*, as well as numerous words with *-er* or *-le* suffixes. It is evident that a great many such words are used to describe precise shapes, patterns, textures and movement; the wealth of association that he observed as early as 1863 in the single word *horn* foreshadows these concerns (see Chapter 2).

The *beakleaved boughs dragonish* of 'Sibyl's Leaves' and other later images seem to have their sources in the tree-descriptions of the earlier part of the Journal. In 1866–7 he is concerned with the *whitebeam* (*Poems*, No. 32), the elm, the chestnut, and other trees. Of the oak, he writes (*JP*, 144): 'the organisation of this tree is difficult', and describes oaks (*JP*, 152) as 'tall and upright, sided well and *ricked* distinctly . . . isles of leaf all *ricked* and *beaked*'. Elm leaves 'do not subdivide or have central knots but tooth or *cog* their woody twigs' – perhaps a forerunner of the *cogged* and *cumbered* of 'The Golden Echo'. A chestnut tree has 'noble long *ramping* boughs'. There is probably more than a suggestion of *romp*, or possibly *rant*, in the tide (of 'The Sea and the Skylark') 'that *ramps* against the shore', but it would be a mistake not to remember the ramps or slanting step-like organization of the chestnut boughs. The waves come in ramps, and as they draw back they leave inclined 'steps' marked by lines of foam. It is characteristic of Hopkins to transfer vocabulary used to describe *solid* or *static* objects or substances to *mobile* or *fluid* substances, or *vice versa*. This is seen most clearly in the water descriptions and cloudscapes of the Journal.

Much of what I shall call 'the vocabulary of inscape' – *skeins*, *flix, curds, combs, rack* and so on – is developed in the early years of the Journal in descriptions of clouds and trees, but his attempts to capture solidity in mobile substances are well exemplified in his rather later wind- and waterscapes, and are heralded in 1868 by his careful observation of a flag in the wind (*JP*, 169). Later he comments: 'indeed a floating flag is like wind visible and what weeds are in a current; it gives it *thew* and fires it and bloods it in' (*JP*, 233). Waterfalls, like clouds, 'are not only *skeined* but silky too'. At a distance 'they are like the wax gutturings [*sic*] on a candle and nearer, losing solidity, like rockets when they dissolve and head their way downwards' (*JP*, 172–3). Again in a waterfall, he observes 'the great limbs in which the water is *packed*' and sees how they are '*tretted* like open sponge or light bread-crumb where the yeast has supped the texture in big and little holes' (*JP*, 177). Here a pattern of moving water is captured in a single state by vocabulary that compares it to a soft but solid substance, and a texture is suggested. Similarly, of waves, he comments, 'the slant *ruck* or *crease* one sees in them shows the way of the wind'. The waves, like napkins, have folds in them.

Solid substances or objects, on the other hand, may be implicitly compared to things in motion. Glaciers preserve in themselves the patterns of a former liquid state and the interaction of wind, water and snow. Speaking of wavy shapings in glaciers he comments (*JP*, 177): 'So water does in fact, wimpling, but these wimplings have the air of being only resultants or accumulations'. Later (*JP*, 178), the snow in a glacier, which is lying in irregular wavy patterns, is memorably compared to 'bright-*plucked* water swaying in a pail . . . a *ruck* of *horned* waves steep and narrow in the gut'. The dialectal *plook* (a pimple), suggested by Norman MacKenzie[9] as the original of *plucked* may be a partial explanation (although I am not convinced, being myself familiar with *plook*); it also suggests a blend of Hopkins's *plash* and *ruck*. The water is *plashed* and *rucked* by the movement of the pail. Mountains also are compared to moving things. 'The mountain ranges . . . have the air of persons and of interrupted activity' (*JP*, 171); ranges can 'run like waves in the wind, *ricked* and sharply inscaped' (*JP*, 180).

Although many of Hopkins's special inscaping *words* appear in them, these quotations are more significant for the development of his fields of imagery in general. The sense of stress or tension that has been noticed as a distinguishing mark of Hopkins's poetry is partly the result of his ability to suggest that mobile substances are somehow captured, 'stalled', caught up, in a particular state, whereas solid stable things have potential motion which is restrained and under stress. The imagery of stanza 4 of 'The Deutschland' originates in the mountain–waterfall descriptions in the Journal. The poet is *soft sift* in an hourglass' (it is mountains in the Journal, 174, that are 'shaped and nippled like sand in an hourglass' as if they are slowly being shaped from their mirror-images above), but at the same time the poet is

> . . . at the wall
> *Fast*, but mined with a motion, a *drift*
> And it crowds and it *combs* to the fall;

Hopkins normally uses *comb* of water. In the Journal (*JP*, 223, 225) he speaks of 'the edge behind the comb or crest' of a wave, and 'the comb of the waves richly clustered and crisped' in breaking (cf. 'crisp combs', *Poems*, No. 68). Ogilvie's dictionary recognizes a verb *comb* 'in the language of seamen, to roll over, as the top of the wave; or to break with a white foam'. In the language of ploughing, *comb* and *drift* may form a system of opposites. Wright (*EDD*) glosses *comb* as the 'ridge' in ploughing; *drift* is the space between furrows, or a trench dug in the ground to convey water.

The imagery of the stanza has become that of the waterfall; the moving sand of the hourglass has become ridged water at the crest of a fall being pushed by intense pressure. In the next line, the water has become poised and steady as Hopkins develops the paradox of the well, in which the water seems immobile although it is continuously fed by underground streams, which like 'Christ's gift' come from the mountain-top and beyond. Typically, he compares the streams of water to *rope* (Note also that *veins* in mountains are normally composed of *solid* metal ore, rather than a liquid).

> I steady as a water, in a well, to a poise to a pane
> But *roped* with, all the way down from the tall
> Fells, or flanks of the voel, a *vein*
> Of the gospel proffer, a pressure, a principle, Christ's gift.

Of mobile things, especially clouds, Hopkins commonly uses comparisons to ropes, cords, skeins of wool and stringy substances. He speaks of a *range* of clouds 'in the N.W., ropy, the coiled folds being taken back across it from top to bottom . . .' (*JP*, 137). It is as if the shifting, vapoury, substance is criss-crossed by cords of rope, tied as a solid object might be. Similar terms are used of waterfalls, but here, often, the sense of tension in linked chains is greater, as in (*JP*, 176): 'a bright *river-tackled* waterfall parted into slender shanks'. Seamen's *tackle* is largely rope, and these slender shanks are *roped* to the river above. But, perhaps, the waterscaped *underthought* of this stanza is best captured in Hopkins's comment on the sea: 'In watching the sea one should be alive to the oneness which all its motion and tumult receives from its perpetual balance and falling this way and that to its level' (*JP*, 225). The sea, like the 'rolling level underneath him steady air' on which the falcon *strides*, exemplifies the paradox of the mobile substance that has potentially the steadiness of a solid. Everywhere in the Journal, the poet is fascinated by this.

The seascapes and windscapes of 'The Deutschland' are in various ways foreshadowed in the Journal, and where obscure, they are partly explained by the Journal. The *cobbled foam-fleece* and the *flint-flake* sea (again the solid texture of a mobile substance) owe something to 'painted white *cobbled* foam' and ' *flinty* waves, carved and scuppled in shallow grooves' (*JP*, 235–6). The *burl of the fountains of air* and *wind's burly* are foreshadowed by the passages where he notices 'the eye-greeting *burl* of the Round Tower' (*JP*, 256, 251) and 'the bole, the burling and the roundness of the world'. *Burl* takes on by association the roundness and firmness of a tree-trunk (*bole*) and the grain of wood (cf. *whorl*) but is also associated with *whirl* and perhaps dialectal *birl* ('*whirl*'), which refer to fast circular motion. Thus, the word unites movement, texture, shape and solidity; the swirling, howling wind is given shape and substance. It is relevant to note that, in his Journal, Hopkins does give substance to the wind, which '*dappled* very sweetly on one's face . . . one could feel the *folds* and *braids* of it . . . a floating flag is like wind visible . . . it gives it *thew* and fires it and bloods it in'. Like the sailor in 'The Deutschland' the wind has *braids of thew*.

Somewhere between the vocabulary appropriate to solid objects (*ranges* of mountains, but applied to clouds; *ricked* trees) and that appropriate to vapours and liquids comes the vocabulary of mobile solid substances like rice, grain or sand. This kind of vocabulary is commonly applied in the poems and Journal to *scapes* of blossom or flowers: *mealed*-with-yellow sallows, leaf*meal*, 'white heaps of *flour*-and-honey blossom, Spanish chestnuts in thickest honey-white *meal*' (*JP*, 145, 168); we have also noted the comparison of 'shaped and *nippled*' mountains to sand in an hourglass. This vocabulary can be applied in the opposite direction – to water, vapour and lightning. So, the Giessbach waterfall falls like 'heaps of snow or *lades* of shining rice', and another 'in discharges of rice or *meal* of which the *frets* or points . . . keep shooting in races' (*JP*, 173, 177). Lightning flashes in 'live veins of rincing or riddling liquid white' in which the implied comparison is to riddling grain or sand through a grating or sieve to separate the finer material from the coarse. Hence, lightning is seen as streaking in numerous long continuous streams, as flour falls in long streams from a sieve. The lightning, which is neither liquid or solid, is given the properties of both. The imagery of *foam*, which is neither quite liquid nor quite solid, may be classed here. The effects of foam are noted in the Journal, as in 'the foam dwindling and twitched into long chains of suds' (*JP*, 223) and applied in the poems to the *drop-of-blood-and-foam-dapple* apple trees, and the *silver-surfèd cherry*. The behaviour of *foam* itself is inscaped in 'Inversnaid', echoing the Journal even to the extent of blending *dwindle* and *twitch* in the portmanteau *twindled*.

The metaphorical transfer of vocabulary from one semantic field to another is a common resource of the language. We can, for example, transfer motion-words like *waves* from sea-vocabulary in which they are commonly applied, to other uses (*waves* in the hair, sound-waves, and even the wave theory of language and dialect dispersal). But in speaking of poetic metaphor we are often content to say that it consists merely of implicitly likening one thing to another, or, to put it more technically, of transferring the vocabulary of one semantic field to another. The basic vocabulary of shape, texture and motion that Hopkins uses to inscape nature explores a deeper level of semantic structure than we normally expect in figurative uses. He does not merely transfer from one semantic field to another to suggest, for example, that clouds may be like string or feathers or skeins of wool. The vocabulary of shape, texture and movement that he develops in the Journal is potentially applicable to anything in God's world. The *broth* of the whirlpool is also applicable to Harry Ploughman's arms, the *ropes* of clouds and waterfalls to his thighs, and the *curds* of cloudscapes to his muscles. This vocabulary may carry the associations of the semantic fields in which it is normally used in ordinary language. When clouds are described as 'curdled and moulded' one word suggests milkiness and another the potter's clay. But it then develops further associations that Hopkins himself attributes to it in the usage of his diaries and Journal; his cloud vocabulary, as we have seen, is transferred to other things, such as a ploughman's muscles; when he uses *horn* of sunbeams or moonbeams, he is suggesting the hard texture, the thrusting motion and the curved shape discussed in his etymologies. The final effect is one of complex sense impression, or of vitality and compression, or of strain and tension, all of which are parts of the special effect of Hopkins's poetry.

Since Hopkins's vocabulary of inscape is to a great extent personal – the basis of a new diction that has little in common with the standard model – it follows that it may sometimes be obscure in use. The exact sense of a word in a particular context may not be quite clear, or we may understand it in a 'normal' sense when it is intended to carry special additional senses peculiar to Hopkins's diction and shaped by his own experience. It is often possible to 'explain' such usages by referring to the Journals and other writings, and this is what various commentaries on Hopkins usually do. Since it is Hopkins's intention to extend the reader's perception of the relation between things and between words and things, to help him to see and feel for himself the wonders of God's creation, we may sometimes think that these occasional obscurities and uncertainties are weaknesses in his technique. But it does not usually matter very much if the full Hopkinsian sense of a particular word and the background to his imagery are not fully perceived at once. The verbal texture of a particular poem or stanza as a whole will usually carry us along and enable us to grasp new inscapes of word and image that we have not previously felt. And if the inscape is then 'dwelt on', it will come through in full. We now mention two such cases: one in which the image is effective, yet the precise sense of a word is not immediately clear; and one in which a simple word may be taken in an obvious sense, although its full inscape is more complex and partly dependent on our knowledge of Hopkins's word-store – the Journal.

In Stanza 26 of 'The Deutschland', as the 'down-dugged ground-hugged grey' gives way first to 'jay-blue' heavens and then to a clear night skyscape, Hopkins speaks of '. . . *belled* fire and the moth-soft Milky Way'. The natural assumption is that he is likening the vault of heaven to the inside of a huge bell, or perhaps its sound; yet, there is little is the imagery of the stanza as a whole to suggest this, and one would prefer if possible to take *belled* as referring to the quality of the 'fire' of evening sunlight or starlight. In 1871–2 there are several journal entries on the effect of the colours of wild flowers. First, the primrose: 'Take a few primroses in a glass and the instress of – brilliancy, sort of starriness: I have not the right word – so simple a flower gives is remarkable' (*JP*, 206). Later, the bluebells (*JP*, 208–9): 'through the light/they came in falls of sky-colour washing the brows and slacks of the ground with vein-blue'. The following year (*JP*, 231), he succeeds in capturing the light-effects of the bluebell's colour: 'Bluebells in Hodder Wood . . . I *caught* as well as I could . . . the level or stage or *shire* of colour they make hanging in the air a foot above the grass, and a notable glare the eye may abstract and sever from the blue colour/of light beating up from so many glassy heads, which like water is good to float their deeper instress in upon the mind'. The *belled fire* is this 'shire of colour', this 'notable glare . . . of light' abstracted from the blue, and transferred in the poem from the flowers to the effect of bluebell-coloured light in the early evening sky. *Bellbright* bodies in No. 159 also have the luminosity of flower-bells.

Weeds in wheels (No. 33) may be taken as weeds growing in circular patterns or even weeds growing in cartwheels which have been abandoned over the winter in the farmyard. But in 1871 Hopkins has a long Journal entry on *Wheel* (*JP*, 211)

> Talking to James Shaw of Dutton Lee, who told us . . . to *sail* as in Sail Wheel is to circle round. This is no tautology, for wheel is not whirlpool but only means, as I think, the double made in the water by the return current where at a spread of the stream caused by the bend or otherwise set or stem of the river bears on one bank and sets the slacker water on its outside spinning with its friction and so working back upstream

The following year, having just described the tumbling and swirling water at Hodder Roughs, he comments that 'a floating flag is like wind visible and *what weeds are in a current*'. The *weeds in wheels* are, I think, suggested by Hopkins's observation of water-currents; weeds grow out from the banks in long straggling lines only to be shaped into curves and semi-circles by the current as it wheels upstream.

Apart from the vocabulary of shape, texture and motion which is used in a complex way by Hopkins, there is a kind of imagery – that of light and shade – which is particularly characteristic and pervades his poetry. This may be seen as an extension of his concern with *texture*, but since it is also relevant to Hopkins's use of colour, it is best treated separately. Characteristically, it involves *difference* or *contrast* of light and shade in the same object or landscape. The key words are *pied* and *dappled*, and the key poem is 'Pied Beauty'. Later in the Journal, Hopkins does occasionally extend this vocabulary into his description of non-visual sense impressions and textures: 'the wind, which was south, *dappled* very sweetly on one's face . . .' (*JP*, 233). However, in the early part of the Journal ('sky *pied* with clouds', *JP*, 135; 1866), and in the poetry, this is a language of light and shade contrasts, and appeals first to the eye. It is so pervasive that we need not discuss it in detail, but note only certain points. The dappled things of Hopkins's world (sunlight and shadow, land-scape 'plotted and pieced', rosemoles) are indeed 'rhymes' of one another. But this vocabulary, like that of shape, texture and motion, is limited. The fact that it can refer generally to all things that are dappled whatever their colours enables the poet to dispense with a detailed vocabulary of colour or hue. The only area of the spectrum for which he has a partly developed colour vocabulary is the range of reds and purples. Here, in the mature poetry, we encounter, for example, *crimson, vermilion, damson*; otherwise, he is content with *blue, green, gold, yellow* and other common terms, modifying them where necessary to *jay-blue* or *bugle-blue*, for example. Such complex structures as *drop-of-blood-and-foam-dapple* (No. 42), while they suggest colour, do not use colour vocabulary, and Hopkins prefers such suggestive figurative structures. Generally, colour vocabulary is subsidiary to his inscaping of light and shade. This is seen in the bluebell passage quoted above, and in the many sunset descriptions of the Journal in which the precise colours (although sometimes mentioned) are subsidiary to quality of light-effects and the concern with shape and texture which is usually present.

This inscaping vocabulary of texture, motion, pattern and shade is a vocabulary of word-*painting* in which precise *hue* is less important than *brightness* and *saturation* (the degree of freedom from dilution with white).[10] In English most of our common colours are defined in terms of *hue*, but some (e.g. *brown*) in terms of *brightness* and *saturation*. *Brown* occupies a range of colour between *red* and *yellow*, but it has low brightness and high saturation. The colour-terms of Old English and other medieval and ancient languages are difficult to translate, partly, it seems, because brightness and saturation may have been more important scales than hue; thus, OE *brun* (the lineal ancestor of *brown*) is indeterminate in hue but high in the scale of brightness. It is often translated by *bright*. OE *fealu* (the ancestor of *fallow*) which is usually translated by *tawny*, is commonly applied to waves. It does not seem to be suggesting that the waves are yellowish in hue, but rather that they are dull (low intensity of brightness) and high in saturation. Homer's 'wine-dark sea' probably had the same degree of *saturation* as dark blue. Chaucer's Prioress's eyes which were 'grey as glass' suggest that for Chaucer the term *grey* had higher luminosity than it has now. Hopkins's *damson* is not so much a hue as a reddish colour with low brightness and high saturation. His concern is with qualities of light rather than with hue. Since Modern English colour-terms are predominantly arranged along a scale of hue, it is important for our linguistic purpose to note that for Hopkins, with his interest in relative brightness and 'texture' of colours, English does not always provide a ready-made vocabulary. The difficulty that he experienced in capturing the precise effects of the bluebell's light, and our difficulty in understanding *belled fire*, are the result of a deficiency in the lexicon[11] rather than a deficiency in the poet. No one has tried harder than Hopkins to communicate sense-impressions for which the language does not provide suitable words.

The inscaping vocabulary of the Journal, limited as it is to series of key words like *quain, rack, braid, curd, thew, dapple* and so on, is, as we have seen, largely responsible for the effects of the imagery of his poetry: for the sense of strain, tension and even torture that has been discerned, for his ability to *catch* (his own word) or *stall* (his own word) in a static form some natural scene, in which vigorous motion is present, and the consequent feeling of tension between that vigorous motion and its *stalling*. The analogies with still photography (a rapidly developing art in Hopkins's day) and with Pre-Raphaelite interests (themselves partly inspired by still photography) are obvious. This vocabulary is constructed in the observation of clouds, trees, flowers, rivers and sea, and largely by transfer of terms from one semantic field to another. Chronologically, we find *skein, rack, curd* first transferred from their normal uses to cloudscapes, *ramp, rick* to treescapes. They are then transferred yet again to other natural phenomena, and the network of words is further extended in the description of whirlpools, waterfalls and the form and *behaviour* of flowers. Finally, in the poetry, the same vocabulary may be extended to other themes, and living creatures may be inscaped in the words originally used by Hopkins for inanimate phenomena. The summit of this art is 'Harry Ploughman'.

'Harry Ploughman' is probably modelled on a painting (Frederick Walker's 'The Plough'), but even if it is not, it is certainly a word-painting.[12] We have already noted that some of the terms used are those previously used for cloudscapes and waterscapes; the tensions between liquid and solid, soft texture and hard, curved shapes and slender, form the underlying pattern of the poem. The octave is infused by *cloudscape* and the sestet is *liquid*. Harry's waist is *liquid*; the plough *wallows* (as if in a liquid). His muscles (*thew/That onewhere curded, onewhere sucked or sank – /Soared or sank*) have the pattern and texture of clouds (which are often *curded* or *curdled*); in places they are sucked in like 'the great limbs of the waterfall in which the water is packed' which are '*tretted* like open sponge ... where the yeast has supped the texture in big and little holes' (*JP*, 177). Harry's *curls* are *windlaced*, as lightning in the Journal *laces* the clouds, and this implies not only that the wind is swirling *through* the curls but that it has somehow laced them *together*. The *furls* (furrows) 'rhyme' the *curls*; they *curl* over in a curved or semi-circular movement like water shooting out (*with-a-fountain's shining-shot*) from a fountain and dropping back to earth. And the furrows shine, as Hopkins had observed in his Journal: 'On the left, brow of the near hill glistening with very bright newly turned sods' (*JP*, 133). The first line sets the pattern of the octave, contrasting hard substances with light, feathery or mobile substances. Harry's arms are 'hard as hurdle' but 'with a broth of goldish flue'; the down on his arms is soft and feathery like clouds or the froth of a whirlpool. The '*rack* of ribs; the *scooped* flank; lank/*Rope*-over thigh' are the vocabulary of cloud shapes – slender lines and curves. The 'knee-nave and barrelled shank' is surely a wheel image, the *nave* being the central part of the wheel and the barrels being the barrel-shaped spokes of old-fashioned wooden cart-wheels. As Harry plods along, the lower parts of his legs are seen somehow as radiating from the knees. The picture of Harry, then, is painted in the octave in curves, circles and lines, and soft textures are attributed to hard, solid muscles and limbs. In the sestet, an impression of vigorous movement, *stalled*, is largely conveyed by compressed imagery of wind and liquids. Even the word *raced*, which we naturally take to refer to Harry's feet racing along the furrows, is (as *race* or *races*) applied by Hopkins to waterfalls.[13]

Harry remains a painting (with little suggestion of colour but with plenty of shape, texture and implied movement), and not a human personality. Hopkins's vocabulary of inscape does not include the inscape of human relations or even of living creatures. When he describes living creatures in his diaries, it is their 'pie-ings' or their shapes and movements that attract him. The lambs (*JP*, 206) 'toss and toss; it is as if it were the earth that flung them, not themselves'. And when he deals in poetry with human relations (as in 'Brothers'), the effect may be forced and artificial, even though the language has its usual strength. His vocabulary of shapes, texture and movement is flexible only within certain limits, and it is most successful when it is applied to natural phenomena and to situations of physical or mental pressure and stress. There are large areas of human experience, and poetic themes, for which it is not ideally suited; some of Hopkins's unfinished pieces are unsuccessful attempts to wed this language to unsuitable themes or genres. Nevertheless, even in these less successful pieces, Hopkins's language can be as intense and expressive as elsewhere; in 'Epithalamion', for instance, the close texture and richness of the language dominates to such an extent that the topic of the poem seems almost to be forgotten. The language, beautiful in itself, overwhelms the theme and form of the poem.

WORD-FORMATION

Hopkins was aware of resources of imagery that were enshrined in common language, and, as we have noted, many of his observa-tions of such imagery in country speech (*flock-of-sheep clouds*, *JP*,

150; *black divers*, *JP*, 221) were of the kind celebrated by Trench (see Chapter 3). Clearly, such terms are preferable to the standard equivalents because they *describe* in themselves behaviour, texture, shape or movement. Much of Hopkins's imagery is suggested to him by, and constructed out of, these *semantic* relations as they are actually exploited by ordinary speakers; his other linguistic devices are also based on characteristics inherent in the language. They are, broadly, of two kinds: phonetic and grammatical.

By exploiting the grammar of the language (specifically its rules of word-formation) he can, as we have seen, create new derivative words by affixation. He is also a master of compounding (which differs from affixation in that two or more free-standing words are joined together). By exploiting phonetic relationships he can suggest echoic effects and a relation between sound and sense. Somewhere between compounding and echoism lies telescoping or blending of words: producing what Lewis Carroll called *portmanteau* words, and which Carroll used, together with other coinings, in 'Jabberwocky':

> 'Slithy' means 'lithe and slimy' . . . You see it's like a portmanteau – there are two meanings packed up into one word . . . 'Mimsy' is 'flimsy and miserable' (there's another portmanteau for you). (*Through the Looking Glass*)

Frequently, the vocabulary of Hopkins's Journal and of his poems is creative in several or all of these ways. Of a given form, we may be able to say that it is derived from dialect, that it is also a derivative or compound belonging to a paradigmatic class (as *leafmeal* is related to *piecemeal*), that it is echoic and at the same time a portmanteau. The effect is often that, whatever its origin in dialect or common English, the word is given associations that it does not necessarily have in common usage, dialectal or otherwise. A word which appears to be a standard word may be pressed into service in a meaning that it does not usually have, and if we are not aware of Hopkins's views on language we may misunderstand it. In the following passage, as we have noted, Hopkins is trying to suggest the movement and *sound* of the sea as it draws back down a shingled beach:

> . . . the strength of the backdraught *shrugged* the stones together and *clocked* them one against the other (*JP*, 223)

In standard use, to *shrug* is used almost always of the shoulders – an association which can hardly be intended here. It is the *sound* of the stones rattling and clicking together that Hopkins wants to emphasize. Clearly, this is for him a nonce-word suggestive of a number of words like *shift, shove, rub, slog, struggle*, from which it is derived as a kind of complex blend. Hopkins prefers *clocked* to *clicked* because the so-called 'broad' back-rounded vowel is phonaesthetically 'larger' than the high front vowel in *click*, to which it is related as a vowelled-off variant (as he relates *flick, fleck, flake* in his diary). Nor is it accidental that it rhymes with *rock, knock, shock*, and it can be seen also as a blend of *click, clip* . . . with *knock* . . . Elsewhere in the Journal, Hopkins describes the petals of carnations as 'powdered with *spankled* red glister' (*JP*, 143), with which compare *sprinkle, spatter, spangle, sparkle*; the glister is *sprinkled* on the flowers, and it *sparkles*. He speaks of '*slubbered* wood in the sea' (*JP*, 184), a word which belongs to the same *sl-* series as the *sloggering brine* of the 'Deutschland', and suggests the sound of the waves lapping and licking against it as well as the slippery, slimy surface of the wood. The word is also listed by Wright as a dialect term. Lightning (*JP*, 233) streaks in 'live veins of *rincing* and riddling liquid white': it causes the onlooker to *wince* as it *races* across the sky, *rending* or *riving* the clouds apart. The clearest example in the Journal of a simple portmanteau is a word which the editors have marked 'thus in MS', possibly considering it to be a mistake. When Hopkins speaks of 'the sun just above, a shaking white fire or waterball, striking and *glanting*' (*JP*, 239), he is using a blend of *slant* and *glint* to describe the oblique rays of the sun striking through the foliage in an irregular way. In *JP*, 181, he describes the stars as '*twiring* brilliantly'; although a verb *twire*: 'peer, peep' and a homophonous *twire*: 'twist, twirl' seem to have existed in earlier English (and Hopkins records *twire* (?) in an 'etymological' list of 1864), the usage is just as well explained as a blend of *twinkle* and *fire*. The 'flinty' waves 'carved and *scuppled* in shallow grooves' (*JP*, 235–6) may be *scalloped, cobbled* and *stippled*, but more probably Hopkins views *scuppled* as a simple diminutive of *scooped*, the two words being related as *wade* is to *waddle* or *brinded* ('Pied Beauty') to *brindled*. And *scoop* (as in the *scooped flank* of Harry Ploughman) is itself part of a system of words that includes (for Hopkins) *scape, shape*, and suggests making or moulding (see Commentary, *s.v.*

-scape). When he speaks of swifts (*JP*, 231) as they 'round and *scurl* under the clouds' one may be supposed to think of the Scots *skirl*, but the word is more probably a portmanteau of *swirl* and *curl*: the spelling is significant, as it is for *rincing* (which is not *rinsing*) and *hawling* ('Deutschland', st. 19), which is not simply *hauling*. Even such a common word as *dappled*, while it may be a derivative of *dab*, may also be taken as a blend of *dip* and *dabble*, especially in the passage (*JP*, 233) that describes the dappling of the wind.

In the poetry, many words – *burl*, *twindle*, *throughther*, and others – may be taken as blends or derivatives of various kinds. Perhaps the most remarkable of these is the word *sloggering* of the 'Deutschland', st. 19. It is one word among many in which the poet is trying to suggest the meaning of a word by its sound and at the same time deriving its force from dialectal associations and from grammatical and phonaesthetic systems within the language. Hopkins's *sl-* list does not include *slogger*, but like Wedgwood he is conscious of end-consonant relationships (*flag*: *flabby*; *flick*: *flip*; *flog*; *flap*: *flop*) and what he considers to be suffixed derivatives (*flutter*, *flitter*, etc., from the *fly* root). Thus, *slogger* can be related to words like *slop* and *slabby*, which are in his *sl-* series, and we may further suggest that *slither*, *slobber*, *slubber* (as in *JP*, 184) are associated.

Commentators have generally taken the dominant sense of *slogger* to be 'to strike hard, assail with blows' (R. V. Schoder). Norman MacKenzie (*Hopkins*, 119) says that '*sloggering* is the colloquial term for the action of a prize-fighter raining blows on his opponent: behind it lies the dialect "*slog*: to strike with great force".' The etymological dictionaries recognize *slog*: to hit hard, to plod (Onions) but *slogger* is taken as an agent-noun: 'one who slogs' (Partridge). I have found no justification for *slogger* as a verb meaning to *slog*. Wright's *EDD* recognizes a Northern dialect verb *slogger*: to hang loosely and untidily – of clothes – and *sloggering* (adj.): loosely-fitting, slovenly; untidy, loosely-built. Wright also records many dialect words of related sound and meaning: *slocher* in Scotland means: to labour under asthma; take liquid food in a slabbering manner; wallow in mud. It is used in Ayrshire of a pig 'slocherin in the glaur [mud]'. In some areas *slidder* may mean to slide or slip; *slobber* can be a noun meaning mud, cold rain mixed with snow, sloppy sleet; *slagger* can mean to besmear with mud, bespatter, bedaub, *slodder* to spill, splash, *slubber* to drink with a gurgling noise, or (as a noun) mud, slush. There is a usage recorded in Norfolk (1855) of *slug* as a heavy surf tumbling in with an off-shore wind or a calm. Clearly, many of these uses are partly or wholly imitative of the sounds involved. Compare also such stand-ard words as *sludge, slush, slither* and the colloquial *slurp.* Hopkins's coining is meant to suggest the sound of the breakers dashing against the ship and then drawing back with a sucking, gurgling noise.

There is also good reason to believe that Hopkins meant the word to be *iterative* or *frequentative* in meaning: to suggest that the waves were lashing constantly against the ship – repeatedly, again and again, at intervals. This depends on the existence within the language of derivational systems in -*er* of the kind pointed out by Wedgwood when he relates *pat, clack* to *patter, clatter* and so on. For Hopkins this -*er* system is in effect a variant of the -*le* system that we have already noticed, and it involves what is phonetically known as *dissimilation.* If the root already contains *l,* then *r* has to be substituted either in the root itself or in the suffix. Thus, numerous small *flecks* are not **fleckles,* but *freckles;* to 'flick' repeatedly is not **flickle,* but *flicker.*

We conclude our discussion of blend-derivatives by observing that, in the poems as well as the prose, a word of standard form (like *shrugged* in JP) may take on the character of a blend in a particular context. Thus the '*tucked* string' of No. 57, while it may well invoke a known sense ('pull, tug'), can also be seen as a blend of *touch* and *pluck.* Similarly, such 'vowelled' series as *roll: reel; rick: rack: ruck,* or rhymed series like *whirl: swirl: burl,* while their individual items may have common standard senses, may also take on by association additional senses or non-standard senses that they do not normally have. Sometimes these phonaesthetic series may also be interpreted as blends (*reel,* from *roll* and *wheel,* for example). Thus, the derivational systems used by Hopkins are often complex; relationships of various kinds may be present in the same word. At best, each of the derivational patterns invoked should add to and enrich the complex 'meaning' of the word.

COMPOUND WORDS

Word compounding is, strictly speaking, part of the syntax of a language in so far as the words joined together in this way bear a syntactic relation to one another. Thus, in English, *blackbird* is a compound of *attributive adjective+noun*; *girlfriend*, *rat poison* (hyphenated or not) are compounds of *noun+noun*, but with a different syntactic relationship between the two items in each word; *breakwater* is a compound of *verb+noun*, with the noun as object of the verb. There is no simple rule in English which states when a compound should be hyphenated and when it should be written like a simple word. Generally speaking, if the meaning of the word is 'idiomatic'[14] (not directly interpretable from the meaning of its parts), and the first item is not inflected, a compound will often be written as a single word. Thus, *blackbird* is a species of bird and is not applied to *any* bird that is black: its conventional sense is not predictable from its form. Such items as *reading-book* and *church steeple* (hyphenated or not) have lexically predictable meanings but are also compounds in that the items cannot be separated by an intervening word. We cannot speak of a **church high steeple*: the sequence cannot be interrupted. Hyphenating practice varies between individuals, between publishing houses, and between British and American English. The definition of a compound word, therefore, does not depend primarily on the presence or absence of a hyphen, but on the *uninterruptability* of the sequence. Hopkins is – at least superficially – inconsistent in his practice: *under he* is as much a single word as *overbend*; *chance-quarried, self-quained, hoar-husked* ('Epithalamion') and many more could all be hyphenated or not: it would make little if any difference. Most important, the presence of hyphens in Hopkins's language does not necessarily mean that we are in the presence of a compound *word*.

This is clearly true when we consider the premodifying phrases that are so characteristic of Hopkins. Sometimes such phrases are hyphenated and sometimes not. When they are, the hyphens are like Hopkins's stress-marks in so far as they are guides to reading. The phrase *sodden-with-its-sorrowing* is hyphenated so that we shall not read the construction as 'sorrowing heart', but as a 'heart *that is sodden* with its sorrowing' ('Deutschland', st. 27). Similarly, the '*dappled-with-damson* west' is not the *damson* west, but the *dappled* west (st. 5), and a '*not-by-morning-matched* face' (No. 59) is a face *which is* not matched by morning. There is a difficult borderline area, of course, in which we are not sure whether a particular structure is best treated as a compound *word* or as a phrase.

Dapple-dawn-drawn (No. 36), unlike the others quoted, does not contain a preposition 'or other inconsiderable word' and can be reasonably viewed as a compound adjective or modifier. However, it contains multiple structural ambiguity. Is the falcon drawn *from* the dawn, or *towards* the dawn, or is it drawn (etched) *in* the dawn, or *like* the dawn (i.e. 'dappled'), or all these things at once? It is most convenient to treat these more complex modifying phrases in Chapter 7 when we discuss syntax.

Bearing in mind, therefore, that there is a fuzzy area between compound words and complex phrases and remembering that, in the last analysis, all compounding is part of syntax, we shall in this chapter specially consider those conventions of compounding which apply to the creation of single words rather than phrases.

Already in the Journal, we can observe the creation of new compounds. In common with his other means of exploiting structural patterns in the language, this is part of Hopkins's purism and *inearnestness*, his avoidance of circumlocution, and his search for the exact descriptive term. The Saxon purists had advocated a return to the 'Anglo-Saxon' conventions in this as in other things, and Hopkins obeyed their precepts splendidly. But it was not chiefly because the words involved were usually early English that he did this: there were deeper reasons arising from the fact that the conventional standard syntax and lexicon was deficient for his purposes of inscape. In July 1866 (*JP*, 143, 144) Hopkins described the 'soft vermilion leather *just-budded* leaves on the purple beech' and the 'strange pretty *scatter-droop* of barley ears'. The *just-budded* leaves and the '*fish-scale-bespattered* sunset' (*JP*, 147) exemplify Hopkins's attempts at syntactic compression and foreshadow *wimpled-water-dimpled* (No. 59) and *dapple-dawn-drawn*. The *scatter-droop* of barley is particularly important for our present purpose. This is a co-ordinating compound: the barley ears scatter and droop *at the same time*. Notice that, if Hopkins had written 'scatter *and* droop', a possible ambiguity inherent in the conjunction would have been introduced. The conjunction may be used as a simple co-ordinator, but it often carries with it the implication of temporal succession (as in stanza 14 and others of the 'Deutschland'), especially when the items joined are verbs of action. Barley-ears scattering *and* drooping seem to do first one thing and then the other. By speaking of a *scatter-droop* Hopkins can suggest that the movements are simultaneous, and even that each move-

ment or pattern is bound up in the other. In this way he catches the inscape of the barley-ears in one movement and one perception of the movement. Such a simple instance typifies Hopkins's art of syntactic compression and justifies it.[15]

In the early 1960s, transformational theory paid considerable attention to the syntax of the noun-phrase, including the formation of compound words. By postulating a deep structure (originally 'kernel sentences') from which the surface form may be 'derived', this approach succeeded in examining compound words with greater subtlety than had been usual previously.[16] Thus, it is perfectly true to observe that, on the surface, *girlfriend, arrowhead, armchair, steamboat, honeybee, gunpowder* and many others consist of *noun+noun*, but the syntactic relations of the items in the compound words are various. For *girlfriend*, we must postulate a deep structure containing the verb *to be* or some kind of 'equals' sign, since it is implied that the girl *is* a friend, or the friend *is* a girl. *Arrowhead*, however, postulates a relationship of possession or attribution: 'the arrow has a head' or 'the head is an attribute of the arrow'. *Armchair* is oppositely constructed. This time it is the second item, *chair*, which 'possesses' arms, and arms are subordinate to, and attributes of, *chair*. A steamboat is *powered* by steam, a honeybee *makes* honey, gunpowder is powder *for use in* guns. The potential structural ambiguities inherent in the surface-structure of such compounds can be linguistically exploited by poets and humorists, as in the *watch-dog* who goes 'tick-tick-woof' (a co-ordinate, as in *scatter-droop*). If we interpret, for example, *snake-poison* on the patterns of *rat poison*, we can make it mean 'poison set down *for* snakes', and we often interpret *witch-doctor* on the pattern of *girl-friend* – 'a doctor who *is* a witch'. In fact, it 'correctly' means a learned man who casts out witches.

Hopkins's co-ordinating compounds often appear in the poetry as adjectives: *kindcold* (No. 159), *rash-fresh* (No. 35), *lovely-asunder, lovely-felicitous, rare-dear* ('Deutschland', st. 5, 31, 35); *wild-worst* (st. 24) probably belongs here too; *white-fiery* (st. 13) is structurally ambiguous[17] in that it may be a derivative of the phrase 'white fire' *or* a co-ordinate 'white *and* fiery'. It has two 'representations' in deep structure. There is no *lexical* ambiguity, and the structural ambiguity may be thought to enrich the verbal texture when the inscape in 'dwelt on', rather than to confuse the reader. Noun+ noun compounds such as *martyr-master* (st. 21), *knee-nave* (No. 71), *heaven-haven* (No. 9, 'Deutschland', st. 35), may be taken as co-ordinates (e.g. 'heaven *and* haven'), but are more probably *copulas* like *girl-friend* ('the knee *is* a nave', and so on). The structural uncertainty or ambiguity is inherent in this type of construction whether it is a Hopkins coining or not; it is not a defect of his art, but a characteristic of current English. Often we find that a simple compound like *foam-fleece*, which seems at first sight to be 'foam *and* fleece' or copulative ('the fleece *is* foam'), may also be interpreted as a subordinating construction with *foam* as an attribute of *fleece*, proposing in effect that the *fleece* has the property of being foamy. This kind of ambiguity prevents us from giving lists of Hopkins's compounds classified according to syntactic types. Too many of them may seem to belong to several types at once.

The compounds we have so far discussed are relatively straightforward. However, in view of the fact that Hopkins's language has been said to be primarily a language of co-ordination,[18] we must emphasize that many of his compounds conceal, in their surface structure, relations of subordination or predication of various kinds. The two terms of the compound are seldom co-ordinate in any sense. Some apparent compounds are simply collocations of *adjective+noun* (*gaygear*, No. 59; *hoarlight*, No. 61; *gay-gangs*, No. 72). These and many others of the same type are written as compounds on the analogy of *blackbird*, *redwood*, etc., in order to indicate the stress pattern that Hopkins requires. *Blackbird* has strong stress on the first syllable and very weak stress on the second, as against *black bird*, which has relatively strong (primary or secondary) stress on both syllables. *Gáygear* (my stress-mark) therefore must take a strong stress on *gay*. The same applies to the very large number of compounds that have *noun modifier+noun*: *rockfire*, (No. 70), *silk-beech*, *waterworld* (No. 159), and others.

In all such *adj.+noun* and *noun+noun* compounds, the first item is subordinate to the second in precisely the same way as an adjectival or adverbial clause is subordinate to a main clause (*silk-beech*: 'beech *which* is made of silk'), but the subordinating relationships in *noun+noun* compounds can be of many kinds. Sometimes the first element is the material out of which the thing is made, as in *silk-beech*, *waterworld*. *Rockfire* and *foam-fleece* seem to fit this category too; yet they are subtly different: *rockfire* seems to be fire *caused* by rock, and in many others this causative relationship seems to hold. *Shadowtackle* (No. 72) is tackle *made* out of shadow, but also *caused* by shadow. *Flint-flake*, however, is not flake *caused* by flint, but *made out of*, or *having the property of* flint. Thus, it can be classed with *silk-beech*, but not with *rockfire*. Such a compound as *girlgrace* (No. 59) is different again: in this case the grace is a possession or attribute of the girl, and the compound can be seen as a derivative of a deep structure paraphrasable as 'the girl has grace'. Note that it is not sufficient to explain it as 'grace *of* a girl'. We could then also argue that *sea-romp* ('Deutschland', st. 17), *anvil-ding* (st. 10), *rockfire*, were 'romp of the sea', 'ding of the anvil', 'fire of the rock' and thereby conceal the subtly different relationships that obtain in each case. A way of explaining such relationships is suggested by Charles Fillmore's Case Grammar.[19] In *sea-romp*, the obvious relationship is that of subject and verb ('the sea romps'), but even this conceals the fact that the relationship is *agentive*: the sea is the agent of the romping. In *anvil-ding* we may paraphrase in the same way: 'the anvil dings'. However, this time the relationship is not agentive. Some linguists would describe it as *ergative*[20] in that the anvil is the object affected, and the true paraphrase is 'someone or something dings (on) the anvil'. Note that *sea-romp* cannot in Hopkins's usage be paraphrased in this way, although *potentially* it could mean that someone is romping on the sea (a mermaid perhaps). Other compounds have *instrumental* force. This is arguable for *anvil-ding*, but more obviously true for *sinew-service* (No. 71), which is service *by means of*, or *using*, sinews. Yet others are *locative*: *womb-life* ('Deutschland', st. 7) and *rutpeel* (No. 72) are 'life *in* the womb', 'peel (pool) *in* a rut'. Many other subtle differences that can be described in terms of case-relationship – *ablative* (motion away from), *illative* (motion into), *partitive*, *genitive of origin*, *objective* and others – are distinguishable in Hopkins's usage of noun-compounds and elsewhere. Where it appears that the form may be interpretable in a number of different ways (as in *rockfire*), the effect is not so much one of uncertainty as of richness and suggestiveness, and subsequent readings (*over-and-overings*) bring out more fully the inscapes. Commonly, however, the poet limits the potential applications of particular items by the context in which he uses them. Thus *sea-romp*, as we have seen, is clearly an action *by* the sea.

One of the most characteristic types of compound used by Hopkins is exemplified by *heavenfallen* (No. 159). In these the form is *noun+participle*, the last used adjectivally and modifying a noun in context (*heaven-fallen* freshness). Again, the formal description conceals a variety of grammatical relationships obtaining within the compounds. *Heaven-fallen* cannot be anything but *ablative* since the verb is *intransitive*; therefore, heaven cannot be an agent, and the freshness has fallen *from* heaven.[21] *Heaven-flung*, however, is not only 'flung *from* heaven' but 'flung *by* heaven': *heaven* is agentive. Similarly, *leafwhelmed* (No. 159), *whirlwind-swivellèd* ('Deutschland', st. 13), *carekilled* (No. 59) are clear agentives, whereas *footfretted* (No. 72) may be agentive or instrumental (the context suggests the latter: 'treadmire toil' frets, i.e. rubs, wears away, 'in it' *by means of* the feet). *Maiden-furled* ('Deutschland', st. 34) is locative, and *care-coiled* (No. 59), *windlaced* (No. 71) are either agentive or *comitative*, or both. While, like the others, these may be paraphrased simply as subject+verb ('care coils one'), the relationship is really an oblique case relationship – 'coiled *with* care' (together with it or bound up in it), 'furled *in* the maiden'. The copulative relationship obtains in *beakleaved* ('the leaves are beaks'), although it may also be interpreted as 'leaved *by* or *with* beaks'.

Like *beakleaved*, most compounds which consist of *adjective+participle* have this copulative relationship. Thus, *plush-capped*, *black-backed* ('Deutschland', st. 8, 13), *hoar-husked* (No. 159), state that the things concerned *have* a black back, plush cap, hoar husk; however, within themselves the compounds are linked by a deep-structure copula and state that the cap *is* plush, the back *is* black and so on. *Lush-kept* differs in that the second item is truly a verb, which in this usage belongs to the class of verbs which take objects plus object-complements, as in: 'they keep it *lush*'; 'they made him *sorry*'. Thus, in the sequence *lush-kept, plush-capped sloe*, the surface similarity (phonetic and grammatical) between the compounds is accompanied by a variation in their deep syntax. This is an aspect of Hopkins's language game, of his 'rhyming', and it is one of the linguistic complexities that help to give richness and strength ('thew and sinew') to his language.

Some readers may feel that our discussion of Hopkins's compounds, incomplete as it is, has been too dryly analytic. They may even feel that it is damaging to go into so much detail. But it is important to understand that Hopkins's conventions of compounding are, like his conventions of blending and phonaesthesia, extensions of linguistic patterns inherent in current English. It is also necessary to emphasize that, like blending and other kinds of derivation and like other syntactic devices that we shall discuss in Chapter 7, compounding is part of Hopkins's compression of language and the elliptical style that so many critics have commented on. Indeed, it is part of inscape. It can be no bad thing to attempt to understand in some detail *how* Hopkins uses the art of compounding, and explanation is surely one of the functions of literary criticism.

WORDS IN CONTEXT

Most of the linguistic devices that we have so far discussed involve exploitation of *paradigmatic* relations within the language. However, no account of Hopkins's vocabulary is complete unless we also consider the distribution of words in context and their sequential relationships in sentences, paragraphs and stanzas. In this chapter, we shall ignore the syntax of sentences and concentrate on the ways in which Hopkins relates the *meanings* of words to one another within the text to heighten his language.

As we have already noted, Hopkins links on the phonetic level pairs or longer chains of words. He may also use a particular phonetic device in a broader way, returning to a particular figure several times in a series of lines or throughout a whole poem (e.g. 'Felix Randal'). His practice on the semantic level is analogous. 'Pied Beauty' is a poem that is organized on the phonetic level in terms of a play on words that end in -*le*. The second element in the disyllables is held more or less constant, while the first syllables are varied in vowel and consonant structure. On the semantic level, it is also organized. The -*le* words, together with the chestnut falls and other things that are dappled, are semantic rhymes, and the whole poem is in effect a definition of *pied* or *dappled*. These are the superordinate terms under which rosemoles, stipples, brindles and so on are grouped as members of the same semantic field. It is hard to believe that Hopkins had not read Ogilvie's dictionary entries on *pied* and *dapple*, as well as Wedgwood. (See Commentary, *s.v. pied, dapple, stipple*.)

In 'Pied Beauty' the relevant semantic rhymes are distributed throughout the poem as an organizing principle. Commonly, however, such semantic series are grouped within the line or at intervals through several lines of a poem. Sometimes, especially in later poems, the semantic relations are relatively obscure and may depend on our knowledge of Hopkins's views on etymology. In 'Heraclitean Fire', *bonfire* in line 9 is taken up by *bonniest* in the next line, probably in the belief that both are from the French *bon*: 'good' (but see Commentary). In 'Sibyl's Leaves', *vast, west, waste* in successive lines are linked etymologically as well as by *skothend-ing* (*west* being wrongly believed to be from the same etymon as the other two); similarly, *equal* and *evening* are quasi-etymologically linked; *trod* and *trade* in 'God's Grandeur' have a common etymology.

Sometimes the etymological play occurs within the same line in a doublet or concatenation, and in the latter type it may be linked to other concatenative devices, semantic or phonetic. In 'a released *shower*, let flash to the *shire*, not a lightning of *fire*' ('Deutschland', st. 34), the first link depends on Hopkins's association of *shire* and *shower* in a series of words with a root meaning 'cut, divide'; the second link clearly depends on phonetic rhyme, but there is also a semantic link between *shire* and *fire* in that Hopkins seems also to have associated his *sheer* series with the sense 'bright, shining' (from older English) and uses *shire* in the Journal in association with the brightness (*belled fire*) of the bluebells (*shire* can even be interpreted as a *blend* of *sheer/fire*). Clearly, this kind of concatena-tive figure is analogous to the phonetic figure that we have called *gradience*, and may be similarly labelled. The gradience in 'Sibyl's Leaves': *earliest stars, earlstars, stars principal*, additionally involves (like *sheer off, disseveral*) a Latin gloss on a preceding English word. *Early* and *earl* were associated by contemporary etymological opinion in a metaphorical transfer of the sense 'prior (in time)' to 'prior (in rank)'. Thus, *earl* continues the notion of 'prior' and adds the notion of 'chief'. Finally *earlstars* is provided with a Latin gloss 'stars *principal*' (from Lat. *princeps*: 'chieftain, prince'), which is itself connected with Lat. *primus*: 'first' and notions of priority in time and space. Frequently, the etymological play applies to *pairs* of words or phrases in close succession. Norman MacKenzie has pointed out that *disremembering, dismembering* ... ('Sibyl's Leaves') are words associated by contemporary philological opinion in a root *men*: 'divide'.[22] We have discussed the complex semantic and etymological play in *sheer off, disseveral* (No. 72), and there are many other simpler examples in such co-ordinate or appositive pairs: '*prized*' and '*priced*', 'Of the *Yore*-flood, of the *year's* fall' ('Deutschland' st. 32), 'Tall sun's *tingeing* or treacherous the *tainting*' (No. 59, from Lat. *tingere*), '*reckon* but, *reck* but . . .' (No. 61; Hopkins may have assumed a connection); '*pool* and rut*peel*' (No. 72; see Commentary). And in other constructions, '*stallion stalwart*' (No. 38), '*Lads* and men her *lade* and treasure' (No. 41), '*degged* with *dew*', invoke real or supposed etymological connections (see Commentary).

Hopkins's etymological or quasi-etymological enrichment does not always involve a pair or series, but may be implicit in a single word and suggested by its association in context with an etymologically unrelated word. *Barbarous* (No. 38), in association with stooks of corn, suggests 'bearded' (Lat. *barba*) as well as its more obvious meaning. More commonly, however, when only a single word is involved, the etymological sense, though usually intended, is submerged. In various poems Hopkins's use of the word *beam* suggests the etymological sense 'tree' or even 'Cross'; *dangerous* (Nos. 36, 62) may invoke the etymological sense 'dominant, mastering, powerful';[23] *hornlight* (No. 61) is best understood as developed from Hopkins's views on the semantic and etymological relationships of *horn*.

But a semantic pair or series need not be formally or historically related by etymology. It is characteristic of the Journal, as of the poems, to use a pair or series of epithets or defining words, as in 'a *stage* or *level* or *shire* of colour'. The effect of such a series is, in effect, for each term in it to help to define the others, and for meaning to be carried forward from one term to the next. In the instance quoted, it is Hopkins's special use of *shire* that is partly defined by *level* and *stage*. In the poetry, such pairs as '*swirling* and *huwling*' ('Deutschland', st. 19) are of this kind, with the notion of swerving almost certainly carried forward and helping to define the unfamiliar *hawling*. Such appositional or co-ordinate pairs are so common in the poems that it is unnecessary to list the more obvious ones. The most extended series are of the kind that appear in 'Pied Beauty' or the octave of 'The Starlight Night'. Such series constitute examples of the device of *variation* (a commonplace of Old English poetry), in that the items in the series all refer to the same thing. Within a single line, the same is true of the first line of 'The Leaden Echo': '*bow* or *brooch* or *braid* or *brace, lace, latch* or *catch* or *key* . . .' or, in 'The Golden Echo': *haggard, care-coiled, care-killed, fagged, fashed, cogged, cumbered*. The items in these lines are sets of synonyms or near-synonyms. We have already suggested that such series are phonetically organized in a *gradience*. Sometimes, however, a *gradience* is organized semantically, or is a mixed phonetic-semantic series. This is common in 'The Leaden Echo and the Golden Echo'. *Winning ways, airs innocent, maiden manners, sweet looks* are semantically connected; *loose locks, long locks, lovelocks* are interconnected semantically and phonetically, but relate back to *sweet looks* phonetically. Finally, *gaygear, going gallant, girlsgrace* are bound together by alliteration, but *gaygear* is related back to *maiden* in the first part of the line because *maidengear* has been used as a compound in the previous line. In one gradience (which is largely phonetically organized) Hopkins proposes that he is a 'Jack, joke, poor potsherd, patch, matchwood'.[24] These terms are by no means synonymous but they are all pejorative in that they refer to mean and common things. This gradience is completed by what amounts to a semantic *contrast*: 'immortal diamond'.

This very widespread tendency to string together words and phrases in pairs and series is largely responsible for the impression that Hopkins's syntax is a syntax of co-ordination, and the device may be extended to include very long phrases or full clauses that are in apposition to one another. Thus, in the 'Deutschland' alone, whereas a series 'the gospel *proffer*, a *pressure*, a *principle*, Christ's gift' is a phonetic-semantic series in which the final term is a superordinate of the others and is defined by them, there are many series which contain longer segments of speech and which are echoes of one another on the grammatical level. Thus 'Take settler and seamen, tell men with women' is co-ordinate just as the word-series are, and 'To bathe in his fall-gold mercies, to breathe in his all-fire glances' is also a co-ordinate pair in which phonetic and grammatical parallelism is obvious. Such devices of extended co-ordination are very different from the norms of Victorian poetic diction, and it is not surprising that critics should particularly notice them and so believe that Hopkins's language is fundamentally a language of co-ordination. We shall see in the next chapter that this is not wholly tenable. What is clear, however, is that the effect of such series (heightened as they are by phonetic devices) is a controlled variation that gives a sense of emotional intensity and immediacy. This immediacy, in turn, despite the artifices involved, gives an illusion of relative closeness to ordinary speech when it is contrasted with most Victorian diction.

CHAPTER 7

'Order and Purpose': Hopkins's Syntax

🐚🐚🐚🐚🐚🐚

As we saw in Chapter 1, critics have often taken the view that Hopkins violates the 'rules' of grammar. Bridges's strictures on Hopkins's omission of relative pronouns and his freedom in 'parts of speech' usage were balanced by an appreciation of his 'rare masterly beauties'. Yvor Winters, however, has gone much further in asserting that Hopkins 'violates grammar as he sees fit'. The view that Hopkins violates grammar is also apparent in the work of David Daiches:

> ... with Hopkins language was a servant, to be bullied and coerced into as immediate contact with the thought as possible. The rules of grammar and syntax were not allowed to stand in the way; if they affected the immediacy of the expression they were ignored ...[1]

Throughout this book we have attempted to understand and explain the nature of Hopkins's poetic diction rather than to condemn it, and we have seen that he believed in *laws* governing *behaviour* in all natural things. We have also argued that Hopkins's attitude to language was based on the belief that it too was a 'natural' thing (a work of God, rather than of Man), and that language *behaviour* was also governed by fundamental *laws*. It is difficult to believe that such a scrupulous man, who set such a store by *laws* and who so revered the orderliness of God's works, could have been so cavalier as to *bully and coerce* the language. Professor Daiches is right about 'immediate contact with the thought', but, as we have attempted to show in previous chapters, Hopkins's use of language is not a violation, but an extension of *laws* or underlying rules that are already present in the language. At best, these critical pronouncements on Hopkins's maltreatment of syntax are exaggerated and misleading; at worst, they show a superficiality in understanding the nature of language and the poet's use of it.

In some cases, one feels, they may be motivated more by lack of sympathy with the man and his ideals than by lack of sympathy with his *language*.

This aside, it would appear (as we have suggested) that strictures on Hopkins's syntax are really objections to his rejection of *continuous literary decorum*. But, as we have also noted, standard Victorian diction itself involves considerable exploitation of a syntax which seems to deviate from ordinary speech (and from prose) just as much as Hopkins does in his 'freedoms'. In the stanza from Tennyson that we quoted in Chapter 4 (page 103) and in Hopkins's early poems, we have seen that the syntactic deviations of this standard diction involve a *foregrounding* against the norms of the standard prose language, and that this *foregrounding* itself becomes standardized. The inversions and archaisms that Hopkins later objected to have in such poetry become part of the *canon*. We tend to accept these marked deviations from ordinary speech because we have become used to them, and when, within the rather stereotyped conventions used, the poet achieves a certain intensity or subtlety of language, we perceive it as elegant or effective. It is also relatively easy to describe in linguistic terms how such poets achieve their effects within the accepted linguistic conventions.

Hopkins, however, created a poetic diction for himself. To describe this and to explain its effects, we require a much deeper understanding of syntax than is displayed by those critics who base their syntax on the prescriptive 'rules' of eighteenth-century grammar. One of the chief insights of modern syntactic theory has been the perception that all language use is in a sense creative. The adult speaker has internalized the rules of his language. These rules are not to be primarily understood as rules imposed from outside by a prescriptive tradition mainly relevant to the writing of prose. They form the basic competence of any speaker to utter 'grammatical' sentences, which are potentially infinite in length and number. Thus, the speaker abstracts from the underlying rules of the language to *create* sentences, and he is able to use these mechanisms to utter sentences that may never have been used before. The fact that language changes at all proves that there is a considerable element of creativity in ordinary language use. Speakers can coin new words and idioms which may or may not become 'accepted'; the massive variation in spoken syntax in time and space also demonstrates that innovation must be continually taking place. For example, the use of positive *anymore*, that Hopkins himself noticed in Ireland and which we have observed,[2] is an innovation in underlying linguistic rules which in the course of time has become characteristic of particular dialects. To put it relatively technically: the element [+ negative] that is a specified feature of the syntax of *anymore* in most dialects (as in 'I *don't* like this town *anymore*') has in these dialects been deleted, so that the item is now indifferently positive or negative. In these dialects, therefore, the rules allow 'I *do* like this town *anymore*'.

Creativity, therefore, is a continuous process in language. Linguists have in recent years fought a number of battles amongst themselves concerning the distinction between *grammatical* and *acceptable*. In Chomsky's earliest exposition of transformational-generative grammar it was stated that such a sentence as *Colourless green ideas sleep furiously* is grammatical, even though it is hard to interpret. Similarly, such a sentence as 'This is Jack, by whom the house that the malt that the rat that the cat that the dog worried, killed, ate, lay in, was built' is grammatical in that it correctly but repeatedly applies the underlying rules of English syntax for transforming active constructions into passive ones. However, both sentences may be considered unacceptable, the first because it is difficult to interpret semantically, the second because of the limitations of human memory. For psychological (not linguistic) reasons, someone hearing this sentence only once would find it impossible to understand. If the sentence is written down, however, it can be interpreted by application of normal syntactic rules if we pore over it for a few minutes. Thus, it is possible for a *writer* to use convoluted syntax and expect his *reader* to be able to interpret it. Much of the prose syntax of the late sixteenth to eighteenth centuries is complicated in this sense, and in more recent times Henry James has used it. In poetry, it is well exemplified in Milton:

> Him haply slumb'ring on the Norway foam,
> The pilot of some small night-founder'd skiff,
> Deeming some island, oft, as seamen tell,
> With fixèd anchor in his scaly rind
> Moors by his side under the lee, while night
> Invests the sea and wishèd morn delays.
>
> (*Paradise Lost*, I, ll. 203-8)

As for Hopkins, a very high level of obvious syntactic convolution is found chiefly in a group of later poems (including 'Tom's Garland'). Where it does occur, our difficulty in comprehension may be aggravated by Hopkins's additional innovations in vocabulary, but his poetry is normally *grammatical* in that it can be interpreted by applying the rules of English grammar. Grammatical complexity or ambiguity are, as we shall see, not the same as being *ungrammatical*. Furthermore, it is reasonable to speak of *degrees* of grammaticality in that an utterance which contains something ungrammatical may still as a whole be *more* grammatical than some other utterance.

One poet who has been much discussed by linguists in recent years is E. E. Cummings, and it may be instructive to compare his poetry briefly with that of Hopkins. In many of his well-known poems (see for example *Collected Poems* II, p. 515), Cummings has introduced a degree of real ungrammaticality in that the word order is scrambled, and it is in places not possible to interpret the syntactic relations with any certainty at all.[3] The 'meaning' has to be interpreted by a complete rearrangement of the lines (e.g. 'with so many bells floating up (and) down'), and when we do rearrange the line in this way we cannot be sure that this is what the poet intends us to do. Even when Hopkins's syntax is at its most difficult, it approaches this degree of ungrammaticality only very rarely and in one particular habit, that of *interruption*; otherwise his syntax, difficult though it may be, follows rules of word-order, ellipsis, inversion and so on for which there are clear models in normal English. Thus, Hopkins's language is always English whereas it may be doubted whether some of Cummings's usages are any language at all. In this sense, Hopkins has more in common with Milton and the tradition than with the anti-grammatical Cummings (who may be thought similar at first sight). In so far as an interpretable grammatical framework is present in Hopkins's poetry together with a daring originality in lexicon, he is more like the nonsense poets and James Joyce. Perhaps it should be added that none of these actually writes nonsense.

The fundamental dissimilarity to Cummings may perhaps be demonstrated by a discussion of a passage in which Hopkins may be thought to approach most closely the *ungrammaticality* of Cummings. The difficulty arises from the fact that a verbal construction is *interrupted*:

> wind
> What most I may eye after, be in at the end
> I cannot . . .   (No. 40)

The verb is *wind eye after*, and the lines can be rearranged to read: 'Whatever I may most wind (my) eye after (i.e. 'follow with my eye': Hopkins explains *wind* in *LB*, 66), I cannot be in at the end'; this makes perfect sense in the context. It is in this habit of interrupting complex constructions that Hopkins approaches the rampant ungrammaticality of Cummings, in so far as he does not always give us clear clues to interpretation. But even here, Hopkins is not truly and completely ungrammatical, and the lines may be thought to be more like the passivization of *the house that Jack built* in that they are difficult to *interpret*, rather than ungrammatical. Hopkins's *a lonely began* (No. 66) is superficially similar to some of Cummings's 'violations' of grammar in that an inflected verb *in the past tense* is here used as if it were a noun. But Hopkins's phrase can be perfectly clearly interpreted as *elliptical* ('a lonely *one who* began') whereas Cummings's usage is not always satisfactorily explained in this way.

Before we examine the kinds of syntax that are most characteristic of Hopkins, we return briefly to the notion of creativity in language and to *acceptability*.

The suggestion that all language use is or may be *creative* involves the perception that poetic language differs from ordinary language not in kind but in degree. In other words it is or should be *current language*, but *heightened*. We have elsewhere noted that figurative and onomatopoetic language, blending, compounding and derivation are all actual or potential in ordinary spoken language. So too is rhyme and rhythm. The language-game is played by children as well as poets, and it is highly relevant to remember that Hopkins knew and appreciated this – most obviously in his association of children's rhymes and weather saws with sprung rhythm. Our explanation of Hopkins's language accords here as elsewhere with his own views on poetic diction – and this is as it should be. Whether Hopkins's usage is *acceptable* is quite another question.

A few years ago it was fashionable for linguists to debate the difference between *grammatical* and *acceptable* as if these were strictly comparable terms.[4] A moment's reflection however will lead us to the conclusion that these are terms of quite different orders. In various ways, one may overlap with the other. *Accept-ability* is social or attitudinal and may be concerned with value-judgement, aesthetics, appropriateness to context and so on. To put it crudely: what is acceptable to one person or one occasion may not be acceptable to other persons or on other occasions. The sentence *I seen it* is not normally acceptable to an English teacher in the classroom, but it is perfectly acceptable when used by a docker in the company of other dockers. Frequently, the reason given for social unacceptability of such a usage is that it is 'ungrammatical', and this of course is not the true reason. Critical attacks on Hopkins's grammar are precisely analogous to this. For various reasons, good or bad, a critic like Winters finds Hopkins's poetry 'unacceptable', and chooses to express his disapproval by attacking the poet's 'grammar'. Since it is not our main purpose in this book to assess the value of Hopkins's poetry or its acceptability, we now return to a discussion of his syntax.

'SPOKEN' SYNTAX IN HOPKINS'S POETRY

In Chapter 1 and in our discussion of the sound-pattern of 'The Deutschland', we have already mentioned the extra range and variety that Hopkins gives to his language by adopting characteristics of spoken usage that other poets would have found unacceptable. In 'The Deutschland' especially, we have suggested that he is able to maintain *an illusion of ordinary speech*. This is partly the result of rhythmic variability, but it is certainly reinforced by the use of 'spoken' syntax:

> But how shall I . . . make me room there:
> Reach me a . . . Fancy, come faster –
> Strike you the sight of it? look at it loom there,
> Thing that she . . . there then! the Master,   (st. 28)

This disjointed syntax communicates well the agitation and indecisiveness experienced in a situation of stress, and it does so by imitating the mixing of questions, exclamations and statements that actually do occur in ordinary speech, though not in well-finished prose or conventional verse. The power of such lines to call up the situation and the emotions appropriate to it is due just as much to the syntax as it is to the information conveyed; outside of metrical considerations the syntax is hardly *heightened* at all, in that it uses very little that is deviant from normal spoken syntax (*strike you* . . . for 'do you strike' seems to be the only deviation).

We have noticed in Chapter 4 several other examples from the 'Deutschland' which capture various speech-styles with little or no deviation from normal spoken syntax. We may add further examples. Notice the sense of resignation in 'Well, she has thee for the pain . . .' (st. 31), exclamation and question in 'The majesty! what did she mean?' (st. 25). Verbless sentences and *run-on* sentences are numerous (as in speech); parentheses and repetitions tend to come in places where prose and conventional diction would forbid them, but where an agitated or uncertain *speaker* would be likely to use them:

> . . . the hurtle of hell
> Behind, *where, where was a, where was a* place?
> ('Deutschland', st. 3)

> I did say yes
> O at lightning and lashed rod;   (st. 2)

> But roped with, *always, all the way down from the tall*
> *Fells or flanks of the voel*, a vein
> Of the gospel proffer . . .   (st. 4)

And in other poems:

> I walk, *I lift up, I lift up* heart, eyes,   (No. 38)

> And *hurls for him*, O half *hurls* earth *for him*

> off under his feet   (No. 38)

> Three hundred souls, O *ulus*! on board   (No. 41)

> Let him *oh*! with his air of angels then lift me . . .
> (No. 45)

> *Where we*, even *where we* mean
> To mend her we end her   (No. 43)

> *When, when, Peace*, will you, *Peace*?   (No. 51)

Sometimes, as in the first two stanzas of 'The Bugler's First Communion', this speech syntax of parenthesis and repetition is mixed with a syntax of compression and subordination of a kind which could only occur in the most carefully constructed written language. We shall discuss this later in this chapter.

In one stanza, 'The Deutschland' also makes extended use of the *tag*-question (which is not usually found in careful prose, and in extended use is rare in conventional verse):

> Ah, touched in your bower of bone,
> *Are you*! turned for an exquisite smart,
> *Have you*! make words break from me here all alone,
> *Do you*! . . .

This passage, in which the poet is addressing his own heart, is somewhat more obviously *heightened* than some others in that the parallelism of the tags calls attention to the language for its own sake; but the pattern of the syntax is clearly that of ordinary speech. Compare, for example, a solicitous friend inquiring 'Enjoying your tea, are you?' Perhaps it is this closeness to mundane language that has made some people so uncomfortable with Hopkins and laid him open to the charge of indecorousness.

Hopkins's 1877–9 lyrics are rich in the 'simple' language of ordinary speech, mixed judiciously as it is with syntactic manipulation: part of the *heightening* of current language that could make it 'unlike itself'. One of these simple lines may well be the best opening line to any of his poems:

> Nothing is so beautiful as Spring –

It is a mere statement, a *declarative* sentence.[5] Like many of the other lyrics of Hopkins's 'Welsh' period, this poem is a celebration of God in nature. However, the *exclamatory* tone of 'The Starlight Night' is perhaps more typical of these poems than the line from 'Spring':

> Look at the stars! look, look up at the skies!
> O look at all the fire-folk sitting in the air!
> The bright boroughs, the circle-citadels there!
> Down in dim woods the diamond delves! the elves'-eyes!

After these six exclamation marks, the octave continues with another five; the first three lines of the sestet have five more and a question-mark in addition. In the first two lines, the word *look* occurs four times. The effect is one of urgency, and the sentence-structure is emphatically speech-like. Phrases and clauses taken individually are no different from those of speech: the effect of heightening in so far as it is due to syntax is achieved mainly by *repetition* of words and syntactic structures. The imperative verbs and other features occur *more often* than they would be likely to occur in any but the most emotional speech.

Like 'Pied Beauty', this poem is largely a list. *Look at* (the poet says) the fire-folk, the boroughs, the citadels, the delves, the elves'-eyes, the grey lawns, the whitebeam, the abeles (poplars), the flake-doves. All these are parallel to, and definitions of, the *stars*. The poem gives one command, and subordinate to it makes a number of statements: *look at* the stars, *which are* fire-folk, circle-citadels and so on. That is almost all it says. A similar simple structure applies to 'Pied Beauty'. The poet exclaims 'Glory be to God for *dappled things*', and the succeeding list of items is semantically subordinate,[6] but grammatically in apposition, to *dappled things*. But whereas the first poem proposes that the *stars* are bright boroughs, circle-citadels, the second poem is logically reversed. In 'The Starlight Night', the superordinate, *stars*, is defined. 'Pied Beauty' proposes the opposite, and it is the rosemoles, finches' wings and so on that are defined by the superordinate *dappled*. But what is important to recognize here is that the rather simple syntactic structure of both poems (based on an imperative in one case and a subjunctive wish in the other) is that of speech. The difference from speech is largely in the subject-matter and content of the lists.

In these poems, the choice of the exclamatory wish or command syntax in the key (first) sentence is what prevents them from being nothing more than statements to the effect that stars are bright boroughs and rosemoles *are* dappled things. But, in general, Hopkins's preference for syntax which is not simply *declarative* has been widely noted. This undoubtedly gives to his poetry something of its intensely emotional quality, despite the fact that the sentence types involved are normal enough in speech. He is much given to the use of interjections: *ah, oh, well, oh well, ah well, alas* (these are not unusual in Victorian poetry, for instance, that of Matthew Arnold). Hopkins probably uses them more thickly than other poets and, since they are characteristic of spoken language rather than written prose, they reinforce the personal tone of his poetry. Speech is more personal, more tied to context, less formal and less public than written language, and Hopkins's interjections help to bring about the sense of immediacy and closeness to situation and speaker that is so palpable in his poetry.

Sudden changes between sentence-types – *statement* (declarative), *question* (interrogative), *command* (imperative) and *exclamation*, together with uncompleted, interrupted, and various kinds of verbless sentences, are very marked. Even in a poem of fundamentally simple structure much of the sense of urgency is brought about by such syntactic changes. 'Ah well!' he exclaims in 'The Starlight Night', 'it is all a purchase, all is a prize'. The Kingdom of Heaven, which he glimpses through the stars, is 'worthy the winning'. Then he goes on to urge the hearer to purchase that Kingdom.

Buy then! bid then! – What? – Prayer, patience, alms, vows.

The logical relations between the parts of this line are not clear on the surface, just as the logic of speech is so often submerged and its sentences ambiguous – to be clarified only by the context of situation in which they are uttered. Hopkins has involved us in a situation fraught with personal feeling. The word *what?* is ambiguous in its syntactic relationship in a number of ways. It may be Hopkins asking us *what* we have said in reply to his urging; it may be the imagined hearer (or Hopkins's *alter ego*) asking *what* he is to buy or *with what* he is to buy it. And the reply comes: 'Buy it with prayer, patience, alms, vows'. That, if you like, is the 'logical' meaning of the line, and it is clear enough despite the ambiguity of the syntactic relations within the line. The illusion of speech and the sense of immediacy and heightened emotion that goes with it could not have been achieved if the 'logic' had been clearly worked out on the surface of the sentence – as in expository prose.

'Hurrahing in Harvest' starts with a statement:

Summer ends now; now barbarous in beauty, the stooks rise
  Around . . .

It continues with exclamations, in sentences that are verbless:

. . . up above, what wind-walks! what lovely behaviour
Of silk-sack clouds! . . .

Again, this is the syntax of speech, and again, Hopkins is communicating an urgency that he could not achieve in standard literary grammar. He is also compressing the meaning. He is not merely saying 'What wind-walks *there are* up above!' He is also urging us again to *look*, as he did in 'The Starlight Night': 'up above' is detached from the remainder of the phrase and placed in a prominent position where it seems to take on something of an *imperative* function as well as being a directional adverb: '*Look up above*! See what wind-walks there are!' The next sentence is in the form of a question:

> . . . has wilder, wilful-wavier
> Meal-drift moulded ever and melted across skies?

No one would actually speak *this* sentence, but the rhetorical question, which seems to ask but actually states a point of view, is a commonplace of speech. Its 'logic' follows on from the previous exclamations and the tone is intimate. 'Here I am, the poet, looking at the beautiful scenery of late summer. I want you to imagine it. *Look at the clouds! Have you ever seen anything so beautiful?*' These last two sentences are natural normal speech, in which they would follow one another almost inevitably. They have the same general syntactic form as the sentences quoted from 'Hurrahing in Harvest'.

These sudden changes between sentence-types, which so often give an impression of thinking aloud, occur very frequently in Hopkins's poetry, and the following examples are only a few of the many that could be quoted:

Felix Randal the farrier, O he is dead then? my duty all
 ended . . .   (No. 53)

Buy then! bid then! – What? – Prayer, patience, alms, vows.
               (No. 3?)

But how shall I . . . make me room there:
         ('Deutschland', st. 28)

> Too proud, too proud, what a press she bore!
> Royal, and all her royals wore.
> Sharp with her, shorten sail!
> Too late; lost; gone with the gale.   (No. 41, ll. 33–6)

With, perilous, O no . . .   (No. 70)

By a grey eye's heed steered well, one crew, fall to; (No. 71)

Often these breaches of 'literary decorum' go so far as mixing direct and indirect speech. The poet seems to be speaking in different voices and from different points of view. In the stanza quoted from 'The Eurydice' (No. 41), the shouts of the sailors are simulated in the third line, and the poet speaks in the fourth. His tone is resigned and the sentences are the verbless *minor* sentences of speech.

As sprung rhythm is firmly based on the rhythm of speech, so this 'broken' syntax is based on speech-syntax. Speech is syntactically much more varied than prose language, just as its rhythms are more varied than those imposed by traditional metre. Thus, Hopkins's syntactic variability is analogous to his adoption of sprung rhythm. It too forms a link between the current language and the heightened language of poetry. But, as we have already suggested, Hopkins's syntactic 'freedoms' are not *caused* by the constraints of sprung rhythm.[7] Both are equally required by the principle that poetic diction shall be based on current spoken language.

Hopkins's *heightening* of language is based on intensity of two kinds, the one achieved by repetition, as in spoken language, and the other by *compression*, which is not so characteristic of speech. His various principles of phonetic rhyme clearly involve *repetition* of like sounds, but also a clustering effect brought about by repetition of particular sounds within lines or stanzas. Similarly, as we have seen, Hopkins achieves *complexity* at the semantic level by exploiting the phonaesthetic suggestiveness of words and by involving more than one 'meaning' in a word. In his semantic series or gradiences, he also arranges words in such a way that each term in the series affects its neighbour and partly 'rhymes' semantically. This of course is a device based on repetition (of meanings). In his syntax also, Hopkins is inclined to use repetition by stringing together words of the same syntactic order. But *heightening* by means of syntax, especially in later poems, is much more commonly brought about by *compression*. This syntactic compression is such a vital part of Hopkins's heightening and such a prominent effect in his poetry that we must discuss it in some detail. In what follows, we shall first consider what Fr Peters has called Hopkins's language of co-ordination (which is rather similar to what we mean by his devices of *repetition* or syntactic *rhyming*). In view of the great *complexity* of much of his syntax it appears that Hopkins's language cannot be *adequately* described as based on co-ordination.

CO-ORDINATION AND REPETITION

It is superficially clear that, especially in his early poetry, Hopkins tends to use sentences which are in traditional terms grammatically *simple*. He also uses *minor* sentences (with no verb), and various kinds of exclamatory and interrogative sentence. When main clauses are linked with other clauses they tend to be linked by co-ordination rather than subordination. Sometimes, as Fr Peters has observed, the co-ordinating conjunction is suppressed: 'Hopkins observes and places facts side by side; the relation is apprehended in the juxtaposition itself'.[8]

Traditional grammar distinguishes *co-ordinating* conjunctions (*and, but, or, nor, for*) from *subordinating conjunctions*. Whereas some of the co-ordinators can be used to link items of various 'ranks' (word, phrase or clause) the subordinators normally link clauses. In a sentence such as 'he was happy when alive' which appears to use a subordinator (*when*) before a word rather than a clause, it is normally said that we are dealing with an *elliptical* clause ('when *he was* alive'), in which subject and verb are suppressed. Otherwise when items that can be subordinating conjunctions appear before words, they tend to be labelled *prepositions*. Clearly, if we define subordinate constructions solely by whether they are signalled in the surface structure by a subordinating conjunction, we may run into difficulties.

There are similar difficulties with co-ordination. If language were entirely 'logical' or mathematical, we could replace *and* by a + sign and *nor* (in some uses) by +*not*. Observe the effect of this in stanza 15 of 'The Deutschland':

> Hope was twelve hours gone;
> +frightful a nightfall folded rueful a day
> +*not* rescue, only rocket and lightship, shone,
> +lives at last were washing away.

It does not work because, underlying the co-ordinating surface structure of the stanza, certain logical or temporal relations between the items are implied. If we were to write a summary prose paraphrase, no one would object to something like this: '*As* night fell, there was no rescue ... *even though* lives were being lost'. The fact that *and*, especially in narrative, is often a *temporal* conjunction is even clearer in:

> night drew her
> Dead to the Kentish Knock;
> *And* she beat the bank down with her bows and the ride
> of her keel   (st. 14)

Here, as commonly in 'The Deutschland', this co-ordinative *surface* grammar is the most effective kind of syntax largely because the passage concerned is *narrative*. *And* constructions are characteristic of spoken narrative. The emphasis is on action and movement, and each movement is as important as the next. To subordinate ('*when* night drew her to the Kentish Knock, she beat down the bank ...') would focus attention on the main clause and suggest that the driving of the ship on to the bank was in some way subsidiary. The poet would by such syntax express an attitude to the events, evaluating one as more important and immediate than the other.

Despite the fact that Hopkins's surface grammar frequently seems to be co-ordinative (with items of the same grammatical status and 'logical' importance linked by a co-ordinator or by simple juxtaposition), we must take issue with Fr Peters's general statement:[9]

> Hopkins used the language of co-ordination. To set off the frequency of this peculiar form of marshalling the phrases side by side without properly joining them together, we should note how very rare subordination is in his poetry. I have counted only about fifteen lines in which Hopkins uses a subordinating conjunction.

The objection to this statement as a characterization of Hopkins's general practice is twofold. It is based first on the acknowledged complexity and difficulty of Hopkins's language. If he had been happy merely to string together words, phrases and sentences, it is reasonable to suppose that his verse would not be as dense and 'obscure' as it often is. The second objection is that Fr Peters implicitly defines *co-ordination* and *subordination* in terms of the occurrence or non-occurrence of particular conjunctions in the surface-form of sentences.

To confine syntactic analysis to a description of the disposition of words and their relations within the surface form of sentences has been much attacked in recent years. It forms the basis of Noam Chomsky's objections to 'immediate constituent analysis' and his proposals for a 'transformational' grammar. In effect, it has been suggested that to confine syntactic analysis to surface structure is simply not illuminating or explanatory; it will fail to apprehend and explain important differences in syntactic relations that actually do exist. We have already touched on this topic in our discussion of compounding in Chapter 6, when we pointed out that compound words of superficially identical syntactic structure may have quite different relations between their components (thus, an *eating apple* is an apple for eating, but a *praying mantis* is not a mantis for praying).[10] The proposed distinction between *surface structure* and *deep structure* is based partly on the fact of ambiguity (Chomsky's example is *Flying planes can be dangerous*), but also on such pairs as *John is easy to please* and *John is eager to please*. In order to explain the different relations within these superficially similar sentences, we must recognize that in one case *John* is the subject in both surface and deep structure (it is actually being proposed that John *is* eager), whereas in the other *John* is only a 'surface' subject. In deep structure *John* is the object of *please*.[11]

As Chomsky points out, this kind of difference has always been perceived by traditional grammarians. It is implicit, for example, in the distinction between 'subjective' and 'objective' genitives. In such a phrase as *the minister's appointment*, we could be speaking of an appointment of someone else *by* the minister or an appointment of the minister *by* someone else. It is similarly implicit in Henry Sweet's distinction between the *grammatical* subject and the *logical* subject, which would account for *John is easy to please* and *John is eager to please*. The difference, however, is that contemporary grammarians insist that deep-structural relations are *linguistic*. They should be handled by any syntactic theory that claims to be explanatory, and should not simply be dismissed as irrelevant to grammar under the rather vague heading of 'logical'. These scholars also differ from traditional grammarians in that they propose *formal* rules (of a broadly 'transformational' kind) which seek to *derive* the surface structure of sentences from underlying deep structures. These formal rules are complex, and technical; the derivation of an ordinary sentence such as 'We expected John to be examined by the doctor' involves a number of underlying sentences, a complex series of instructions for deletion and permutation of elements, together with instructions for *embedding* elements in their proper place in the final sentence.[12]

In this book, bearing in mind that the object of our interest is not linguistic theory but the poetry of Hopkins, we do not aspire to the high formalism of strict transformational theory. But it appears that the insights of this theory offer us the best way of describing simply, and in an informal way, what Hopkins actually does with English syntactic rules. All critics have perceived that Hopkins's language is dense and grammatically complex, that he inverts word-order and indulges in ellipsis and omission of certain kinds of words. He is also given to embedding sentences and phrases in a complex way within other sentences and phrases. Although he extends the rules for ellipsis, permutation and embedding beyond what is normal in ordinary usage, the fact remains that we can describe what he does in these terms. Virtually all his usage can be brought within the orbit of transformational rules, and thus shown to be rule-governed – to have a 'logic' of its own.

Before we go on to argue that Hopkins's language is in effect a language of *subordination*, we return to Fr Peters's discussion of Hopkins's syntax and to those surface features of Hopkins's usage that are truly co-ordinative. Peters's account of Hopkins's syntax is brilliant and discerning. It is marred only by his assumption that syntax is a superficial thing. In effect, Peters's account of Hopkins's co-ordinate sentences contradicts his own point that Hopkins's language is co-ordinate, since, as he so clearly shows, the relations obtaining between co-ordinate clauses or adjacent simple sentences are often logically complex. As he notes:[13]

> . . . this syntactical parity does not stand for a corresponding parity in the poet's mind. Thus there is nothing less than disparity, or contrast, expressed in the following lines (italics inserted):

> Away in the loveable west
>   . . .
> I was under a roof here, I was at rest,
>   *And* they the prey of the gales
>   ('Deutschland', st. 24)

Fr Peters then suggests that, if we were to express this by a sub-ordinating conjunction, the language would not be heightened but *lowered*. As far as it goes, this is probably true, here as else-where. Even if we were to substitute *yet* for the first *and* in the following, there would be a change:

> They fought with God's cold –
> *And* they could not and fell to the deck
>
> ('Deutschland', st. 17)

The co-ordination is more effective, and it is helpful to ask why. It could be argued that the suppression of a logical connection between the clauses is justified in a purely descriptive narration. Hopkins is saying that these things happened, but not presuming to say why, in the same way in which his Journal describes the *behaviour* of flowers without presuming to know God's reasons for making them *behave* in the orderly way that they do. It is the sense of wonder again. We marvel at God's creation, and although we may try we cannot explain it. But if we look at the quotation again we shall see that the words themselves provide the answer to our linguistic problem. Hopkins did not choose *yet* because he did not mean *yet*. There is nothing strange or unexpected or contrastive in the idea that 'they' could not fight against *God's* cold. *Of course* they could not do so successfully; it is God who disposes. But a linguistic purist would hardly approve of using this cliché *phrase* (*of course*) in poetry that aimed to get the maximum meaning from words. When Hopkins does use *of course* in No. 35 ('Why, it seemed of *course*; seemed of *right* it should'), *course* is a *word* with full meaning, not part of a phrase meaning 'naturally'. In 'The Deutschland', st 17, we may read: 'Of course they could not, and so, as a result, they fell to the deck'.

Thus, Hopkins's preference here and elsewhere for the co-ordinating conjunction is seen to be justified in a number of ways. Co-ordination (parataxis) is frequent in speech and in narrative, whereas a subordinate clause structure is frequent in logical argument or 'spoken prose'. What is important about clause-linking *and* is the quasi-objectivity of the effect; logical, temporal and attitudinal relations that the poet has in mind are apparently suppressed, and the language becomes all the more rich and suggestive for that. Clause-linking *and*, therefore, is a surface effect in Hopkins's poetry and is most commonly found in narrative, where it is either temporal in meaning, or 'logically' subordinating, or both.

True co-ordination (without these deeper 'logical' implications) in Hopkins's work is found chiefly at the level of the *word* or *phrase*, not the clause. In descriptive or narrative passages, it commonly links *two* or *three* items of related meaning or sound, or both. The following examples are all from 'The Deutschland' (my italics):

> . . . giver of breath *and* bread   (st. 1)

> The dense *and* the driven Passion, *and* frightful sweat
>   (st. 7)

> Wiry *and* white-fiery *and* whirlwind-swivellèd snow (st. 13)

> The flange *and* the rail; flame,
> Fang, *or* flood . . .   (st. 11)

> And canvas *and* compass, the whorl *and* the wheel
> Idle for ever to waft her *or* wind her with . . .   (st. 14)

> And the inboard seas run swirling *and* hawling
>   (st. 19)

> Five! the finding *and* sake
> *And* cipher of suffering Christ   (st. 22)

This simple co-ordinative grammar is the grammar of current language and is related to the effect of 'thinking aloud' we have noticed in Hopkins's poetry. He seems to be searching around for the right word, and if the first one he uses does not fully capture the inscape, he adds another and then another. If this were done without skill, such phrases would seem to be random and disorderly. But in the examples quoted and in many others, Hopkins's faith in the orderliness of language is rewarded. Note that in every case the effect achieved is one of a unity of sound and sense. The words thus linked, besides being grammatically parallel, are related by phonetic or semantic devices (or both), of the kind discussed in Chapters 5 and 6.

In extreme cases, we encounter multiple co-ordination within simple phrases. Again, the paradigmatic example is the first line of 'The Leaden Echo', where a simple noun-phrase within a relatively simple sentence ('Is there nowhere known some *key* to keep back beauty?') is extended to eight items, related, as we have seen, in sound and meaning: '*bow* or *brooch* or *braid* or *brace, lace, latch* or *catch* or *key* . . .'

Series such as this are not always linked in surface structure by a co-ordinating conjunction. When the conjunction is absent the distinction between co-ordination and apposition is difficult to discern. There are rules in normal English allowing the suppression of co-ordinators in series; normally only the last two items are linked by a co-ordinator. Thus, we say *bacon and eggs*, but *Tom, Dick and Harry*. Premodifying adjectives in particular tend to lose co-ordinators, and it is not always clear in ordinary use whether such series are truly co-ordinate or not. Hopkins is very much inclined to suppress the conjunction even between the last two items in a series.

In Hopkins's usage, there are many instances where it would make no difference logically whether the conjunction were used or not. Thus, if we inserted *and* between the items marked off by slants in the following, the difference would be rhetorical or rhythmic. The items are of the same grammatical status. All are adjectival, and most are participial adjectives:

> . . . so haggard at the heart/ so care-coiled/
> care-killed/ so fagged/ so fashed/ so cogged/
> so cumbered . . . (No. 59)

Despite the absence of *and*, this series and many others like it seem to be co-ordinative series, rather than appositive.[14]

But there can be very subtle logical differences between series that seem to be co-ordinate and series that seem to be appositive (both being devices of *repetition*). This can be demonstrated by referring to the structure of 'Pied Beauty', which is built up by a series of constructions that are appositive to *for dappled things*. If we were to insert the word *and* before each item in the series that follows in ll. 2–8, the items would become mutually exclusive. This would apply even if *and* were inserted only before the first appositive; underlying *and* would then be 'understood' in all the following items. The items listed would not then be *dappled things*, but other things additional to *dappled things*.

Normally, when Hopkins gives a list of simple or compound words or phrases linked by *and* (or *or* in 'on turf *or* perch *or* poor low stage', No. 39), all the items are mutually exclusive, and this often applies even when the conjunction is suppressed. For the present argument, we conclude that Hopkins is fond of co-ordination when the items are words or phrases rather than clauses, but we shall see that there may still be considerable grammatical complexity within the structure of single items in series. Hopkins's various uses of grammatical parallelism within sentences are analogous on the syntactic level to the devices of phonetic and semantic concatenation that we have discussed. We may refer to these devices (chiefly co-ordination) as *repetition* to differentiate them from devices of *compression* which we take to be more basic to Hopkins's syntax. It is relevant at this point to draw attention to the fundamental difference between Hopkins's devices of repetition and those of other poets.

It is very unusual to find in Hopkins's work the kind of syntactic and lexical parallelism that we find in the successive lines of the following (my italics):

> Too quick despairer, wherefore wilt thou go?
> *Soon will the* high Midsummer pomps come on,
> *Soon will the* musk carnations break and swell,
> *Soon shall we* have gold-dusted snapdragon
> Sweet-William with his homely cottage-smell . . .
> (Matthew Arnold, 'Thyrsis')

Nor do we find an 'echo' syntax carrying over from one stanza to the other, as in this:

> Now as I was young and easy under the apple-boughs
> About the lilting house and happy as the grass was green . . .
> About the happy yard and singing as the farm was home . . .
> Under the new made clouds and happy as the heart was long.
> (Dylan Thomas, 'Fern Hill')

This kind of obvious parallelism derives from the *canon* that Hopkins rejected. Something like it is found in early poetry such as 'Heaven-Haven' (in which the two stanzas are syntactic echoes) and in the refrain-like devices of his occasional and later unfinished verse. As we saw in Chapter 5, Hopkins's *rhythms* (unlike those of Tennyson's song from 'The Brook') are not carried over as parallels from one stanza to another. The rhythm of each stanza is individuated within it. Much the same applies to Hopkins's syntactic parallelism. There are *lines* in which a marked and fore-grounded syntax is echoed in the two halves (*frightful a nightfall* . . . *rueful a day*; *Our heart's charity's hearth's fire, our thought's chivalry's throng's Lord*). Otherwise, parallelism is exploited within the sentence or phrase by imitating the chance repetitions of speech (*Here he will then, here he will* . . ., No. 159), or by syntactic co-ordination and apposition. This avoidance of conventional parallelism and preference for repetition of like syntax *within* the phrase or sentence is a distinguishing mark of Hopkins's poetry.

SYNTACTIC COMPRESSION

Important as syntactic repetition is in Hopkins's poetry (especially in helping to suggest spoken syntax), the syntactic devices by which he builds up the dense verbal structure of most of his poetry are better described as *compression*. Everyone agrees that his style is 'elliptical'; many complain that words are left out or put together in the wrong order. This density of language can be best explained as based on what are nowadays called rules of *sentence-embedding*.

In recent linguistics, what is traditionally called subordination is said to be brought about by embedding. Thus, if we take a simple sentence: *John wears galoshes*, we may embed a subordinate clause and produce: *John, who is fat, wears galoshes*. To put it in another way, we can say that the sentence contains two pro-positions: *John wears galoshes* and *John is fat*. Although these two sentences are equally main clauses, the complex sentence *embeds* one in the other, thereby making the embedded clause subordinate. Normally, a subordinate clause will contain information which the user considers to be subsidiary to the content of the main clause and which the hearer perceives as subsidiary. Transformational grammar would propose that the complex sentence is derived from underlying forms that we have informally represented as two simple sentences. But the embedding process involves the application of *rules*: in this case rules of deletion of an underlying *noun phrase*, John, and the *substitution* of a WH- form (in this case *who* is required; *which* would be either ungrammatical, unaccept-able, or deviant). In other derivations, rules involving *transposition* and *addition* might also be required.

Now, if instead of saying 'That man, *who is fat*, wears galoshes,' a speaker says 'That *fat* man wears galoshes', transformational grammar would propose that these sentences are synonymous and that therefore they have the same *deep structure*. The derivation of the second sentence involves the application of additional rules requiring the deletion of underlying forms here represented as relative pronoun and verb, and the transposition of the adjective to a premodifying position. Thus, while a traditional or 'surface-structure' approach would label the first sentence *complex* and the second *simple*, a 'deep-structure' approach perceives both sentences as complex. Clearly, the complexity would be greater if we were to expand to something like 'My fat, greedy, penny-pinching brother, John, wears galoshes'. Here, the main proposition is: 'my brother wears galoshes'. But incorporated into the sentence structure in subordinate roles, we find also: *my brother is John, my brother is fat, my brother is greedy, my brother pinches pennies.*

One of the most characteristic features of Hopkins's syntax is multiple modification especially within the noun phrase. He is particularly fond of premodifying constructions of the kind typified by the German *das hinter der Kirche stehende Haus* ('the behind-the-church-standing house').[15] Although such constructions are extremely rare in English prose (which favours elaborate clausal modification), they are rather more readily tolerated in speech, where they may occur as nonce-formations or rise to the status of idioms. The *never-to-be-forgotten occasion* is only slightly less complex than Hopkins's *'not-by-morning-matchèd* face' (No. 59), and then only superficially so. In Hopkins's poetry, these pre-modifiers may consist of a participial construction of the kind discussed, or of a series of constructions, some being single words (adjectives, noun-modifiers, possessives) and others phrasal. They can usually be paraphrased by converting one or more of their elements into clauses and transposing these to a postmodifying position. The *rolling level underneath him steady air* is (in prose) *the steady air which is rolling and which is level underneath him*. The noun phrase states that the air is *steady*, that it *rolls*, that it is *level* and that it is underneath him. Hopkins deletes the 'underlying' grammatical elements (*which, is,* possibly *and*), and orders his adjectivals in such a way that one of them at least is made clearly subordinate to another (*level underneath him*). His method is to compress what might otherwise be a series of clauses, and this syntactic compression is clearly one of the reasons why critics have spoken of a sense of strain and tension in his verse and one of the reasons why we can speak of a rich verbal texture. Hopkins's habits of omitting 'grammatical'[16] words and transposing elements in the sentence are most coherently explained by recognizing that the poet is extending sentence-structure rules of current English in which ellipsis and transposition are required. Let us consider some further examples of noun-phrase structure.

The first two lines of 'The Windhover' contain appositive constructions, but the appositive items are themselves grammatically complex. While the appositive structure proposes that the *minion* is the *dauphin*, is the *falcon* (and could be coded as $X+Y=Z$, *minion+dauphin=falcon*), the first two noun phrases are 'genitive' or possessive constructions. *Morning's minion* need not detain us; the *dauphin* is the *dauphin of the kingdom of daylight*. This prose re-ordering resolves the syntactic ambiguity that is normal in such noun-phrase constructions (cr. *the stout major's wife*: this does not worry us in practice if we already know either that the major is stout or that his wife is stout). The phrase should not be read as if it were *daylight's dauphin*. Hopkins's syntactic compression, limited though it is in this instance, requires of us an effort if we are to interpret it correctly. The third noun-phrase, *dapple-dawn-drawn Falcon* is highly compressed and multiply ambiguous. Even a simple analysis on transformational lines would have to postulate at least two underlying sentences with various derivational rules. The falcon is *drawn* from, by, with or to, the *dawn*, and the dawn is *dappled*. Both sentences are, or can be construed as, passives, which are derivationally more complex than active sentences in that they involve a greater number of rules of ellipsis, transposition and so on. At the deepest level, therefore, each of these sentences consists of a noun-phrase+verb-phrase structure (represented informally as the *dawn draws the falcon* and X *dapples the dawn*). Rules are then applied to convert these into passives, followed by further rules deleting some of the features of passive sentences, and rules of transposition required for embedding the subordinate construction into the main one. This account, although inadequate, is enough to demonstrate that Hopkins's noun-phrase constructions tend to be very complex and involve a high degree of compression. In accordance with the rules of deriving noun-phrase modifiers from underlying clauses, much of the grammatical apparatus that would help us to interpret the relationship between the words has been suppressed.

Similar to *dapple-dawn-drawn* is *wimpled-water-dimpled* (No. 59). Elaborate pairs or series of noun-modifying constructions are found here (*wimpled-water-dimpled, not-by-morning matchèd face*), and elsewhere. One of the most extended is:

> The heaven-flung, heart-fleshed, maiden-furled
> Miracle-in-Mary-of-flame
>
> ('Deutschland', st. 34)

Here the head-phrase has the surface ambiguity characteristic of all such constructions. If we take the modifiers within it as co-ordinate, it may be read as the *Miracle* which is *in Mary* and which is *of flame*. This phrase as a whole is then premodified: the *Miracle* is *flung* from (or by) *heaven, fleshed* in the form of a *heart* and *furled* in a *maiden*. Clearly, such a construction, although it involves co-ordination, carries with it an order in which elements are sub-ordinated to one another. That its heightened effects are brought about by syntactic compression and transposition is evident when we try to paraphrase it as a prose sentence.

Similar to *kingdom of daylight's dauphin* are series of genitive premodifiers, as in:

> Our heart's charity's hearth's fire, our thought's chivalry's throng's
> Lord.
>
> ('Deutschland', st. 35)

It is obvious that such series imply an order of subordination, but not immediately obvious what that order is. Hence, these com-pressed premodifying structures are more difficult to comprehend than postmodifying constructions would be. We may paraphrase: the *hearth's fire* of our *heart's charity*, the *Lord of the throng* of the *chivalry* of our thoughts. The two parallel structures are shown to conceal a possible difference of underlying grammar. The second appears to mean the large number (*throng*) of our most noble (*chivalry*) thoughts. Whereas it involves successive subordinations (each item in succession being subordinate to the next), the first half-line is binary; it has a head-phrase (*hearth's fire*) and a modify-ing phrase, each phrase having further modification within itself.

Structures of this kind, whether they consist of adjectives, participial phrases, compound words, genitives, noun modifiers or

other attributives, are technically known as left-branching constructions. Postmodifying constructions, which may consist of
single words, phrases or clauses, are known as *right-branching*.
Extended left-branching constructions tend to be more compressed
and more difficult to comprehend than *right-branching* ones partly
because the adjectival clauses that underlie them have undergone
more deletions in the course of derivation. We can re-write
wimpled-water-dimpled . . . face as 'a face *which is* dimpled by wimpled
water' and further as two sentences 'Water *dimples* the face' and
'X *wimples* the water'. It is obvious that Hopkins makes frequent
and extended use of such premodifying constructions. When he
uses postmodification, the difficulties may be less severe, but they
still exist.

They exist in extended right-branching constructions such as
Miracle-in-Mary-of-flame, where the correct analysis could con-
ceivably be *Mary-of-flame* rather than *Miracle- . . . of-flame*. But
right-branching, unlike left-branching, constructions can often be
clauses, and when this is so it is less likely that the language will be
compressed and difficult. Hopkins does use relative clauses,
sometimes fully marked by the relative pronoun (my italics):

The swoon of a heart *that* the sweep and the hurl of thee trod
('Deutschland', st. 2)

Wording it how but by him *that* present and past,
Heaven and earth are word of, worded by? (st. 29)

. . . a sovereignty *that* heeds but hides . . . (st. 32)

The fine delight *that* fathers thought . . . (No. 76)

Sometimes, the clause is unfinished:

Thing *that* she . . . There then! the Master
('Deutschland', st. 28)

But he is very much inclined to suppress the linking relative pronoun. When it is the object of the relative clause, this is normal in
speech and permissible (though less normal) in prose. In Hopkins's
usage it is sometimes unremarkable, but in long and complex
sentences it can lead to some difficulty in construing the sentences.
The treasure never eyesight got ('Deutschland', st. 26) is 'easy' enough,
but not *manmarks treadmire toil there footfretted in it* (No. 72) or
the following extended phrase:

... lovely-felicitous Providence
Finger of a tender of, O of a feathery delicacy, the breast of the
Maiden could obey so, be a bell to, ring of it ...
('Deutschland', st. 31)

The difficulties are not *caused* by the suppression of the relative
pronoun (which is 'understood' after *delicacy*), but they are not
helped by it. The noun phrases of which *Providence* and *Finger* are
the head words (the second phrase interrupted between the two
adjectives *tender* and *feathery*) are in apposition. One, or the other,
or both, are modified by the relative clause: *(that) the breast of the
Maiden could obey so.*[17]

Those who complain about Hopkins's language have been more
inclined to notice the very few instances[18] in his poetry where the
relative pronoun is suppressed even when it is the subject of its
clause:

What was the feast followed the night
Thou hadst glory of this nun?   ('Deutschland', st. 30)

Squander the hell-rook ranks sally to molest him;
(No. 48)

... Here! creep,
Wretch, under a comfort serves in a whirlwind ...
(No. 65)

Note that in such examples the effect is that the object or complement of the main clause is placed immediately before the verb of
the subordinate clause, and there is a tendency to read them as if
they were subject and verb in the same clause. The noun of one
clause is *attracted* to the other clause and takes on a dual syntactic
function. Hence the difficulty, and the tendency to avoid this
construction in careful prose. But Hopkins is, as always, consistent.
He had observed this construction in current English *speech*, in
children's rhymes, in Elizabethan and later literature and in
Scottish or Northern dialect (in which, for example, 'There's a
draught would freeze ye!' is a normal construction). Their own
inferior powers of linguistic observation do not entitle certain
critics to claim that Hopkins's usage is 'ungrammatical'.[19]

Hopkins's omission of relative pronouns in these instances and
elsewhere is consistent with his general tendency to seek the

maximum compression of language. Hopkins could have written 'What was the feast *that* followed the night . . .' or 'What was the feast follow*ing* the night'. In either case, the result would have been the addition of a syllable with a purely diacritic or *marking* function. This would have clarified the syntax, but would have added no *meaning* to the line. We shall later discuss some of the more obvious effects of Hopkins's suppression of grammatical markers.

We have so far been concerned with the syntax of noun phrases. We now extend our discussion of Hopkins's syntactic compression to take some account of the verb phrase. This, like the noun phrase, can be extended by embedding within it a series of co-ordinates or appositives, or by introducing modifiers (subordinate clauses or phrases). But Hopkins is more inclined to introduce multiple modification of nouns than he is of verbs, and his extended sentences normally show in the verb less complexity of this kind.

This sentence, in which there is some complexity in the verb phrases, is one of his longest:

> A bugler boy from barrack (it is over the hill
> There) – boy, bugler, born, he tells me, of Irish
>   Mother to an English sire (he
> Shares their best gifts surely, fall how things will),
>
> This very very day came down to us after a boon he on
> My late being there begged of me, overflowing
>   Boon in my bestowing,
> Came, I say, this day to it – to a First Communion.

The sentence contains a subject phrase in the first line (*a . . . boy*) and a verb phrase in the fifth line (*came down to us*). Otherwise, there are modifying clauses and phrases, modifiers within modifiers, and repetitions. There is a *reprise* of the subject (line 2) and a *reprise* of the verb (line 8). The subject is modified within the phrase (*bugler*), the noun phrase is then postmodified by a prepositional phrase (*from barrack*) and the object of the preposition is then itself postmodified (*it is over the hill there*). The surface grammar of this last modifier is that of a parenthetical sentence in apposition, but it is no less a modifier for that. The advantage of seeing it this way is that we observe this sentence to be embedded inside a series of constructions. It is not merely a loose appositive, but has its logical place in the sentence. Hopkins prefers *it* to *which* (or simply *barrack over the hill* there) because he is imitating colloquial speech. Here as elsewhere he involves us more intimately in the situation by doing this; it is as if we are asking him where the *barrack* is and he replies to us. The second to fourth lines (despite the preference for *he* rather than *who*) are also modifiers of the noun phrase. In effect, they say: 'the boy is a bugler, *who* tells me *that* he was born of an Irish mother to an English sire, *whose* best gifts he shares'. Hopkins again achieves a colloquial effect without abandoning the underlying logical structure. The clause subordinate to the verb *tells* appears on the surface as a parenthesis.

Whereas the first stanza is an expansion of the subject, the second is an expansion of the verb. The verb *came* and its *reprise* are modified by a time adverbial (this . . . day); otherwise their syntax is that of the normal complementation of the verb of motion. The bugler *came* (down) *after a boon*, and *to a First Communion*. Hopkins omits the relative in the clause modifying *boon*, and characteristically avoids the subordinate adverbial clause of time. We could paraphrase: 'the bugler came after a boon *which* he begged of me *when I was lately* there'. He prefers a complex nominal phrase introduced by a preposition: *on my late being there*, where *being there* is a nominal. In the modifier *in my bestowing* he similarly prefers the phrase (with no finite verb) to the clause. Although it is not our main business to evaluate Hopkins's success in using such a syntax, it is worth pointing out that the final effect of these lines is a rather odd blending of speech-like immediacy with a degree of syntactic compression not typical of speech. It may be that the poet's search for intensity through syntactic compression has pulled him in a different direction from his anxiety to maintain the illusion of ordinary speech.

We may summarize by noting that Hopkins prefers complex noun phrases to complexity of the verb phrase. Adverbial clauses (and sometimes noun clauses) which modify the verb may be (as in the above example) *nominalized;* just as relative clauses are normally converted into premodifiers within the noun-phrase. Since we cannot list all examples of both types, we may draw attention to typical examples of both.

Compression of underlying adverbials is clear in (my italics):

> . . . How a lush-kept plush-capped sloe
> Will, *mouthed to flesh-burst,*

Gush! – flush the man, *the being with it, sour or sweet,*
Brim, in a flash, full! ('Deutschland', st. 8)

Mouthed to flesh-burst may be paraphrased: '*when it is* mouthed to flesh-burst', and the compound *flesh-burst* is derived by trans-formational rules from an underlying temporal clause in which *burst* is a verb ('*when* the flesh bursts'). The effect in such a com-pound is to override and make irrelevant the distinction between noun (*a burst*) and verb (*to burst*). *The being with it* may be a phrase in apposition to *man*, but it may also be a nominalization of a conditional clause. The sloe flushes the man brim-full, *whether it is* sour *or* sweet.

In this instance (*flesh-burst*) and in many others, the compound word is seen to achieve the greatest compression of syntax. This is so whether, as here, the compound is a *noun* derived from an underlying verbal construction, or whether, as in the great majority of cases, it is adjectival. The 'towery city' of Oxford (No. 44) is *cuckoo-echoing, bell-swarmed, lark-charmed, rook-racked, river-rounded.* All these adjectival modifiers are derived from clauses by trans-formational rules and embedded in premodifying positions. They state that cuckoos *echo in* Oxford, larks *charm* Oxford, and so on. The underlying clauses from which the compounds are derived are not all precisely the same in syntax and, as we pointed out in Chapter 6, the effect of controlled variation in apparently similar compounds may be thought pleasing. However, it is clear that in order to explain Hopkins's methods we must invoke rules of syntax.

In certain later poems, the intensely compressed and elliptical sentence-structure can depart very far from the syntax of speech. The link with current language is, however, still important to the poet, and he tries to suggest it by using uncompleted constructions (*with, perilous, O no,* No. 70) and vowel elisions that might occur in speech (*Sure, 's bed now,* No. 70; *'S cheek crimsons,* No. 71). But the sentences, particularly the noun phrases in them, are multiply complex.

Geoffrey Hill[20] has commented on the disjointed *rhythm* of 'Tom's Garland' and has pointed out that, by the 1880s, Hopkins's prose style had become similarly tortuous and disjointed, as in: '. . . something must be sacrificed, with so trying a task, in the process, and this may be the being at once, nay perhaps even the

being without explanation at all, intelligible'. This comes from a
letter that we quoted in Chapter 1, in which Hopkins is defending
obscurity in language where it results from complexity in thought.
Syntactically, this prose follows the same principles as the poetry.
Hopkins prefers nominalizations (*the being at once* rather than 'that
it should be at once') to clauses, and he interrupts his phrases with
long parentheses. The (*finds his,*) *as at a rollcall,* (*rank*) of Harry
Ploughman contains a modest interruption compared with *nay
perhaps even the being without explanation at all*. What Mr Hill perceives
as disjointed rhythms in the poetry is clearly also an effect of compressed, elaborate and inverted syntax.

The syntax of this sentence is hardly that of current language:

> . . . Low be it: lustily he his low lot (feel
> That ne'er need hunger, Tom; Tom seldom sick,
> Seldomer heartsore; that treads through, prickproof, thick
> Thousands of thorns, thoughts) swings though . . .
>
> (No. 70)

The main sentence has inversion within itself (read: 'he swings his
low lot lustily though') and is interrupted by a long parenthesis
which is linked to the main sentence by the appositive relation
between *Tom* and *he*. The other propositions are subordinate to
and modifying *Tom*, and may themselves contract subordinate or
co-ordinate relationships (*He, Tom, who* never need feel hunger,
who is seldom sick and seldomer heartsore, and *who, being* prickproof, treads through thick thousands of thorns, *which are*
thoughts). Tom is not bothered by sickness or anxiety and does
not *think* very much. At various points we have to supply relative
pronouns, linking verbs (the verb *to be*) and conjunctions. But the
whole construction is perfectly grammatical, compressed though
it is.

One of the *effects* of these syntactic manipulations is to throw
into sharp relief the word *thick*. This effect is something beyond
strict grammar: it is neither ungrammatical nor anti-grammatical.
Thick is a rhyming word, separated from the construction of which
it is a part by a line-ending. In various poems, Hopkins manages to
throw an important word into focus by suggesting some detach-
ment from its sentence relations. In this instance the word is both
part of the syntax and not part of it at the same time. In its strict
sentence-relation it must be construed with *thousands*; but *thick*

thousands and *thick thorns* come to the same thing. However, it is clearly not only the thorns that are thick, but also Tom's *boots*. Tom's boots are *prickproof* but, according to the syntax here, *Tom* is also prickproof. Thus, Hopkins implies that *Tom* is also thick (insensitive and mentally dull). The word *thick*, therefore, is a key-word placed in a prominent position because it related directly to the whole theme of the poem. Physical thickness of natural objects (*thorns*) suggests the thickness of an attribute of the man (his *boots*), and finally the dullness, toughness and insensitivity of the man himself. Hopkins's syntactic manipulations succeed splendidly in foregrounding an important element in the *thought* of the whole poem and justify his claims in the letter about necessary obscurity in language.

This compressed syntax also seems to be more successful than in the long sentence we have discussed from 'The Bugler's First Communion', because its heightening or foregrounding of language seems to be of a more consistent type. Hopkins is not riding two horses at once: there is no attempt in this sentence to suggest the paratactic syntax of ordinary speech (although the colloquial word *though* is preferred to the 'literary' *however*). The current language is heightened by syntactic devices *to any degree* so that it becomes *unlike itself*. The heightening is ultimately in the sound and feel and flavour of the words; the elliptical syntax eliminates grammatical markers which have no flavour. Words are savoured for their own sake. Some are positioned in such a way that they can be detached altogether from their syntactic relations and thus take on a wider significance in the poem.

It is in these late poems also that Hopkins is moved to his most daring experiments in what appears to be *compounding*. As we have observed in Chapter 6, however, such constructions as *with-a-fountain's shining-shot* are not strictly compound *words*. They are the ultimate in syntactic compression of modifying *phrases*. The *furls* (furrows) along which Harry's feet (*broad in bluff hide*) race with the plough are *shot with the shining of a fountain*. They shoot up from the earth, as if they were water, shining like water, and then curl over back to the earth again, like a fountain. However compressed and difficult such syntax may be, it is a remarkable achievement to *inscape* the quick movements, the texture, sheen and the shape of the furrows as economically as Hopkins has done here. Indeed, it is only by compressing the syntax that he can capture so many instantaneously perceived effects in a unity. In order to inscape, he must try to override the syntactic distinction of *subject* (actor), *verb* (action) and the thing affected (*goal* or *object*). An inscape, being an instantaneous perception of a state, must unify the perceiver, the perceived and the perception; it must try to avoid ascribing causes, temporal succession or results. When change or development is perceived or suggested, then the inscape is *sided on the slide* – a series of successive inscapes (*JP*, 211).[21] This means that it is the normal grammar of the *verb* (the implications of time and attitude[22] that the finite verb carries within it, and its relationship to 'subject' and 'object') that must particularly be overridden. As we have seen, Hopkins uses nominalization and compound derivatives, rather than finite verbs, very frequently indeed.

In 'Harry Ploughman', Hopkins extends his customary *interruption* of sentences and phrases to interruption of the word itself. He describes this as a 'desperate deed', but it is all attempted in the cause of inscape. *See his wind-lilylocks-laced* can be rewritten as *See his lilylocks windlaced* (i.e. 'laced by the wind'). But this destroys the unity of this small inscape, which suggests the perceived inseparability of the wind and the locks. Like the floating flag of the Journal (*JP*, 233), the locks are 'wind visible and what weeds are in a current; it gives it thew . . . and bloods it in'. The interrupted compound foregrounds the perception that the wind and the locks are inseparable; and action is indifferently performed by either and indifferently affects either. Objects and motion are all one; things 'and the relations of things' (*JP*, 125) are unified. Hopkins felt that this 'desperate deed' was not 'an unquestionable success'. Perhaps it is not, but it is consistent with his search for inscape.

PARTS OF SPEECH

We do not take the view in this book that a language is merely a list of *words*, classified according to their membership of 'parts of speech' categories. We have preferred to consider that the syntax of a language is built up on the grammar of *noun-phrases* and *verb-phrases*. It is usually clear whether Hopkins is using one of these or the other. The transfer of a particular *word* from one 'part of speech' to another is not in itself the secret of Hopkins's manipulation of syntax. It is a resource of ordinary English in which the most common words (including many of those listed in Hopkins's early diaries) are often indifferently noun and verb (and sometimes adjective, adverb or preposition as well). This is a resource which is particularly fruitful in a language with few inflections. In English (as opposed to Latin or, to some extent, German) words are not necessarily defined by their shape or endings as belonging to one class or another. Hopkins exploits this just as he exploits aspects of rhythm, or vowel and consonant structure, which happen to be poetically useful aspects of the language in which he is writing.

We have already seen that *nominalization* is a favourite syntactic device. But when single *words* are transferred from one class to another, there is again a tendency for Hopkins to *nominalize* other parts of speech rather than make verbs out of nouns. For many reasons, however, it is difficult to be precise about this. First, we cannot always be certain that in ordinary language, a particular word belongs primarily to one particular 'part of speech' class. Are *hush, flush, brace, braid,* primarily nouns or verbs in ordinary usage? What part of speech is *round*? Second, Hopkins's transfers are often unremarkable, since a great many verbs are *commonly* transferred to the noun class and vice versa in ordinary English. Yet, it may be important to notice that Hopkins makes such transfers more commonly than would be the case in ordinary English. Thus, it is *sweep* and *hurl*, not sweeping and hurling, in 'The swoon of a heart that the *sweep* and the *hurl* of thee trod' ('Deutschland', st. 2). Third, because of the relative lack of inflections in English, sentence functions have to be indicated by position and by grammatical *markers* (*the* 'marks' nouns; auxiliaries such as *do, must,* may 'mark' verbs, and intensifiers such as *very, quite,* may 'mark' adjectives). When such markers are omitted and the word-order rearranged, it may be impossible or irrelevant in a given case to say that a word belongs to one part of speech and not another.

In this simple instance, Hopkins uses inversion:

> And frightful a nightfall folded rueful a day
> ('Deutschland', st. 15)

The word-order suggests at least two kinds of construction that differ from the normal noun phrase. One is the *many a day* construction, which is of very limited use in English; the other is the transposed predicate adjective construction (as in *Lovely the woods . . .*, No. 34). The effect is to suggest not only that the night-fall was *frightful*, but that the manner of its falling and 'folding' was *frightful*. That is to say that the 'adjective' takes on *adverbial* colouring and seems to refer to the whole event as well as the *nightfall*. A more complex instance is:

> . . . why wouldst thou rude on me
> Thy wring-world right foot rock? . . .   (No. 64)

Here the word *rude* seems to be singled out. The absence of gram-matical markers makes it indifferently adjective, adverb or noun in apposition (or a verb?), but it clearly suggests *the manner of* the action. *Wring-world right foot* is 'derivationally' complex. Under-lying it is the proposition that the foot *wrings* the world. It is pointless to worry whether *wring* should be labelled as nominal, verbal or adjectival in surface structure. The construction is best explained as a *nominalization* of an underlying clause that contains a verb (*wring*).

In such subordinating structures as this, 'parts of speech' classification often becomes irrelevant or misleading. In some co-ordinating constructions, however, the uncertainty as to whether particular words are nouns, verbs or adjectives may cause difficulty in reading. Consider the following passage:

> Delightfully the bright wind boisterous | ropes, wrestles, beats earth bare
> Of yestertempest's creases; | in pool and rutpeel parches
> Squandering ooze to squeezed | dough, crust, dust; stanches, starches
> Squadroned masks and manmarks | treadmire toil there
> Footfretted in it . . .   (No. 72)

In the first line here, *ropes* is defined as a verb by its sequential co-ordinate relations with the verbs following. The words *parches*, *stanches* and *starches* give difficulty. Sequentially it is possible to read *rutpeel parches* as a noun-phrase. Similarly, *stanches* and *starches* seem to take on something of the quality of nouns because they follow a sequence of nouns. On the other hand, *manmarks*, which looks like a noun, *may* at first be read as a compound verb with *treadmire toil* as its object. In fact, *parches* appears to be a verb: the wind, in pool and rutpeel, *parches* the *squandering ooze* to squeezed *dough*, then to *crust*, then to *dust*. The wind also *stanches* and *starches* the *squadroned masks and manmarks* which *treadmire toil* has *foot-fretted* 'in it'. The difficulty in construing *manmarks* arises from the suppression of a relative pronoun, and the general difficulty arises from suppression of other grammatical markers.[23]

Although full noun-like status is not quite achieved by the verbs in this passage, there is a suggestion in the way that they are loosened from the syntax that *parches*, *stanches*, *starches* are things as well as acts. Sometimes Hopkins goes further, and words which are normally verbs or adjectives are clearly marked as nouns. In the 'Deutschland', we find, for example, the compound *flesh-burst* as a noun, where there must be a verb *to burst* in the deep structure. The following instances, however, are more clearly foregrounded (my italics):

> . . . a vein
> Of the gospel *proffer*, a pressure, a principle, Christ's gift.
> ('Deutschland', st. 4)

> . . . the *achieve* of, the mastery of the thing!   (No. 36)

> But ah, but O thou *terrible* . . .   (No. 64)

> . . . leaves me a lonely *began*.   (No. 66)

> By groping round my *comfortless* . . .   (No. 69)

These are unambiguously nouns, and are easily 'explained' by ellipsis. In *proffer*, *achieve*, *comfortless*, it can be said that Hopkins has omitted the normal suffixes (-ment, -ness) that would make them clearly nouns. In normal English, adjectives in direct address require the addition of a 'dummy' marker *one*; in *thou terrible* the marker is deleted. The 'noun' *began* is the residue of a relative clause and its antecedent; *one who* is deleted. As has been pointed out, this is similar to the expression *also-ran*, and its derivation is, we propose, the same.

One obvious *effect* in all these instances is *compression*. Purely grammatical elements which have little or no referential meaning are omitted, and the 'thew and sinew' of the language is strengthened. But Hopkins's habit of nominalizing verbs and clauses has another very important effect. The *gospel proffer* inscapes the action and the idea. The action of offering, thrusting forward, Christ's gift is far more palpably present than it would be if a noun or verbal noun had been used. Similarly, if we substitute *achievement* for *achieve*, we seem to be speaking of something pale and abstract, something completed and at a distance from the act and motion of the falcon. But this *effect* of immediacy and activity is also present in cases where nominalization is uncertain or ambiguous. *The combating keen* of the 'Deutschland' (st. 25) may be either *noun* (*combating*)+*adjective* (*keen*) or the other way round. Whichever it is, the effect is to compress and to foreground the word *keen* in such a way that the sharpness and coldness (and perhaps shrillness) are more immediately 'felt'. We may say much the same for the verbs that *almost* become nouns in 'Heraclitean Fire', and for countless other instances where motion and action are compressed in a noun, a modifier, a compound, or a word which has been partly loosened from its normal verbal use and seems to take on a quality of tangibility – to be an action and a thing at the same time. The aim and the effect of this is similar to the effects of the imagery that we discussed in Chapter 6, where we saw that, by associating the imagery of fluids (motion) with solid and stable substances, Hopkins attempts to capture (in one perception) motion in stable things, and by the opposite process, solidity in mobile things. Motion and act are normally in the verb rather than the noun.[24] The poet tries to override this difference and suggest the qualities of both verb and noun in the same word or phrase.

Some of Hopkins's most subtle manipulation of the parts of speech occurs when the poet retains the word in its normal noun or verb use, but at the same time exploits rules of *sub-categorization* within that part of speech. This is where the grammar of the finite verb is most obviously relevant in Hopkins's poetry. Nouns may be sub-categorized as common or proper, concrete or abstract, 'mass-nouns', or 'count-nouns', animate or inanimate, human or non-human, and so on. They usually belong to several of these sub-categories at the same time; thus *water* for example is common, concrete (yes!), a mass-noun, inanimate and so on. Where such distinctions appear in surface-structure they are normally signalled by the presence or absence of a determiner (article), and one of the chief uses of the article is to convert proper nouns into common, abstract into concrete, and mass-nouns into count-nouns. Deletion of the article has the opposite effect. However, *verbal* sub-categorization is more complex. Verbs may be classified quasi-semantically into verbs of action (*kick*), motion (*swim*), sensation (*see*), 'private

state' (*know*), performative (*promise, declare*) and many more. To a
certain extent these differences appear in surface structure. For
example, action and motion verbs normally take the present continuous form when they refer to present action rather than habitual
(*he is eating his dinner now*, but *he eats his dinner every day*), whereas the
other classes mentioned take the 'simple' form for present state
reference (*I know George Smith*, not **I am knowing George Smith*).
It is a fact of English grammar that verbs of action and motion
have no unambiguous *instantaneous* form, and poetic diction has
traditionally used the simple present for this purpose. In normal
use, the *instantaneous* present (as against the *habitual*) is only used
for demonstrations and descriptive commentaries of present action
(*I take the eggs and break them*; *Smith centres the ball, but the goalkeeper
intercepts*). Hopkins often uses the simple form to capture this
immediacy: 'I walk, I lift up, I lift up heart, eyes' (No. 38). He
also uses it in the 'poetic' way. 'Summer ends now' (No. 38) is not
habitual or instantaneous. In 'normal' English we would say
'Summer is ending now'. 'The stooks rise around' in the same
poem, however, suggests that Hopkins is describing something
static, permanent and motionless, as if it were a painting. It also
suggests the 'eternal truth' usage of the present tense, as in 'the
sun *rises* every morning' or even 'oil *floats* on water'. It is not
surprising that Hopkins favours the simple present in his poetry,
since instantaneous action/perception, or being, or behaving, are
the essence of inscape. But the lack of an unambiguous verbal
form in English to capture instantaneous states or actions is one
of the reasons why a special vocabulary of inscape has to be
evolved.[25]

English verbal usage is, however, very much more complex
than the foregoing discussion would suggest. Apart from these
quasi-semantic classifications, the verb can also be classified in
terms of tense and mood; and it may be active or passive in form.
But in sentence structure the relationships which are clearly most
important in Hopkins's poetry are the relationships of the verb
with its subject on the one hand and its complement (object,
subject complement or verb-of-motion complement) on the other.
Such relationships may be subsumed under the term *transitivity*.
Transitive verbs take a direct object; normally they are verbs of
action; their subject is the actor or agent and their object the *goal*
or the thing affected. This relationship is clear in such a sentence

as *John opens the door*. Here the verb is transitive, and this can be demonstrated by the fact that it can be converted into the passive, in which agency is signalled by a prepositional phrase introduced by *by*: *the door is opened by John*. But agency is much less clear in a true intransitive such as *die* or *vanish*. If we say *John died*, we can hardly define the subject here as being the agent. The *dying* is something that *has happened* to John. John is *affected*. Obviously, the sentence cannot be converted from active to passive, since the *meaning* is hardly active to begin with.[26]

Hopkins in his search for inscape is often anxious to avoid making a distinction between agent and the thing affected – a distinction which the subject-object grammar of English sentences tends to force upon us. In the world of Hopkins's Journal things *behave*, and in order to emphasize the objectivity of the description it is often necessary to avoid assuming that one thing is the actor or agent and another the thing affected. In the poetry, Hopkins often omits the object of a transitive verb or, conversely, manages to suggest that an intransitive verb has a concealed object of some kind. The effect is really to override the distinction between the actor and the thing affected.

In the following example a transitive verb is used without a direct object:

> . . . has wilder, wilful-wavier
> Meal-drift *moulded* ever and melted across skies?
>
> (No. 38)

To *melt* can normally be intransitive, but to *mould* is transitive: one must mould *something*. In this instance, however, the meal-drift is presented as the thing affected by the moulding. The poet manages to suggest by using meal-drift as the subject of an intransitive that it may be both actor and acted upon at the same time. What he really does is to avoid definitely assigning agency and effect, and allow us to contemplate the states and movements as *behaviour* of the clouds. His choice of grammar here is an important aspect of his compression of language and his achievement of inscape.

Conversely, he can use an *intransitive* verb where there is nevertheless a suggestion that an object is understood. In *there must/ The sour scythe cringe* ('Deutschland', st. 11), we have already suggested that *cringe* (an intransitive) has become a transitive, and that we are to understand that the scrythe 'cringes' someone or something.

Note that, if we were to substitute *bend* for *cringe*, it would be unambiguously intransitive, for the reason that the verb *to bend* can be either. That is to say, you can bend *something*, or simply *bend* (intransitive or implied reflexive). It may well be that Hopkins thought that *cringe* 'originally' meant 'to bend' (see Commentary), but whatever his main reason for using it, his choice of the word *cringe* is effective foregrounding. It seems to be transitive and intransitive at the same time. The scythe bends, and the crop bends before it. In the background, of course, is the image of the reaper who bends to the scythe.

There are many more instances of this apparent manipulation of transitivity in Hopkins's poetry.[27] Sometimes the effect is clear. The blue-bleak embers of 'The Windhover' that '*gash* gold-vermilion' are understood to gash *themselves*, to split open. But at the same time, since *gash* is normally transitive, we are aware of an allusion to the wounding of Christ on the Cross, in which case we have to understand an implied transitive use. In other poems, the precise interpretations are less clear, partly because the verbs concerned may seem to be nouns, but, if they are verbs, then they may be felt to be partly or wholly loosened from the syntax of transitivity. Harry Ploughman's cheek 'crimsons; curls wag or crossbridle, in a wind lifted . . .'. *Crossbridle* seems to be a verb, intransitive in form. The clouds of 'Heraclitean Fire' '*chevy* on an air-/built thoroughfare'. To chevy is to *tease*, and one normally teases *something*. In the same poem, there are several verbs that can be taken as transitives *or* intransitive; thus, 'in pool and rutpeel *parches*/ Squandering ooze . . .', the verb *parches* is given such prominence that it may momentarily be taken as a noun and then as an intransitive verb ('the wind *parches* in pool and rutpeel') with *squandering ooze* . . . as a separate phrase. Finally, we will probably take it as transitive with *squandering ooze* as object. In such uses, and in uses where a verb that can be both transitive and intransitive is used ambiguously ('God's most deep decree/ Bitter would have me taste . . .', No. 67), the effect is to overrule or obscure the difference between the agent and the thing affected. The general tendency to suppress possible objects of 'transitive' verbs is part of Hopkins's compression of language.

As Hopkins extends the uses of verbal sub-categories and manipulates verbal relations, so with the noun he achieves certain effects by variable use of the determiners (articles). In Chapter 1 we noted several instances of suppression of the determiner. To take only one: the effect in 'sheer plod makes plough down sillion/ Shine', is, I think, obvious. It is not a particular plough or sillion that is involved, but any plough or any sillion. The count-nouns take on the generalizing qualities of mass-nouns or abstracts. It is a universal (a 'law') that plough and furrows shine as the earth is turned over.

Conversely, in 'The Deutschland', st. 4, a noun that is normally a mass-noun is given an article: 'I steady as *a* water in a well'. The effect is again clear. The substance (water) becomes a specific instance of water, more tangible, more 'solid'. The imagery of the stanza as a whole strengthens this: the water is steady and stable in the well, like a pane of glass. In English, this simple device of adding or deleting the determiner is a powerful rule of the language in use, in the active and passive competence of all speakers. When Hopkins manipulates the grammar of determiners, or the grammar of transitivity, or when he nominalizes verbs, adjectives and subordinate clauses, he is merely using rules which are already present in the language, sometimes extending them to lexical items to which they do not 'normally' apply. In so doing he explores the inscape of words and their relations to other words, and he creates for us new perceptions, new relationships, new inscapes. Since inscape requires some suspension of our assumptions about cause and effect and a quasi-objective attempt to describe states and behaviours as instantaneously perceived, it is not surprising that to achieve the right effect, the poet often over-rides the normal subject–object relations of the transitive verb of action. Similarly, since inscaping implies some perception of general or universal laws in particular instances of them, it is not surprising that the syntax of mass-nouns and count-nouns is manipulated. Finally, there is clearly a relationship between syntactic devices and the imagery of fluids and solids that we discussed in Chapter 6, in which Hopkins attempts to 'catch' mobility and action actually *within* the thing perceived. The tendency is for motion and action (normally signalled by verbs) to be inscaped into the noun; therefore, nominalization is a major device in Hopkins's syntax. His syntax, like his phonetic and lexical devices, is emphatically part of inscaping.

Looking out of his window one winter day, the poet 'caught' inscape in 'random clods and broken heaps made by the cast of a broom'. Inscape *is* order and the perception of it in natural things and in language. To unite in language that order and its perception was Hopkins's life's work. 'All the world is full of inscape', he exclaimed, 'and chance left free to act falls into an order as well as a purpose.' Language, like nature, has this order and purpose. Hopkins used it with a sense of wonder, and in an orderly and purposeful way.

Coda: 'In-Earnestness'

I T may seem odd to some readers that a book on Hopkins's language should contain very little reference to events in the poet's life. We have said little about his religious conversion, his priestly vocation, his English patriotism, and the various periods of his life spent in different regions within these islands (in Wales and Ireland as well as in various parts of England). Naturally, our excuse for these omissions is that this has been a book on Hopkins's language, and that is sufficient in itself to form the subject-matter of many books.

Nevertheless, we would agree that a man's language is part of his being and behaving and cannot in reality be wholly separated from the man himself – his attitudes and his beliefs. What we would claim is that the study of the sources and form of Hopkins's *language* is the best and most reliable method of approaching an understanding of the man. In the language alone, we have had to notice and resolve certain paradoxes. Hopkins rejected archaism, yet often used language that seemed to be archaic; he rejected inversion, yet often inverted word-order; he condemned 'Victorian English', but he based his diction on 'current language'; nevertheless, in many poems he seems to have departed very far from current language. We have attempted to explain that these inconsistencies and others are only apparent inconsistencies, and that they arise naturally from the poet's single-minded preoccupation with exactitude in the language used to 'catch' most effectively and memorably the orderliness of the world.

But critics have been much exercised by other seeming inconsistencies about Hopkins, and their views have ranged from those who feel that he was virtually saint-like – a model of goodness, sincerity and modesty – to those who feel that he was an unhappy tormented creature continually torn between priesthood and poetry. To Brigid Brophy and her co-writers:

Hopkins's is the poetry of a mental cripple. Sympathize as one might with his confusion, with the absurd struggle that went on within him between priest and poet, it is impossible not to end by feeling completely exasperated with the disastrous mess he made of his life.[1]

One of the underlying assumptions of this book is that such views have to be rejected as nonsense, simply because there is very little in Hopkins's writings that justifies the belief that the struggle of his life was any more 'absurd' than the mental struggles of other men. On the contrary, the dominant impression of the diary and Journal (to which we have mainly referred and which are his personal records) is one of joy and vitality. That peculiar obstinacy that seems to have been part of his character seems only to have enriched his mental life; without it he could hardly have persevered so single-mindedly in his poetic creativity in the absence of really helpful criticism. Even the depression that attended his later 'banishment' to Ireland seems in no way remarkable to one who has lived through similar times in the same country.

The key-words that unite Hopkins's poetic language and his character are the words *purism* and *in-earnestness*. There is nothing particularly neurotic about these qualities; they do not have to be unrelieved by humour and joy. As we have tried to show, the wonder of language and of natural creation were sources of joy for the poet, and in his poetic creation there was a considerable element of 'game' that is not inconsistent with seriousness. His *purism* and *in-earnestness* are also relevant to his patriotism, his religious conversion and his priestly vocation. These were pursued with the same zeal and dedication as was the 'game' of language, and if they were sometimes accompanied by intellectual arrogance or intolerance, that too was consistent with his purist impatience with *language* that seemed to him to be less *in-earnest* than his own. Who is to say that he was wrong, or that his single-mindedness did not bring its own mental and spiritual rewards?

Hopkins's attitudes to language, as we have presented them, seem to be entirely consistent with his attitudes to other things. Our own single-minded concentration on this remarkable language is justified, if only because it is for his poetry, rather than for his piety and patriotism, that Hopkins is chiefly remembered.

A Commentary on Words used in Rare, Special or Non-Standard Senses in Hopkins's Poetry

🉑🉑🉑🉑🉑🉑

SINCE it is not usually possible to give a single precise definition to unusual words or to words used in unusual ways, this commentary seeks to make available to the reader information on etymology, dialectal uses, and relevant details from the diary and Journal. Hopkins's associative series of the kinds discussed in Chapter 5, 6 and 7 are also mentioned where relevant. In this way, it is hoped that the reader's appreciation of the rich semantic associations of Hopkins's vocabulary will be assisted. References under each item are given to all relevant occurrences in Hopkins's mature finished poems (1876–89) and also to early and unfinished work, where it seems to be important. For abbreviations, see 'Abbreviations used in the Text' p. ix.

ASUNDER (*lovely-asunder*, 'Deutschland', st. 5): Richardson (*Philology*, 48–9) . . . originally from Anglo-Saxon *Sond*; i.e. Sand . . . (incorrect etymology – see Ch. 2, p. 43). Wedgwood connects *sunder* with ON *sund*, swimming, and with *squander*, to scatter, waste. 'The dashing abroad of a liquid affords the most lively image of scattering in fragments.' This word, although archaic and 'literary' in St.E, is current in provincial dialect.

BEACON ('Deutschland', st. 29, No. 72): In No. 72, association of *beacon* and *beam* suggests reference to Cross. In *JP*, 179, H notes: 'They enclose the head of the cross in a triangle . . . it looks like a beacon at sea', speaking of churches in the Rhone Valley. In OE the words *beacen* ('sign') and *beam* ('tree') are used frequently of the Cross, as in *The Dream of the Rood*, l. 5: . . . *beama beorhtost. Eall þæt beacen wæs/ begoten mid golde* ('the brightest of "trees". All that "sign" was overlaid with gold').

BEAM ('Deutschland', st. 14, Nos. 40, 72; *beam-blind, trambeams*, No. 46; *hornbeam*, No. 159, *whitebeam*, No. 32, *JP*, 147): In compounds whitebeam, hornbeam, etym. sense 'tree' (OE beam) is preserved. Nautical use, emphasized by Ogilvie and Wedgwood, found in 'Deutschland'. *Beam-blind* (No. 46) clearly refers to the 'beam in thine own eye' (Matt. vii), but the senses 'ray of light' and possibly 'Cross' may also be present. *OED* recognizes obsolete meaning 'rood-tree or cross' and cites *beam-light* (1720) as 'a lighted candle placed before the rood'. The sense 'ray of light' probably dependent on sense 'beam of wood'. Onions traces this sense to OE *byrnende beam* (pillar of fire) and compares development of Lat. *radius* > 'ray'. H uses word of cloudscapes, etc., in *JP* referring to shape of cloud rather than rays of light. Reference to Cross important in No. 72; see s.v. BEACON and discussion in Chapter 6.

BELL ('Deutschland', st. 31, Nos. 29, 57; *belled*, No. 28; *bell-swarmed*, No. 44; *bellbright*, No. 159): Richly suggestive of sound, curved shape and quality of light, the last association derived from 'bells' of flowers (see especially *JP*, 231, and discussion, Chapter 6). Wedgwood considers words for 'bell' in several languages to be imitative of sound of bell; especially relevant to No. 57, in which the 'name' of the bell is its sound (see Chapter 2). Here, as in Nos. 44 and 159, association with flower-bells may also be present.

BLEAR ('Deutschland', st. 11, Nos. 31, 46, 60): In Standard English, forms of this word are usually used in reference to the eyes. Provincial 'to expose oneself to the cold', and *bleared* (of milk, porridge): 'thin, of a bluish colour' help to account for *blear share* ('Deutschland'). Association with *blue* likely in view of Hopkins's interest in etym. and phonaesthetic series, and Barnes's BL- list (see Chapter 3). Otherwise, notion of blinding or obscuring is dominant, as also in *blur* (No. 72).

BOLE (No. 41, st. 16; *beechbole*, No. 71): Frequent in *JP*: 'I marked the *bole*, the burling and roundness of the world' (*JP*, 251), where association with roundness made clear by the context. A technical and provincial term for tree-trunk. Phonaesthetic reasons to prefer it to 'trunk': it rhymes with *roll*, *scroll* and is homophonous with *bowl*.

BONFIRE (No. 72): Wedgwood thought origin of *bon-* was in Welsh *ban* 'high, lofty', but it is certainly OE *ban-fyr* 'bone-fire'. H may have connected *bon* with Fr. *bon* 'good', and is probably playing on this etymology in *bonniest* (No. 72, following line).

BONNY (*beadbonny*, No. 54; *bonniest*, No. 72): Scots dialect: handsome, fine. Possibly from Fr. *bon* (Onions). See also BONFIRE.

Bow ('Deutschland', st. 14: of ship; No. 57, inner arc of bell; No. 59: of string, lace, ribbon; *bow-bend*, No. 36; cf. *boughs*, of tree, in No. 32 and elsewhere): In 19th century *bow* (curve), *bow* (of ship), *bow* (to bend from waist), *bough* (of tree) usually considered to have same etymology, to be from OE *bugan* (to bend). Thus in Ogilvie. Richardson says *bow* (*sic*) of tree so called because it bows or bends from stem or trunk. H clearly interested in curved shape, and *bow-bend* is a quasi-etym. doublet.

BRACE (Nos. 47, 59): Many meanings (including nautical) given by Ogilvie all involve notion of tightness, tension, strengthening.

BRAID ('Deutschland', st. 16, No. 59): In *JP*, 190, H notes North-country usage 'not ... at random but in braids' ('in rows'). Frequently used in journal of long, stringy cloud-shapes, etc. Ogilvie has *braid* (verb) 'to weave'. Dictionaries otherwise unhelpful. See Chapters 3 and 6.

BRANDLE (No. 48): Schoder glosses: 'shake, rock, make totter' and Gardner and MacKenzie suggest 'shake'. Seemingly associated with *brandish*. H likely also to have associated with *brand* (archaic: 'sword'). Ogilvie has *brangle* 'to wrangle, to dispute contentiously, to squabble'. Transfer of a probable intrans. verb to transitive use would not trouble H (see Chapter 7).

BROTH (Nos. 54, 71): Ogilvie: 'In America the word is often applied to foaming water, and especially to a mixture of snow and water on the highways, which is called *snow-broth*.' Part of H's foam and waterscape vocabulary, clearly associated with *froth*, etc.

BUCK ('Deutschland', st. 16; cf. *buckle*, No. 32). Ogilvie connects it with *beak* ('from thrusting') and takes underlying sense to be 'ram, thrust'. H possibly associated *buck* and *buckle* with OE *bugan* 'bend' (cf. Bow), and might have associated *buck* with *buckle* on the pattern of *brinded*: *brindled*, etc. (see Chapter 6). This would favour 'collapse, bend under stress' as interpretation of *buckle* in No. 32.

BURL ('Deutschland', st. 16, *burling*, No. 157, cf. *wind's burly*, st. 27): 'The burl of the fountains of air' has multiple associations: (1) roundness, as in *JP*, 251 (see s.v. BOLE), 256, 'the eye-greeting burl of the Round Tower'; (2) strength, as in *JP*, 256 (cf. a *burly* man); (3) noise and tumult, cf. Scots *burl* 'a crowd, a tumult' – Wright; Ogilvie believed *burl(y)* 'obsolete or nearly so' but noted that *hurly-burly* was common 'in vulgar use'; (4) circular motion or pattern, cf. *whirl*, *hurl*, *swirl*, etc., and Scots *birl* ('whirl'). Wright recognizes northern use: 'to twirl round, to spin, to make a noise like the rapid twirling of a wheel'. See also Milroy, *TLS* (26 September 1968), p. 1090.

BURN (No. 56): Stream, rivulet, brook, in Ireland, Scotland, Northern England.

CATCH ('Deutschland', st. 26, No. 36): In Journal (several times) and in No. 36, to observe, understand and succeed in describing some-thing accurately, to 'catch' an inscape. See, for example *JP*, 204 (and Chapter 3): '. . . film in the sheet, which may be *caught* as it turns on the edge of a cloud . . .'. This is accompanied by a drawing, which 'catches' it. The 'throng that *catches* and quails' ('Deutschland') besides suggesting that people are 'catching' at one another, may owe something to provincial 'of water: film over, begin to freeze; of wax, melted fat, etc.: to congeal, grow thick' (Wright). This last is an intransitive use.

CHEVY (No. 72): 'To pursue, chase, hunt about; to tease, worry' (Wright); also *chivy* or *chivvy*: 'tease'. Commonly trans.; H's use is intrans. MacKenzie (*Hopkins*) states that *chevy* entered language about 1830.

COGGED (No. 59): Common dialectal meaning of *cog*, 'to deceive, cheat', still current in Ireland, especially in children's usage. Most commentators accept this meaning, which has its origins in the practice of *cogging a die* ('to secure it, so as to direct its fall', Todd). H, however, is alluding to the cog or tooth of a wheel when he speaks of elm-leaves (*JP*, 152) which 'tooth or cog their woody twigs'. Both weighting a die and cogging a wheel suggest impeding, hindering or controlling. The context in No. 59, 'so fagged, so fashed, so cogged, so cumbered' suggests 'held back, hindered'. Sound associations with *haggard*, *fagged*, etc., in context and potentially with *clog* ('fetter, hamper, encumber' – Onions), tend to confirm this.

COIL (Nos. 22, 64; *care-coiled*, No. 59): In *JP* (often cloudscapes) and poems, derived from notion of coiling rope (*coils* of hay also a provincial usage). In No. 22, 'coils, keeps and teases simple sight' seems to associate coiling *in*, of rope or string, with teasing *out*, of thread or some such fine material which has become entangled. Wright gives 'enfold in a snare, to ensnare' for *coil*. This is relevant in No. 64, as is Scots and Northern 'noisy disturbance, stir, confusion, bustle' (Wright, Ogilvie). Shakespeare's 'this mortal coil', *Hamlet*, III. i. 67, doubtless relevant.

COMB (Nos. 2, 56, 68, 76, 149, 'Deutschland', st. 4, 14): Dialectal uses meaning crest or ridge fully justify H's use in poems and *JP* (13 times in *JP*, according to Bremer, *ES*, 1970). Wright has: 'furrow† or strip of ground turned up by the plough; an unturned ridge or balk left in ploughing; a crest, ridge of a hill', etc. Scots equivalent, *kaim*, is 'a name generally given to a ridge of hills'. Ogilvie recognizes nautical 'to roll over, as the top of a wave; or to break with white foam'. In 'To R.B.' (No. 76), it may mean 'filling to the crest, to the utmost', as Bremer suggests.

CRINGE ('Deutschland', st. 11): Milward comments that in the expression 'there must/ the sour scythe cringe', the verb is applied 'to the instrument instead of the agent: properly speaking it is the mower

---

† Wright uses *furrow* loosely; in ploughing the 'ridge' (higher part of 'furrow') is often distinguished from the 'furrow' (lower part, where the plough has turned the soil out and upwards).

who *cringes* or stoops to his scythe. Or perhaps it is used in a causative sense "make to cringe . . .".' Ogilvie recognizes a transitive verb 'to shrink, to contract, to draw together, a popular use of the word'. The etymology is OE *cringan*, variant of *crincan*, to yield (Partridge). Hopkins, however, almost certainly connects it with a series: *crook, crank, kranke, crick, cranky*, 'Original meaning crooked, not straight or right, wrong, awry' (*JP*, 5) and connects the series with *horn* (*JP*, 4). Under *cringe* Todd gives *crank, crinkle, crook*, etc., as etymologically connected. Ogilvie gives *crimpled*, 'contracted, shrunk'. The notion of *bending* is dominant in H (but see also Chapter 7).

CRISP (Nos. 35, 68, 159): H normally means *curled* rather than 'brittle, friable'. See Todd 'curled; indented, winding; or alluding to the little wave or *curl* . . . which the gentlest wind occasions on the surface of waters.' *JP* (e.g. 142, 144, 154) use *crisp/crispy/crisping* of clouds and water.

DAPPLE ('Deutschland', st. 5, Nos. 28, 36, 37, 42, 44, 49, 56, 61): A key word in H, associated with *pied, fleck*, etc. Todd thought that it was related to *apple* (cf. No. 44). Ogilvie thought it allied to *tabby* (this is etymologically unlikely) 'and from dipping or to Welsh *davnu* to drop'. *Streaked*, according to Ogilvie, is not its true signification; it means *spotted*. Partridge: 'presumably a diminutive of ON *dapi* a pool . . . "a small splash".' H undoubtedly connects it with *dip* and *dab* and probably with other -*le* words, such as *dimple* (see, for example, *JP* 233, and Chapter 6). *Dabs*, used of cloudscape *JP*, 142: 'a grey bank with moist gold dabs and racks'.

DEGGED (No. 56): MacKenzie (*Hopkins*) suggests this is a northern dialect word meaning 'to sprinkle'. Barnes's connection with *dag*, 'dew or mist', (also mentioned by MacKenzie) is probably right. Scandinavian (Icelandic) *dögg* (from **daggw-*) is 'dew', and early Scand. influence on northern dialect is very heavy indeed.

DING (*anvil-ding*, 'Deutschland', st. 10; No. 159): Clearly imit. and associated with *fling, ring* series and *din, dint* (q.v.) series. Ogilvie recognizes Scots: 'drive, to beat, to strike, to overcome . . . to descend, to fall with violence. The phrase *It's dingin on* is applied to a fall of rain, hail or snow.' Wright similar; Claxton (E. Anglia) additionally recognizes 'throw, hurl', which seems to fit context in No. 159: 'down he *dings/* His bleached . . . wear'.

DINT (*firedint*, No. 72): Provincially usually a blow, shock. Wright recognizes also 'vigour, energy'. Ogilvie connects it with *din, ding*. Common in ME alliterative poetry from the North (e.g. *Sir Gawain*). In standard use, survives only in expression 'by dint of'.

DOWN-DUGGED ('Deutschland', st. 26): MacKenzie(*QQ*, 501) points out probable source in Müller's *Lectures*, II, 353–4: 'the rain clouds are spoken of as cows with heavy udders', and refers to *CD*, 73, where Dixon had described 'white precipitate clouds ... like a herd/ Of deep-uddered cows'. H remarked that the image was Aryan in origin.

DRIFT ('Deutschland', st. 4, No. 48): Etym. closely connected with *drive*, but not with *drip*, *drop*. Wright recognizes provincial usage: 'a strip or line from one end of the field to another; the space between furrows; a trench cut in the ground resembling a channel dug to convey water to a millwheel'. See also s.v. COMB.

EARLSTARS (No. 61): Association of *earl* with *early* probable in view of Richardson's etymology. Modern dictionaries generally give *earl* as etymology unknown or uncertain. See also MacKenzie (*QQ*, 500).

EQUAL (No. 61): As MacKenzie points out (*QQ*, 499), early 19th century dictionaries accepted that *even* (equal) and *even* (evening) were of identical origin. I was taught at school that *evening* was so called because it was a time of *equal* balance between day and night.

FAGGED (No. 59). Wright has: 'to grow weary, flag, droop; labour, struggle ...' and *fagged out*: 'frayed, ravelled, worn at the edge' (cf. also *fadge*: 'burden'). Ogilvie also has *fag-end*, 'the untwisted end of a rope'. In *JP*, 237, H speaks of grass 'not healthily tanned like hay, but as if fagged, drained, baked.'

FASHED (No. 59): Wright: 'to trouble, afflict; to inconvenience, vex; to weary' hence ' *fashed*: troubled in mind; sorry, grieved; weary'. H (*JP*, 5): 'Fash. Don't fash yourself. Scotch. Connected with *fessus*, *fatiscor*'. Ward (*JP*, 504) derives it from OFr. *fascher*, which is not connected with Lat. *fessus*, *fatiscor*.

FETTLE (No. 53): Wright gives many provincial uses all more or less clearly connected with 'repair, mend; prepare, make ready'.

FLECK (No. 60): Ogilvie: 'to spot, to streak to stripe; to variegate; to dapple'. Part of H's 'dapple' vocabulary and connected by him with *flick*, *flake*, etc. (see *JP*, 11, and Chapter 2). Cf. also *freckled* (No. 37), *flix*.

FLITCH (*flitches*, No. 56): Richardson thinks the sense 'side of bacon' is perhaps from *flake* 'in its consequential application to a broad flat piece or portion, separated from a solid body'. H also connects *flitch* with *flake*, etc. (*JP*, 11). In 56, *flitches of fern* perhaps suggested by *groins* in previous line (on which see *JP*, 179: 'daylight glazes the groins with gleaming rose-colour').

FLIX (common in *JP*, of clouds; *flixed*, No. 60): Wright relates it to *fleck*, *flick*, *flitch*, Ogilvie to *flax*. Wright: 'fluff, dust, collected into a light down'.

FLUE (No. 71): Relevant sense in Ogilvie: 'soft down or fur; very fine hair'. H would surely connect *flick*, *fly*, *etc*. (*JP*, 11), and *fluff*.

FOLD ('Deutschland', st. 15, Nos. 37, 43, 60, 61): In *JP* commonly of landscape, with implied comparison to folds in a garment (cf. *creases*, No. 72). 'Br Sidgreaves has heard the high ridges of a field called *folds* and the hollow between the *drip*' (*JP*, 191). In No. 37, cf. also a three-yearly system of agricultural rotation (S. England): first, *fallow*, then *fold* (i.e. sheep grazing), finally, *plough*.

FOREFALLS (No. 41, st. 2): MacKenzie (*Hopkins*, 65) notes a Hampshire usage: 'steep valleys pitching down to the sea'.

GANG (*gay-gangs*, No. 72): Ogilvie: 'properly, a going; hence a number going in a company . . .' H uses it in this etym. sense.

GEAR (No. 37): *Not* a recent slang word for *dress*, etc. Common for 'dress' and 'equipment' for centuries. A slightly technical ring in that it is commonly applied in naval, farming, or angling or sporting contexts. Spenserian origin need not be invoked, as MacKenzie (*Hopkins*) comments. Cf. also *gaygear*, *maidengear* (No. 59).

GNARL ('Deutschland', st. 23; No. 41): Apart from connection with 'gnaw, bite at' (Wright), sound-association with *snarl* may be relevant. Ogilvie, under *gnar*, *gnarl* gives 'growl, murmur, snarl'.

GULLY (*gullies*, v., No. 41, st. 16): Wright gives 'to swallow, gulp'.

HAWLING ('Deutschland', st. 19): MacKenzie refers to OED *hawl* as variant of *haul* with one of its meanings: 'Of the wind: to change direction, shift, veer'. The sense of 'swerving' is taken up from the neighbouring word 'swirling'. H may well have preferred the spelling *hawling* because it also suggests *howling* – a spelling-blend.

HORN (*horns*, No. 50; *hornlight*, No. 61; *hornbeam*, No. 159): Early etymological note (*JP*, 4; 1863) shows H's concern with etymological relationships but also with shapes and textures suggested in various uses of this word (see esp. Chapters 2, 6). Common in Journal, referring to shape of tree-boughs or sun's rays in e.g. *JP*, 141: 'great towering clouds behind which the sun put out his shaded horns . . .' For *hornlight* see also *JP*, 201 (of an aurora): 'dull blood-coloured horns . . . yellow-rose light', and Chapter 6. H believed *corona*, *crown*, *crane*, *heron*, *corn*, *kernel* and many more were associated etymologically. See Chapter 2 and Ward (*JP*).

KEEN ('Deutschland', st. 25): In 'combating keen' apparently a noun-like use. Apart from usual senses (Wright: 'sharp, severe' of weather), the Scots, Irish and Northern sense 'cry of lamentation over a corpse' (Wright) also seems to be suggested.

LADE (No. 41, st. 3): In Scots dialect precisely *load*. Compare H's 'lade and treasure' with Burns, 'Tam o'Shanter': 'As bees flee hame wi' lades o' treasure/ The minutes winged their way wi' pleasure'. Otherwise relevant dialectal senses are commonly a measure, an instrument for loading, a ladder, a frame projecting from a waggon to give greater width (for loading?) (see Wright). Note 'lads' in same line, of unknown etymology, but connected by Ogilvie with *lade*, with an 'original' sense 'throw'. H may well have made this connection. See also *JP*, 173: (waterfalls) 'like heaps of snow or *lades* of shining rice'.

LOUCHÈD (No. 58): H wrote to Dixon (*CD*, 109): 'a coinage of mine and is to mean much the same as *slouched, slouching*'. As Bridges noted, it is in Wright, who recognizes Northern, Midland and South-Western use: 'slouch, bend the back in walking, walk awkwardly'.

MAMMOCK (No. 70): Amongst dialectal meanings listed by Wright are: 'to squander, dissipate, waste, leave carelessly about; to disarrange, crumble, throw into confusion; to break or cut into pieces, crumble, tear, mangle'.

MARCHES (No. 72): The sense 'border, boundary' may be relevant; etym. connected with *mark*.

MEAL (*mealed*, No. 32; *mealdrift*, No. 38; *leafmeal*, No. 55): There are two separate words: (1) a measure (archaic), a repast, from OE *mæl*, mark, sign, measure, fixed time; (2) powder of ground grain or pulse (etym. connected with *mill* and the idea of grinding): Onions. Ogilvie thought *mellow* also connected. H combines both senses in *leafmeal*, formed on the analogy of *piecemeal*, but frequently uses *meal* in *JP* in the sense of soft, powdery substance, e.g. *JP*, 168: 'Spanish chestnuts in thickest honey-white meal'.

MESS (*May-mess*, No. 32; *messes*, No. 41, st. 10): Etymologically probably connected, through Lat. *missus*, with *Mass* (religious sense), but see Onions. Archaic and dial. senses: a dish of food, a number, a large quantity. Wright quotes: 'There's a mess of apples uppa that tree' (cf. H's *May-mess like on orchard-boughs*). Nautical use, e.g. *messmate*, may have influenced H in No. 41. Cf. also *JP*, 184: 'some simple gilded messes of cloud'. For H, *mass* (quantity, bulk) and *mess* would certainly be variants of the same word.

MINION (No. 36): Trench (*On the Study of Words*, 78) bewails the degeneration of meaning in this word, which formerly meant merely 'a favourite (man in Sylvester is God's dearest minion)'. Ogilvie (see MacKenzie, *Hopkins*) derived it from Welsh *main*, 'small', with related *mwyn*, 'tender, gentle'. H, in his Welsh period, may well have been influenced by its Welsh 'ring'; there are many Welsh words (though usually plurals) that end in *-ion*. The word is from French, but possibly ultimately Celtic (see Onions).

MOULD (Nos. 40, 41, 53, 59, 60, 145): H seems to transfer verbal use 'to shape' to noun use. This happens also in dialect where 'to be of good mould' can mean to be well shaped (of children or young animals) – Wright. Otherwise, *mould*, as noun, in modern English is usually 'ground, soil (esp. for a grave)'. OE *molde* meant 'earth'. See Chapter 7 for verbal use in No. 38.

NAVE (knee-nave, No. 71): 'The thick piece of timber in the centre of a wheel, in which the spokes are inserted; called also the *hub* or *hob*'. N. White (*HQ*, 1975) has suggested a connection with dial. *neaf*, *neave*, 'fist', but see Chapter 6.

PASHED (No. 61): Wright recognizes amongst other meanings: 'to smash, shatter, break in fragments ... of rain or water: to come down suddenly or heavily ... a soft, rotten, decayed or pulpy mass'. H clearly associates it in *JP* with *splash* ('*pashes* of grass' – *JP*, 243), and in 'a *pash* of soap-sud coloured gummy bim-beams' (*JP*, 233), there appear to be further associations with rhyming or near-rhyming words (*rash, mash, mass*). In No. 61, context suggests that the notion of mixing or mingling is dominant, and collocation with *steeped* suggests that an association with liquid substances is invoked. But, since the context also concerns the variegation of evening settling down into the blackness of night, Ogilvie's obsolete meaning 'to strike; to strike down' may also be relevant. H uses *plash* for 'splash' in his early poetry (No. 2, l. 102).

PEEL (*peeled*, 'Deutschland', st. 26; *rutpeel*, No. 72): Certainly a dialect form of *pool* (Wright) varying with *pill* (a pool, creek, running stream). 'Pied and *peeled* May' is a month of clouds and showers resulting in the formation of small pools of water in fields, roadways, etc.; *rutpeel* is left by the rain in ruts caused by cartwheels on unpaved roads. (Wright notes that *to do one's peels* is 'to make water, urinate').

PIED ('Deutschland', st. 26; No. 37 (title); *betweenpie*, No. 69): Together with *dappled*, favourite word in *JP* for 'particoloured, variegated'. In May 1866, H describes a sky '*pied* with clouds' (*JP*, 135). The month is significant; see under PEEL. In No. 37, *pied* is extended to many objects not normally described thus; cf. Ogilvie: 'if the spots are small, we use *speckled*. This distinction was not formerly observed, and in some cases, *pied* is elegantly used to express a diversity of colours in small spots. "Meadows trim with daisies pied" *Milton*.' *Betweenpie*, No. 69, is a verb, with *pie* a back-formation from *pied*. Cf. *JP*, 232: 'white pieings' on pigeons; and see *Poems*, 290. *Betweenpie* is to 'intervariegate', as Bridges suggested.

PITCH ('Deutschland', st. 16, No. 65; *pitchblack*, No. 56): Only in 'pitched past *pitch* of grief' does there seem to be a connection with Hopkins's *inscape* uses of this word. Clouds (*JP*, 203–4) 'lurch' into 'some particular *pitch*' (state of being *and* doing – see Milward, p. 85, and *SD*, 151) and their tufts are 'quained' 'in forepitch or in origin' (former state of being and doing). Ogilvie connects *pitch* with *pike* and *peak*: 'literally, a point ... hence any point or degree of elevation ...

size, stature ... the point where a declivity begins ... descent, slope ...'. For H to prefer *pitch* to 'degree, state' etc., is part of his Germanic purism. Cf. Barnes's *pitches of suchness* for 'degrees of adjective comparison' (see Chapter 2). In H's terms of inscaping, *pitch* is allied to self, haecceitas and inscape itself – 'simple positiveness ... And such "doing-be", and the thread or chain of such pitches or "doing-be's" ... is self, personality' (*SD*, 151). For H, *being* is not a stative quality, but positive and active.

PLOUGH: In 'fold, fallow and plough' (No. 37), may be 'section of ploughed land'; cf. Wright: 'the quantity of land which one plough can till' (obsolete). But see s.v. FOLD.

QUAIL ('Deutschland', st. 24; No. 71): Ogilvie gives: 'sink or languish, to curdle, and to crush or quell'. The meaning 'curdle, coagulate' (as in milk) may be relevant in 'Deutschland', where the neighbouring *catch* (q.v.) may also have similar associations ('congeal, freeze over'). Ogilvie's meanings, 'sink, curdle', also seem relevant to the imagery of 'Harry Ploughman' (No. 71). See Chapter 6.

QUELL (Nos. 43, 48): From OE *cwellan*, 'kill', which may possibly be the origin of some senses of *quail* also. Part of H's *qu-* vocabulary, with *quail, quench*, and *squander, squadron, squeeze* (No. 72).

QUAIN (*selfquainèd*, No. 159): Etym. related to *coin, coign* (Fr. 'corner'), and used in *JP* in description of shapes. 'And if you look carefully at big pack-clouds overhead you will soon find a strong large quaining and squaring in them ...' Also applied to rocks and mountains, the word suggests bulkiness, squareness, weight. Things which are *burly* (No. 159, previous line, and see s.v. BURL) may be *quained*.

RACE (Nos. 41, 47, 60, 71, 102): Many dialectal uses include 'a range or series of anything' (Wright). Used in *JP* of clouds, waterfalls, etc. *JP* vocabulary used in No. 102 'As the fine morsels of a dwindling cloud/ That piece themselves into a *race* of drops' (written in 1864). Quick motion often implied, of liquid or vapour (see Chapter 6, note 13).

RACK (Nos. 43, 54, 58, 61, 71): Ogilvie connects it with *reach*; hence, 'something used for stretching, something in which things are spread out for use'. He also mentions 'framework' or 'frame': 'we say, a *rack* of bones' (cf. *rack of ribs*, No. 71). As a second word, he glosses *rack*: 'vapour; hence, thin, flying broken clouds' (cf. H's cloudscapes), and *reech, reek*, (*JP*, 204, of vapour). Wright recognizes a similar dialectal use: 'flying clouds', etc., and mentions phrases: *the rack of the weather*: 'track in which clouds move; *the rack rides*; used of clouds when driven by the wind'. It may also mean 'rain' and figuratively 'foam' on the sea. It can also mean *rick* (*ruck*) or *stack* (of hay or corn). In No. 58 ('o'ergives all to rack and wrong'), H may be suggesting *pain, torture* (Ogilvie, Wright). In No. 43 ('hack and rack the growing green'), there is surely a connection with homophonous *wrack*, and *wreck*. Wright notes dial. alternation of *rack* with *reck*. See also *reck, rank, ruck, wreck* and cf. *rick* (in *JP*), *rake*.

RAMPS (No. 35): Wright recognizes: 'romp, prance, rage violently' and 'of milk: to become ropy'. Onions thinks *romp* is perhaps an alternant of *ramp* (cf. *sea-romp*, 'Deutschland', st. 17). Second word *ramp*: 'an inclined plane' (Onions) also relevant (see Chapter 6).

RANK (Nos. 43, 48, 71; *ranked*, Nos. 59, 159; *rank-old*, No. 141): Arrange in ranks; a row, series, line. But cf. Wright: 'thorough, utter, close together, thick-set; strong, great, formidable'. Suggestion of quasi-etymological association in *ranked wrinkles*, No. 59.

RASH ('Deutschland', st. 19; No. 152, C; *rash-fresh*, No. 35): In dialect: 'brisk, hale, hearty; eager, quick, impetuous; ... hot-tempered, severely harsh' (Wright). Also 'a squall of rain'. Applied to water in Nos. 28, 152 and in context of sea in No. 35.

REAVE (Nos. 51, 58): 'Rob, steal, plunder' (Wright), but cf. *reeve* (possibly relevant especially in No. 58).

RANDAL (No. 53): Mariani says 'of Anglo-Saxon origin and means a shield as well as a strip of leather placed on the heels of a shoe. Both meanings reinforce one another here'. OE *rand*: 'shield' is probably too archaic to be relevant, but Ogilvie mentions the '*rand* of a shoe' from *rand*, 'border, edge, margin'.

RANDOM (No. 53): Wright cites usages from Lancashire and Cheshire (Felix Randal's locality): 'irregular stone, rubble'. 'A random wall is one built of stones of various shapes and sizes, in contradistinction to a "coursed" wall ... Random flags are flags of all sizes, not ranked.' Also in Ogilvie. Etym. through Romance from Germanic *rand* ('shield'); oldest meanings in English are 'impetuosity, great speed or violence' (Onions).

RECK (Nos. 31, 58, 61, 70, 152): Heed, regard for, care for. Ogilvie: 'This verb is obsolete unless in poetry ... primary sense ... in the phrase "it recks me not", that is it does not strain or distress me, it does not *rack* my mind; it is not estimated by me; or, I care not'. MacKenzie comments on association with Lat. *rectus*, English *right*, mentioned by Ogilvie, and clearly relevant in No. 61, where *right* is a neighbouring word; *rack* also occurs a few lines later. OE *recan*, to tell, narrate, is related by Ogilvie to Lat. *rego*. 'The primary sense is to strain. Care is a straining of the mind. See *rack* and *reckon*.'

RECKON (No. 61): Still commonly used in much of England in the sense 'count, enumerate'; this probably relevant in No. 61, differentiating *reckon* from *reck* ('to care').

REEL (Nos, 22, 58, 141; *reeling* (water), No. 152): Surely phonaesthetically connected by H with *roll*, but with a 'smaller', 'thinner' sound. See Chapter 2 and references to Firth and R. Brown. Cf. context in No. 141 'with a tide rolls reels/ Of crumbling, fore-foundering, thundering all-surfy seas in'. The tide *rolls in* (large) the *reels* (small) of surfy sea.

REEVE ('Deutschland', st. 12; No. 63): Ogilvie (*reeving*): 'In marine language – the pulling of a rope through a block'; *reeve*: 'to pass the end of a rope through any hole in a block . . .'.

RIVELLING (*rivelling snowstorm*, No. 41): Ogilvie has 'to contract into wrinkles; to shrink; as *rivelled* fruit; rivelled flowers'. Like *cringe* (q.v.), used to suggest that those who are affected by the snow-storm are *rivelling*, as well as the storm itself. H no doubt associated *rivel* with *rive* (this word is also in No. 41): 'to tear, split', with diminutive or iterative sense (see Chapters 2, 6 and s.v. DAPPLE *et al.*). It also clearly suggests *shrivel, swivel* (cf. 'Deutschland', st. 13), *drivel* and even *drizzle*. Ogilvie thinks *rivel* allied to *shrivel* and *ruffle*.

ROAD ('Deutschland', st. 35; No. 53): *All road* in No. 53 used to give northern flavour to the language. Wright lists idiomatic phrases *any road, no road, in the road, out of the road* (for 'way'), but *all road* is not listed. *Roads* ('Deutschland'): a place where ships may ride at anchor at some distance from the shore.

ROPE ('Deutschland', st. 16, No. 63; *ropes* (verb), No. 72; *roped*, 'Deutschland', st. 4; *rope-over*, No. 71): Ogilvie: 'to draw out or extend into a filament or thread, by means of any glutinous or adhesive quality. Any glutinous substance will *rope* considerably before it will part'. Part of H's wind and water imagery, by which he imparts solidity and tension to non-solid substances (see Chapter 6). Cannot be connected with old past participle of reap, as has been suggested. In No. 72, the bright wind 'ropes, wrestles'; it spins out, extends itself, 'coils' into circles, and so on.

ROSEMOLES (No. 37): For *mole*, Schoder glosses '(dialectal) spot, stain, as on cloth'. Onions gives obsolete 'discoloured spot' now specialized to 'spot or blemish on the human skin'. This is common British English usage.

RUCK (Nos. 22, 59): 'Fold, wrinkle, crease . . . a ridge' (Wright); cf. *ruck* and *wrinkle* (No. 59); also 'a mass, number . . . pile, heap, rough bundle . . . hence *rucking* (*a*) a drift; (*b*) fleecy white clouds'. This sense relevant in No. 22. It is also a dialectal alternant of *rick* ('a haystack, etc.') H in *JP* often uses *ricked* (e.g. of oaks, *JP*, 168) in the sense 'folded, wrinkled, ridged', and, for H, *rack* when used of clouds may also be associated with *ruck*: 'pile, bundle'.

RUTPEEL (No. 72): See s.v. PEEL.

SAKE ('Deutschland', st. 22; No. 45): See *LB*, 83, where H explains:

'*Sake* is a word I find it convenient to use . . . It is the sake of "for the sake of", *forsake, namesake, keepsake*. I mean by it the being a thing has outside itself, as a voice by its echo, a face by its reflection, a man by his name, fame or memory, *and also* that in the thing by virtue of which especially it has this being abroad, and that is something distinctive, marked, specifically or individually speaking, as for a voice and echo clearness; for a reflected image light, brightness; for a shadow-casting body bulk; for a man genius, great achievements, amiability, and so on. In this case (No. 45) it is, as the sonnet says, distinctive quality in genius.' Ogilvie connects *sake* (wrongly) with *seek, essay* and Latin *sequor* 'follow'. The idea that *sake* is something that 'follows', or goes with, a man or object, could possibly have been suggested to H by Ogilvie's etymology.

SALLOWS (No. 32): Willow-trees.

-SCAPE (*lovescape*, 'Deutschland', st. 23): H clearly associates *-scape* compounds (*inscape, offscape, lovescape*) with idea of shaping, making, forming. Eng. *shape* is from OE *scieppan*, Gmc **skapjan*. ON *skap* is cognate. *Landscape* is from Dutch *landschap*, and extended to *seascape*, etc., in vocabulary of art. But see Müller (*Lectures* I, p. 256): 'Thus *scape* in *landscape*, and the more modern *ship* in *hardship* are both derived from the same root which we have in Gothic, *skapa, skop, skopum*, to create; in Anglo-Saxon, *scape, scop, scopon*'. H clearly associates *sk-* words with *sh-* words in *JP*, 25; for him *scoop* (e.g. No. 71), *scupple* (*JP*) may be associated with *scape, shape*.

SHEER (Nos. 36, 41, 64, 65, 72): See Chapter 6 and s.v. SHIRE. Onions recognizes obsolete *sheer*: 'bright, shining; thin, fine; mixed, unqualified'. The word is probably an alternant of dialect *shire*: 'clear, pure, mere, thin, weak' (Onions). To *sheer* (of a ship) is identical with *shear*: 'cut', probably also *sheer* (noun): 'curve of a ship' (Onions). In Nos. 36 and 72, word associations of both cutting and shining; the latter sense dominant in No. 64.

SHIRE (No. 25; 'Deutschland', st. 34): Probably, together with *sheer*, H associates this word with cutting and division, and also with light or brightness. Although modern opinion derives it from a word meaning 'care, official charge' (Onions), the nineteenth century accepted derivation from OE *scieran*, to cut. Thus Ogilvie, who also associated *share* and *shear*. Trench, 329–30, comments: '"Shire" is connected with "shear", "share", and is properly a portion "shered" or "shorn" off'. H (*JP*, 12) lists *shear, share* and others, and comments '*Shire*, a division of land? *Shore*, where the land is cut by water? *Shower*, cf. shred, a fall of water in little shreds and divisions'. H is wrong about *shower* and *shire*, and possibly wrong about *shore*. Of mountain ranges, H later comments: 'they express a second level with an upper world or *shires* of snow' (*JP*, 171). Of bluebells (*JP*, 231), he speaks of the 'level or stage or *shire* of colour they make hanging in the air a foot above the grass'. The *starry shire* of No. 22 is a level or division which is also bright. Cf. OE *scir*: 'bright, shining', with which at least one modern sense of *sheer* (pure, transparent) is associated (see Milroy, *CS*, 1971). In No. 28 ('A released shower, let flash to the shire'), there is quasi-etymological play. Christ is to descend upon England, gently, as a *shower*, upon the *shire* (possibly first upon the upper divisions and levels of the world: the 'starry shire', the *shire* of the mountains, and so on). H clearly does *not* mean the counties (shires) of England. See also SHEER.

SHIVE (No. 159; *shivelights*, No. 72): Ogilvie recognizes 'obsolete' *shive*: 'a slice'. Wright records it as current dialect: 'a slice of anything edible ... a piece of wood shaved or splintered off ... a splinter'. *Shiver*: 'a fragment, chip', prob. associated, both by etym. and by H. Cf. also *sliver*.

SHOCKS (STOOKS) (Nos. 8, 32): Piles of sheaves set up endwise in the field to dry. H also uses *stooks* (No. 38). See *JP*, 200: 'stooks (which the Devonshire people call shocks)', and *JP*, 209 (of bluebells): 'with a *shock* of wet heads.' *Shock* (stook) and *shuck* (thick mass of hair) are of uncertain origin. Onions does not connect them, but H may well have done so.

SILLION (No. 36): Certainly Fr. 'furrow turned over by the plough'. Schoder: '(*dial.* spelling for "selion") a strip or ridge of land between two furrows dividing plots in the open field system, a "narrow land"'. .

SKILL ('Or as Austin, a lingering-out sweet skill', 'Deutschland', st. 10): A reference to the gradual conversion of St Augustine of Hippo to Christianity. Etymologically connected to Lat. *scire* 'to know', with a basic IE sense 'divide'. A good historical example of metaphorical transfer from concrete to abstract use (see Chapter 2). H knew this. See *JP*, 25: '*skill*, originally I believe to divide, discriminate'; he connects it with *shell, shilling, school,* shoal, *scale, keel,* and Lat. *scindere*. Wright lists dialect uses: 'a proof, trial; to understand, comprehend, judge, discriminate, to know how to deal with; to prove, test'. He also distinguishes a second word *skill*: 'to shell, separate from the husk' (from Scand. *skilja*: to part). *Skill* is a variant of the same root. In H's list, *school* (of boys) and *keel* are certainly not related to *skill* (see Ward, *JP*, 521).

SLOGGERING ('Deutschland', st. 19): Certainly imit., belonging to phonaesthetic series (*slither*, etc.), a derivative (*slog*, etc.), and a blend. *Slogger* recorded by Wright: 'hang loosely and untidily' (in northern use). Complex associations suggest the meaning: 'dashing (against the ship) repeatedly and drawing back with a sucking gurgling noise'. Firth mentions that some have suggested that *sl-* words suggest salivation. See Chapter 2 and discussion of *sloggering* in Chapter 6. Cf. (dialect uses from Wright): *slagger*: besmear with mud; *slog*: a haze, fog; a slough quagmire; to walk laboriously through mud; *slodder*: mud; to splash; *slubber*: daub, besmear (cf. *JP*, 184); *slobber*; *slocher*: labour under asthma; take liquid food in a slabbering manner; wallow in mud; *slidder*: 'slide, slope'; *slag*: soft, wet; *slopper*: slobber; *sludder*: any wet viscous substance; *slug*: a heavy surf tumbling in with an offshore wind; and many more. Also *slosh, slush, slorp, slurp, slig, sludge.*

SMART ('Deutschland', st. 18, 19; No. 63): *Smart* (of weather): 'severe, sharp'. Dorset: 'smart weather' – a severe frost (Wright). A *smart* is a sharp pain. Ogilvie connects *smart* with Lat. *amarus*, bitter, Onions with *mordere*, bite.

SQUANDER (Nos. 48, 72): In Northern dialect, to scatter (see Wright, Schoder). See also s.v. ASUNDER.

STIPPLE (No. 37): An art term derived from Dutch (Onions, Partridge): to paint or engrave in dots. A frequentative (iterative) of Dutch *stippen*. Partridge adds that *stip* is probably a variant of Gmc words exemplified by English *stick*. See discussion of *-le* words, Chapter 6.

TACKLE (No. 37): Wright: 'gear, implements, machinery, harness'. Ogilvie 'primary sense is . . . put in order'. Cf. *tack* (of a ship) and see also *gear, trim.*

THEW ('Deutschland', st. 16; Nos, 49, 71): A favourite in the Journal and poems in the sense 'brawn, muscle, sinew'. This application depends largely on Scott's revival of Shakespearean uses of *thew* in the sense 'vigour'. Scott misapplied the word to 'muscle'. Originally in OE 'custom, habit; virtue; in plural, bodily powers'. See Onions.

THORP (No. 42): An archaic word common in Victorian poetry for 'hamlet, village'. Common in place names.

THROSTLE (No. 42): Common dialectally for 'song-thrush'; an *-le* diminutive.

TRAMBEAMS (No. 46): Tram is basically a beam, bar or shaft. Ogilvie comments that a tramway, a plate railway, is prepared 'by forming the wheel tracks of smooth *beams* of wood . . . plates of iron'; these would seem to be *trambeams*. Schoder comments that 'silk threads used in weft' are called *trams*, hence the idea here is probably of wavy silk-like beams, but H may mean *straight*, not wavy, beams of light. See also BEAM.

TRIM (No. 37): Possibly from OE *trymian*: strengthen, confirm (*trum*: strong). Widely used in traditional crafts and industries in the sense 'proper array or equipment'. Wright notes *trim* (noun): 'the whole number of lobster or other fish pots set out in one place'; Ogilvie:

'the state of a ship ... by which she is well prepared for sailing'. *Gear*, *tackle* and *trim* are near-synonyms (Ogilvie gives 'gear' for *trim*). Barnes calls the art of speaking *speech trimming*: 'the putting of speech into trim; *trim* being a truly good form or state'.

TRUCKLE (No. 46): Wright gives 'trundle, roll' as one meaning, and H is probably thinking of *track* in this word and in *tram-* (see s.v. TRAMBEAM). Ogilvie recognizes 'yield obsequiously'. Schoder accepts this second meaning, but both are probably relevant. The 'to-fro ... trambeams' both *trundle* and *yield*.

TUCKED (No. 57): Wright mentions for *tuck* 'the beat or sound of a drum or trumpet ... a pull; a jerk; a tug'. Not etym. identical with *touch*, but H would probably associate the two. There may also be a portmanteau relationship to *touch* and *pluck* (see Chapter 6).

TURF (No. 39): Warwickshire: 'a sod or piece of turf cut from a common or the wayside to put into a lark's cage'.

VAST (No. 61; *vastness*, No. 72; *vasty*, No. 60): Etymologically certainly connected with waste (Lat. *vastus*); etymological play on *vast* ... *waste* in No. 61. See also WEST.

WAKES (No. 74): Keep watch; be or keep awake.

WEST (in No. 61): Ogilvie: 'probably signified decline or fall, or departure ... In elements it coincides with *waste*' (quoted by MacKenzie, *QQ*). Involved in etymological play on *vast* and *waste* in No. 61.

WHORL ('Deutschland', st. 14; *whorled (ear)*, No. 22). Probably etym. identical with *whirl*, but normally restricted to technical uses in *botany*, *conchology*, etc. Common in JP, and Wright recognizes 'eddy, whirlpool'. In No. 22, the ear is likened to a shell; significantly, *shelled* occurs a few lines later in reference to eyes. In 'Deutschland' the reference is to the screw-propeller of the ship, which was lost. Suggests circular *pattern* rather more than *motion* (contrast *whirl*).

WIND¹ (No. 40: 'wind/ what most I may eye after'): H writes (*LB*, 66): 'I mean that the eye winds/ only in the sense that its focus or point of sight winds and that coincides with a point of the object and winds with that. For the object, a lantern passing further and further away and bearing now east, now west of one right line, is truly and properly described as winding.' Paraphrase 'what I may most wind my eyes after' and note how the verb is used both of observer and observed, thus inscaping the event.

WIND² (e.g. 'Deutschland', st. 13, 14): H may have made some connection between the verb to *wind* and *wind* ('air in motion'), which he had heard pronounced with the *i* long (*JP*, 227), as it still is by some speakers in Co. Donegal, Ireland (personal observations, 1975–6). In st. 13, therefore, the rhyme *unkind-wind* (air in motion) is not an archaism. In the next stanza 'to wind her with' may mean to 'turn her to the wind (i.e. breeze)' rather than merely 'turn in circles'. See Ogilvie: 'To wind a ship, to bring it round until the head occupies the place where the stern was, so that the *wind* may strike the opposite side.'

WRECK ('Deutschland', st. 17; Nos. 41, 68; *wrecking*, 'Deutschland', st. 9; cf. *shipwrack*, 'Deutschland', st. 31). Although Onions does not treat them as directly etym. connected, *wrack* and *wreck* in the senses connected with wreck and wreckage are normally felt to be doublets. *Wrack* in the sense 'retributive punishment' is derived by Onions from the same root as *wreck* (OE *wrecan*: drive). These words may take on associations with *reck, rack, ruck*, etc. (q.v.).

Notes

CHAPTER I

1. Reviews and Sturge Moore's revision are quoted from W. H. Gardner, *Gerard Manley Hopkins (1884–1889) a study of poetic idiosyncrasy in relation to poetic tradition,* 2 vols. (London, 1944, 1949) which discusses in detail the critical reception of Hopkins's poetry.
2. Robert Bridges's *Preface* to the first edition of Hopkins's poems (1919), quoted from *Poems* (4th ed.), p. 239.
3. F. R. Leavis, *Gerard Manley Hopkins: Reflections after Fifty Years,* The Hopkins Society, Second Annual Lecture (London, 1971), p. 3.
   According to Tom Dunne, *Gerard Manley Hopkins: A Comprehensive Bibliography* (Oxford, 1976), articles on 'The Windhover' number 76 up to 1970. Up to 1968, there were 294 dissertations on Hopkins.
4. F. R. Leavis, 'Gerard Manley Hopkins', *New Bearings in English Poetry* (London, 1932), reprinted by Penguin Books (Harmondsworth, 1950), pp. 119–43.
5. For references to these important studies, see Bibliography.
6. G. H. Hartman, 'The Dialectic of Sense-Perception', in G. H. Hartman (ed.), *Hopkins: A Collection of Critical Essays* (Englewood Cliffs N.J., 1966), p. 122.
7. See discussion of left-branching as against right-branching constructions, in Chapter 7 (pp. 212–13).
8. *Gerard Manley Hopkins and the Victorian Temper* (New York, 1972), p. 4.
9. Louis James, *Fiction for the Working Man* (Harmondsworth, 1974), pp. 202–4.
10. 'Politics and the English Language', in *Shooting an Elephant and Other Essays* (London, 1953); variously reprinted.
11. This is not to say that some nineteenth-century poets and scholars were not interested in experimental metres and rhythms. In various

ways, Coleridge, Bridges and Patmore pursued these interests. It has been suggested by Norman MacKenzie, *Hopkins* (Edinburgh and London, 1968), pp. 106–7, that Hopkins's theory of sprung rhythm was indebted to an essay by John Addington Symonds: 'The Blank Verse of Milton', *Fortnightly Review*, Dec. 1874, pp. 767–81. The earliest major poem in English in syllable-timed rhyming couplets is *The Owl and the Nightingale* (ed. E. G. Stanley, Manchester, 1972), written in the late twelfth century.

12. It is now reprinted with an introduction by Robert W. Gutman as *Volsunga Saga* (New York, 1972).

13. Basil Bernstein's theories regarding language difficulties in education are based on the contrast between 'restricted code' which is context-tied and 'elaborated code' which is context-free. See, for example, Bernstein, *Class, Codes and Control*, 3 vols. (London, 1971, 1972, 1975), and for a discussion, M. Stubbs, *Language, Schools and Classrooms* (London, 1976). 'Spoken prose' is a term coined by David Abercrombie. See his 'Conversation and Spoken Prose', *Studies in Phonetics and Linguistics* (London, 1965), pp. 1–9.

14. For an introduction to these topics, see, for example, Randolph Quirk, *The Use of English* (London, 1962), and references therein, particularly the notion of speech as 'phatic communion' – a term coined by the anthropologist Bronislaw Malinowski.

15. In recent years linguists have paid considerable attention to the study of speech in context, and its variability in relation to social and contextual factors. See especially W. Labov, *Sociolinguistic Patterns* (Philadelphia, 1972); Dell Hymes (ed.), *Language in Culture and Society* (New York, 1964); P. P. Giglioli (ed.), *Language and Social Context* (Harmondsworth, 1972); J. B. Pride and J. Holmes (eds.), *Sociolinguistics* (Harmondsworth, 1972). British linguists have used the word *register* for language variation according to occasion of use. On this see M. A. K. Halliday, A. McIntosh and P. Strevens, *The Linguistic Sciences and Language Teaching* (London, 1964), especially Chapter 4, and the work of R. Quirk, D. Crystal and others.

16. 'Gerard Manley Hopkins: An Idiom of Desperation', in John Wain, *Essays on Literature and Ideas* (London, 1966), pp. 103–31. See p. 116.

17. J. D. O'Connor, *Phonetics* (Harmondsworth, 1973), pp. 197–8, 238–9.

18. Kenneth Sisam, *Fourteenth Century Verse and Prose* (Oxford, 1920).

19. 'Hopkins' Sprung Rhythm and the Life of English Poetry', in N. Weyand (ed.), *Immortal Diamond* (London and New York, 1949), pp. 93–174.

20. *Gerard Manley Hopkins: A Critical Essay towards the Understanding of his Poetry*, 2nd ed. (Oxford, 1970). See especially pp. 62ff. and p. 87.
21. See, for example, John Lyons, *Introduction to Theoretical Linguistics* (Cambridge, 1968), pp. 403, 427, 448ff; F. Palmer, *Semantics* (Cambridge, 1976), pp. 17, 35–6, 61–3.

CHAPTER 2

1. Alison Sulloway, op. cit., pp. 68–9.
2. Preface to *A Dictionary of the English Language* (1755). Reprinted in W. F. Bolton (ed.), *The English Language, Essays by English and American Men of Letters* 1490–1839 (Cambridge, 1966), pp. 129–56. The quotation is from p. 150.
3. In terms of Prague School theory, as discussed in Chapter 4, this corresponds to a distinction between the *utilitarian* and *aesthetic* 'functions'.
4. William Barnes, *Outline of English Speech-Craft* (London, 1878).
5. Ibid.
6. H. M. McLuhan, 'The Analogical Mirrors', *Kenyon Review* (1944), reprinted in G. H. Hartman (ed.), *Hopkins: A Collection of Critical Essays* (Englewood Cliffs, N.J., 1966), pp. 80–8. The quotations are from p. 81. W. H. Gardner, op. cit., Vol. 2, p. 399.
7. Quoted from O. Jespersen, *Language, Its Nature, Development and Origin* (London, 1922), p. 29.
8. See Hans Aarsleff, *The Study of Language in England, 1780–1860* (Princeton, 1967). Kemble's remark is quoted from p. 201.
9. Richard M. Dorson, *The British Folklorists: A History* (London, 1968), p. 62.
10. But see Alan Ward's commentary: 'Philological Notes', *JP*, 499–527.
11. See further discussion of such etymological series in Chapter 6.
12. See Commentary, and discussion of *sloggering* in Chapter 6.
13. Nirad C. Chaudhuri, *Scholar Extraordinary: The Life of Professor the Rt. Hon. Friedrich Max Müller, P. C.* (London, 1974), p. 185.
14. Max Müller, *Lectures on the Science of Language*, First Series (London, 1861), p. 36. For further discussion of Müller's views, see Chaudhuri, op. cit., pp. 177–201, and J. Milroy 'Hopkins' Victorian Language', *Hopkins Quarterly* I (January 1975), pp. 167–81.
15. Max Müller, *Selected Essays on Language, Mythology and Religion*, Vol. 1 (London, 1881), p. 33.
16. N. Chomsky and M. Halle, *The Sound Pattern of English* (New York,

1968). Historical rules of lengthening, shortening and fronting of vowels have for a long time been well recognized and documented by historical linguists. Recently, phonologists have been much interested in *natural* and *unnatural* phonological changes and relationships such as we here discuss. See L. M. Hyman, *Phonology: Theory and Analysis* (New York, 1975), e.g. pp. 153–85.

17. Jespersen, op. cit., p. 52.
18. Müller, *Lectures*, I, especially in the early chapters, emphasizes not only the endless variety of language, but the sense of *wonder* and curiosity that has motivated speculation about language and investigation of its forms.
19. Ralph Waldo Emerson, reprinted in W. F. Bolton, op. cit., p. 191.
20. R. C. Trench, *On the Study of Words*, 20th ed. (London, 1888), p. 6, and see pp. 46–72.
21. Hensleigh Wedgwood, *Dictionary of English Etymology*, Vol. 1 (London, 1859), pp. iii–xx.
22. Quoted by Jespersen, op. cit., p. 414.
23. Ibid., p. 415.
24. Ibid., pp. 396–411. Jespersen's (1920) criticisms of linguistic science are worth quoting: 'It is so preoccupied with etymology with the origin of words, that it pays much more attention to what words have come from than to what they have come to be. If a word has not always been suggestive on account of its sound, then its actual suggestiveness is left out of account and may even be declared to be merely fanciful. I hope that this chapter contains throughout what is psychologically a more true and linguistically a more fruitful view.' To judge by Hopkins, such a view is *poetically* fruitful too.
25. Since Noam Chomsky's exposition of transformational syntax in *Aspects of the Theory of Syntax* (Cambridge Mass. 1965), the view that linguistic descriptions should match 'the intuition of the idealized native speaker–hearer' has been accepted by many linguists.
26. See J. R. Firth's chapter 'Phonetic Habits' in *Speech*, reprinted in *The Tongues of Men and Speech* (London, 1964), pp. 180–8, especially pp. 184–7.
27. Roger Brown, *Words and Things* (New York, 1958), pp. 110–54.

CHAPTER 3

1. Quoted by Jespersen, op, cit., p. 41.
2. W. A. M. Peters, *Gerard Manley Hopkins: A Critical Essay towards*

the Understanding of his Poetry (London, 1948; 2nd ed., 1970), pp. 141–2.

3. E. R. August, *Word Inscapes: A Study of the Poetic Vocabulary of Gerard Manley Hopkins*, unpublished dissertation (University of Pittsburgh, 1964), pp. 24–5, 29, 38.

4. Relevant work by Cobbett, Hazlitt and De Quincey is reprinted by W. F. Bolton, op. cit.

5. See Aarsleff, op. cit., pp. 191–210; Giles Dugdale, *William Barnes of Dorset*, pp. 83–4, 267–75; Norman MacKenzie, *Hopkins* (1968), p. 113.

6. Reprinted in Dugdale, op. cit., loc. cit. The quotation is from pp. 268–9.

7. Henry Sweet, *The Practical Study of Languages* (1899), reprinted by Oxford University Press (London, 1964), pp. 244–5.

8. T. Kington Oliphant, *The Sources of Standard English* (London, 1873). See pp. 215, 317, 319, 323.

9. MacKenzie, op. cit., p. 118.

10. Peters, op. cit., p. 64.

11. See, for example, articles by J. Braidwood, G. B. Adams and R. J. Gregg in *Ulster Dialects: An Introductory Symposium* (Holywood, Co. Down, 1964). A Hiberno-English Dialect Survey, under the direction of G. B. Adams, M. V. Barry and P. Tilling, is now under way. Early results of a study of variation in Belfast speech have appeared as *Belfast Working Papers in Language and Linguistics*, Vol. 1 (Belfast, 1976), comprising articles by J. Milroy, L. Milroy and R. Maclaran.

12. Trench, op. cit., p. 63.

13. Ibid., pp. 329–30.

14. Ibid., pp. 223–4.

15. *Transactions of the Philological Society* (1860), p. 16.

16. On Ruskin's influence, see Sulloway, op. cit., pp. 68–9 and elsewhere. The use of the term *law* rather than *rule* by Hopkins and by nineteenth-century linguists is itself interesting, and owes much to the use of the term in physical science. Modern linguists prefer the term *rule*.

17. On 'positive anymore' in the USA see W. Labov, *Where do Grammars stop?* Georgetown University Monograph Series on Language and Linguistics, No. 25 (1972), and Donald Hindle, *Syntactic Variation in Philadelphia: Positive Anymore*, Pennsylvania Working Papers on Linguistic Change and Variation, Vol. 1, No. 5.

18. A. McIntosh, 'Linguistics and English Studies', in A. McIntosh and M. A. K. Halliday, *Patterns of Language: Papers in General,*

Descriptive and Applied Linguistics (London 1966). On the syntax of inscape, see below, Chapter 7.

19. MacKenzie, op. cit., pp. 112–24.

CHAPTER 4

1. Paul Garvin, *A Prague School Reader on Esthetics, Literary Structure and Style* (Washington, D.C., 1964), pp. vii–viii.
2. Hopkins, of course, did not think that such things were really random. 'All the world is full of inscape and chance left free to act falls into an order as well as a purpose' (*JP*, 230).
3. Jan Mukarovsky, in Garvin, op. cit., pp. 21–2.
4. Mukarovsky, op. cit.
5. Wain, op. cit.
6. F. De Saussure, *Cours de Linguistique Générale*, 5th ed. (Paris, 1955). English translation by Wade Baskin, *Course in General Linguistics* (New York, 1959).
7. See the excellent discussion by E. L. Epstein, 'Hopkins's "Heaven-Haven": A Linguistic-Critical Description', *Essays in Criticism* (1973), pp. 137–45.

CHAPTER 5

1. Susanne Langer, *Feeling and Form* (London, 1953).
2. S. W. Dawson, *Essays in Criticism* XIX (January 1969), draws attention to Hopkins's indebtedness in his rhythms to the Anglican tradition of chanting psalms. Geoffrey Hill, *Agenda* X–XI (1972–3), comments that the achievement of sprung rhythm is 'its being "out of stride" if judged by the standards of common (or running) rhythm, while remaining "in stride" if considered as procession, as pointed liturgical chant . . .'
3. See particularly Yvor Winters, 'The Poetry of Gerard Manley Hopkins', in his *The Function of Criticism* (London, 1962), a reprint from *The Hudson Review* I (Winter 1949) and reprinted in Hartman, *Hopkins*.
4. See, for example, N. Chomsky, *Aspects of the Theory of Syntax* (Cambridge, Mass., 1965), pp. 3–15.
5. Amongst many excellent treatments of Joyce's language, see for example Anthony Burgess's book in The Language Library, *Joysprick* (London, 1973). For comparison of Hopkins with Joyce, see pp. 90–2, p. 178.

6. Modern phoneticians would broadly agree with Hopkins's perceptions about relationships within series of consonants. In English *p*, *b*, *f*, *v* are related in that they belong to a *labial* series: the lips are 'the place of articulation'; within the series, *p* and *f* are *voiceless*, where *b* and *v* are *voiced*; *p* and *b* are related in 'manner of articulation': both are *stop* consonants or *plosives*, whereas *f* and *v* are *fricatives*. Distinctive feature theory, based on Prague School linguistics, has achieved very subtle analysis of such relationships. and forms the basis of modern 'generative phonology'. See Erik Fudge, *Phonology* (Harmondsworth, 1973) for relevant readings, and Hyman, op. cit. Hopkins's phonetic analysis could have been made possible by his own unusual powers of observation, but it is likely that he had read something about it in Müller's *Lectures*.

7. For a full discussion of these complex skaldic metres, see G. Turville-Petre, *Scaldic Poetry* (Oxford, 1976).

8. Quoted from J. Hall (ed.), *Selections from Early Middle English* (Oxford, 1920), pp. 94–5, ll. 26–31. I have introduced modern punctuation and expanded the abbreviation for *and*.

9. Old Norse skaldic kennings can be amazingly far-fetched. In Egill's *Hǫfuðlausn*, poetry is 'the sea of Oðinn's breast'. But Hopkins's poetry, unlike that of the skalds, is not court or ceremonial poetry; what is acceptable in one style or tradition may not be acceptable in another. I accept Hopkins's *kenning* for the same reason that I find it acceptable that Cleopatra's barge '*burn'd* on the water' (*Antony and Cleopatra*, III. ii. 200) – not literally but metaphorically. Shakespeare here uses *burn'd* as the last term in an alliterative and rhyming series: *barge, burnished, burn'd*.

10. A phoneme is a *distinctive* segment of sound; substitution of one phoneme for another is capable of bringing about a distinction in meaning, as in substitution series such as *tin, ten, tan, ton, tone . . .,* etc.

CHAPTER 6

1. This depends on a 'contextual' approach to meaning such as that advocated by J. R. Firth. See, for example, Firth, *Papers in Linguistics 1934–1951* (London, 1951); for a discussion of *dark night* see p. 295. This approach has been criticized because meaning is defined too widely. See John Lyons's discussion, 'Firth's Theory of "Meaning"', in C. E. Bazell *et al.*, *In Memory of J. R. Firth* (London, 1966). Firth's emphasis on the tendency of words

to pick up associations from the 'collocations' in which they are frequently used is nevertheless highly relevant to Hopkins's language.

2. Despite Professor Mariani's valuable contributions to Hopkins studies, the following (on *Sibyl's Leaves*) is a clear example of what I mean: 'This blending of evening into night is mimetically captured in the digraph and vowel chiming and smooth blending of word into word in "*Ear*nest, *ear*thless, *equal*, attun*ea*ble". But the dental stops work against a too easy blending. There is a pause and then a chiming at the other end of the alphabet with "*v*aulty, *v*oluminous, . . . stupen*dous*",' P. L. Mariani, *A Commentary on the Complete Poems of Gerard Manley Hopkins* (Ithaca and London, 1970), pp. 199–200. Confusion of spelling with sound ('digraphs', 'alphabet') leads to great uncertainty as to what is meant by 'dental stops', and to general vagueness. Reacting against this kind of thing, some critics have denied that sound symbolism has much importance at all. See F. W. Bateson, *English Poetry*, 2nd ed. (London, 1966), pp. 1–32.

3. *JP*, 137, 141, 142, 143, 174, 175, 182, 218, 231, 233, 235. Firth, *The Tongues of Men and Speech* (London, 1966), p. 193, considers *le* sounds in 'iteratives or frequentatives' to be amongst the most interesting 'affective' sounds in English and Germanic languages generally.

4. Labials are speech sounds articulated by the lips. Of these, *b* and *p* are labial *plosives*. The corresponding fricatives, *v* and *f*, are in English *labiodentals*. In contemporary phonological theory change or variation between, for example, *b* and *v* would be described as a 'natural' rule, one which is likely because of the close relationship between the sounds concerned. See Hyman, op. cit., loc. cit.

5. See my discussion of these relationships in J. Milroy, 'Gerard Manley Hopkins: Etymology and "Current Language"', *Critical Survey* V (Winter 1971), pp. 211–18.

6. In a letter to Bridges (*LB*, 44) Hopkins jokes: 'Your letter cannot amuse Father Provincial, for he is on the unfathering deeps outward bound to Jamaica'. Apart from the pun (father=priest), the syntactic relations here differ subtly from those of 'The Deutschland'.

7. For a fuller explanation, see Lyons, *Introduction to Theoretical Linguistics*, pp. 73–81.

8. For a full discussion see Adrienne Lehrer, *Semantic Fields and Lexical Structure* (Amsterdam and London, 1974), pp. 15–45, 95–130.

9. MacKenzie, op. cit., p. 115.

10. For a discussion of the semantics of colour, see Lyons, *Introduction to Theoretical Linguistics*, pp. 429–33.

11. Of course this 'deficiency' in the semantics of colour is not an *absolute* deficiency in the language. The absence of precise *words* for degrees of brightness and saturation can be made good by periphrastic and metaphorical usage, but only with difficulty.

12. Hopkins refers to *word-painting* in a letter to Bridges in 1887 in which he also discusses 'Harry Ploughman' (*LB*, 267). It seems as if Bridges may have referred somewhat scathingly to the poem as a word-painting. Hopkins deplores the current fashion of despising word-painting and adds: 'Wordpainting is, of all the verbal arts, the great success of our day ... and this I shall not be bullied out of'. He was extremely interested in contemporary painting and much admired Millais. See Jerome Bump, 'Hopkins, Millais and Modernity', *Hopkins Quarterly* II (1975), pp. 5–19.

13. The *Concise Oxford Dictionary* lists 'Channel of stream (esp. in comb., as *mill-*)' as one of the meanings of *race*. See Commentary.

14. Some linguists have used the term *idiom* in a very broad sense. By C. F. Hockett's definition (*A Course in Modern Linguistics*, New York, 1958, pp. 303–30), Hopkins's word-coinings (*lovescape, leafmeal, American-outward-bound*) would all be described as idioms. However, Hockett recognizes the special 'idiomaticity' of 'phrasal compounds' such as *blackbird, blackboard* as against *black bird*, etc. The accompanying pattern of reduced stress on the second constituent is recognized as a marker of 'idiomaticity' (pp. 316–17).

15. Syntactic co-ordination is further discussed in Chapter 7.

16. See R. B. Lees, *The Grammar of English Nominalizations* (The Hague, 1963). Many of the examples used here are from Lees (see pp. 113–75).

17. Structural or syntactic ambiguity in noun phrases is further discussed in Chapter 7. See N. Chomsky, *Aspects of the Theory of Syntax* (Cambridge, Mass., 1965), e.g. pp. 21–2, R. B. Lees, 'A Multiply Ambiguous Adjectival Construction in English', *Language* XXXVI (1960), reprinted in W. F. Bolton and D. Crystal, *The English Language*, Vol. 2 (Cambridge, 1969).

18. Peters, op. cit., pp. 78–86.

19. C. Fillmore, 'The Case for Case', in E. Bach and R. T. Harms (eds) *Universals in Linguistic Theory* (New York, 1968). Fillmore proposes that the *underlying* relationships between nouns and verbs can be stated in terms of a limited array of 'cases'. In both *John kicked the ball* and *The ball was kicked by John, John* is 'agentive' and *the ball* 'objective'. In *The hammer broke the window, The window was broken*

by the hammer and *John broke the window with the hammer*, *hammer* is 'instrumental', but *John* remains 'agentive'.

20. An *ergative* case is the case of the thing affected, in those languages which indicate it in surface-structure. See Lyons, *Introduction to Theoretical Linguistics*, pp. 341–2, 350–71. In English it may be recognized as a deep-structural case relationship. Thus, in *John moves the stone* and *The stone moves, the stone* in both sentences may be considered ergative. See also our discussion of Hopkins's manipulation of transitivity in Chapter 7.

21. Heaven cannot 'fall' something, but it *can* 'fling' something. See also the discussion of transitivity in Chapter 7.

22. MacKenzie, 'On Editing Gerard Manley Hopkins', *Queen's Quarterly* LXXVIII, No. 4 (Winter 1971), p. 500.

23. See J. Milroy, 'Gerard Manley Hopkins: Etymology and "Current Language",' *Critical Survey* V (1971), pp. 211–18.

24. According to Peters (op. cit., p. 167), the link between *joke* and *potsherd* is a suppressed allusion to Job, 'the type of man in deepest misery. But Job irresistibly called up the potsherd with which he scraped his wounds . . .' Underlying conceptual links are typical of Hopkins. See also our discussion of *thick* in 'Tom's Garland', Chapter 7.

CHAPTER 7

1. David Daiches, 'Gerard Manley Hopkins and the Modern Poets', in his *New Literary Values* (Edinburgh, 1936), p. 30.

2. See Chapter 3, pp. 89–90 and note 17.

3. Cummings's poetry and other matters of relevance here have been discussed from a linguistic point of view by J. P. Thorne, 'Stylistics and Generative Grammars', *Journal of Linguistics* I (1965), pp. 49–59, 'Poetry, Stylistics and Imaginary Grammars', *Journal of Linguistics* V (1969), pp. 147–50, R. Fowler, 'On the Interpretation of Nonsense Strings', *Journal of Linguistics* V (1969), pp. 75–83, R. R. Butters, 'On the Interpretation of "Deviant Utterances",' *Journal of Linguistics* VI (1970), pp. 105–10, and J. Aarts, 'A Note on the Interpretation of "he danced his did",' *Journal of Linguistics* VII (1971), pp. 71–3.

4. By 1965, linguists were beginning to avoid the term *acceptability* and preferred to speak of *deviance* or *deviant utterances*, apparently ruling out the 'social' aspect of use. See Chomsky's discussion of 'degrees of grammaticalness' in *Aspects of the Theory of Syntax*, pp. 148 ff.

5. We assume here the traditional distinction of sentence types into declarative, exclamatory, interrogative and imperative sentences (for statements, exclamations, questions and commands). We also recognize the special grammar of exclamatory 'wish' sentences (*Long Live the King! Glory be to God . . .*), and Bloomfield's surface-structure distinction between *major* sentences (which contain a finite verb) and *minor* sentences, such as *Just coming! Not to worry!* (which are verbless). See L. Bloomfield, *Language* (New York, 1933).

6. The semantic relations involved are those of *hyponymy* or *inclusion*. Hopkins is proposing that the dappled items are included within the class of *dappled things*, as, for example, tulips are included within the class of flowers. See Lyons, *Introduction to Theoretical Linguistics*, pp. 453 ff.

7. Compare Chapter 5, pp. 115–16 ff.

8. Peters, op. cit., p. 78.

9. op. cit., p. 86.

10. See R. B. Lees, op. cit., loc. cit.

11. For the distinction between 'logical' and 'grammatical' subject, see, for example, Lyons, *Introduction to Theoretical Linguistics*, pp. 343–4, and for 'surface' and 'deep' structure, see Chomsky, *Aspects of the Theory of Syntax*, pp. 16 ff. and note 12.

12. Chomsky, *Aspects of the Theory of Syntax*, loc. cit. and pp. 128 ff. A rule for what we have called *permutation* or 'transposition', merely states that in a given case $X+Y$ is to be 're-written' as $Y+X$. Thus, 'hardly *John had* finished' becomes, by a normal rule, 'hardly *had John* finished'.

13. Peters, op. cit., pp. 81–2.

14. The difference between *apposition* and *conjunction* is, broadly speaking, that in appositive series (e.g. *George, my cousin*) the items closely modify or define one another and are closely logically connected. In a conjunctive series, such as *bacon and eggs*, this is not so. But when the conjunction is suppressed, this distinction may not always be clear.

15. Hopkins's knowledge of contemporary philology (see Chapter 2) is probably relevant here. See William Barnes, *A Philological Grammar* (London, 1854), p. 243: 'In Mongolian, for want of a relative pronoun, the place of the relative pronoun and the verb of the relative clause is taken by a participle. The speech-form "the girl who danced" is "the having-danced girl". "The book which thou gavest me" is "thy to-me given book". "The apple which fell from the tree" is "the from-the-tree fallen apple".' Compare 'not-by-morning-matched face' (No. 59).

16. 'Grammatical' words, also called 'function' words, are discussed by C. C. Fries, *The Structure of English* (London, 1957), pp. 87 ff. They are those which are relatively 'empty' of referential meaning, and used chiefly to 'mark' 'full' words and their relationships. In Lewis Carroll's *Jabberwocky* they are retained, whereas the 'full' words are nonsense words.

17. Many other 'regular' omissions of the relative pronoun are listed by Peters, op. cit., pp. 125–8.

18. Peters (op. cit., p. 128) lists also the following, supplying the relative pronoun in square brackets:

> Save my Hero, O Hero [who] savest . . .

> O well wept, mother [you who] have lost son;
> Wept, wife; wept, sweetheart [who] would be one . . .   (No. 41)

> . . . the outward sentence [which] low lays him . . . here . . .
> (No. 45)

> They were elseminded then . . . the men [who]
> Woke thee . . .   ('Deutschland', st. 25)

> . . . I have put my lips on pleas [that]
> Would brandle adamantine heaven . . .   (No. 48)

> . . . with a love [that] glides
> Lower than death . . .   ('Deutschland', st. 33)

19. Although dialectal syntax has not been sufficiently studied for us to be sure, it would appear that there are precedents (for Hopkins's usage) in dialect literature or speech in all the cases quoted, except possibly 'Squander the hell-rook ranks sally to molest him', where the relative clause modifies a *direct object*. Otherwise – in direct address, after indirect objects, object-complements, objects of prepositions, and especially after complements of the verb *to be* – suppression of the relative pronoun seems to be grammatical in many dialects.

20. Geoffrey Hill, 'Redeeming the Time', *Agenda* X–XI (1972–3).

21. In 1870 (*JP*, 199), Hopkins observes movement and change in chestnut trees tossed by the wind 'without losing their inscape'. He then comments: 'Observe that motion multiplies inscape only when inscape is discovered, otherwise it disfigures'. Note also the convenient ambiguity of the word *discover*, which could be said to *inscape* 'discovery' by the observer and 'revelation' by the object perceived.

22. Verbs in English are obligatorily inflected in finite forms for

tense, but there are also considerable overtones of *aspect* (reflecting the user's perception of, and point of view to, the event) in choices made within the verbal paradigm. Some so-called tense forms require aspectual choices between *continuous* and *non-continuous* forms, *perfective* ('I have gone') and *non-perfective* ('I went'), and so on. The choice of infinitives or participles may partly obscure such distinctions, but they are particularly useful for obscuring the *active v. passive* distinction.

23. In this quotation, the word *delightfully* is an important inscaping word because of its syntactic ambiguity. The *delight* referred to is simultaneously an *attribute* of the wind and an *effect* on the observer.

24. 'Notional' definitions of the 'parts of speech' normally describe the verb as an 'action-word' or something of the kind, whereas the noun is a 'thing-word' or 'the name of a person, place or thing'.

25. Hopkins's difficulties with the normal assumptions of traditional grammar – that words stand either for *things* or the *relations of things* – are discussed by McIntosh in *Patterns of Language*, pp. 51–2. One of the inscaping words by which Hopkins tries to overcome the requirement to distinguish between *being* and *doing* (*state* and *action* or *movement*) is *pitch*, on which see Commentary.

26. For a full discussion of transitivity and its relation to *ergativity* (see Chapter 6, note 20), see Lyons, *Introduction to Theoretical Linguistics*, pp. 350–71. Note that a true intransitive is a 'one-place' verb, whereas a transitive is a two- or three-place verb. An intransitive (e.g. 'die') *cannot* take an object, whereas a transitive verb can have 'object-deletion'. Thus, in *John eats at the Ritz*, 'eats,' is still a transitive, although its object (e.g. 'dinner') is deleted.

27. In 'mild night's *blear-all* black' (No. 46), *blear-all* is at the same time 'blinding' all, but also 'obscure' to all people and obscuring all things. See also Commentary, s.v. BRANDLE, CATCH, ROPE (as verb), RIVELLING, WIND (eye after).

CODA

1. Brigid Brophy *et al.*, 'Gerard Manley Hopkins: Poems', in *Fifty Works of English Literature We Could Do Without* (London, 1967), pp. 97–8.

Select Bibliography

〰〰〰〰〰

I CHIEF REFERENCE WORKS

BORRELLO, ALFRED, *A Concordance of the Poetry in English of Gerard Manley Hopkins*, Metuchen, N.J., 1969.

DILLIGAN, R. J., and BENDER, T. K., *A Concordance to the English Poetry of Gerard Manley Hopkins*, Madison, Wis., 1970.

DUNNE, TOM, *Gerard Manley Hopkins: A Comprehensive Bibliography*, Oxford, 1976. Complete to about 1970.

THOMAS, ALFRED and others (eds), *The Hopkins Research Bulletin*, published annually by The Hopkins Society (London, 1970–6). This contains annual bibliographies of work on Hopkins.

II COMMENTARIES ON THE POEMS

McCHESNEY, DONALD, *A Hopkins Commentary*, London, 1968. A commentary on the main poems 1876–89.

MARIANI, PAUL L., *A Commentary on the Complete Poems of Gerard Manley Hopkins*, Ithaca and London, 1970.

MILWARD, PETER, *A Commentary on Gerard Manley Hopkins's 'The Wreck of the Deutschland'*, Tokyo, 1968.

MILWARD, PETER, *A Commentary on the Sonnets of Gerard Manley Hopkins*, Tokyo, 1969.
A commentary on 31 sonnets.

III STANDARD BOOKS ON HOPKINS

GARDNER, W. H., *Gerard Manley Hopkins: A Study of Poetic Idiosyncrasy in Relation to Poetic Tradition*, 2 vols., London, 1944, 1949; 2nd ed., 1962.

LAHEY, G. F., *Gerard Manley Hopkins*, London, 1930.

MacKENZIE, N. H., *Hopkins*, Edinburgh and London, 1968.
A brief but excellent introduction.

PETERS, W. A. M., *Gerard Manley Hopkins: A Critical Essay towards the Understanding of his Poetry*, London, 1948; 2nd ed., 1970.
  An excellent study of H's language in relation to inscape.

PICK, JOHN, *Gerard Manley Hopkins: Priest and Poet*, London, 1942.

PICK, JOHN (ed.), *A Hopkins Reader*, London, 1953.
  A selection of prose and poetry, chiefly valuable as a convenient selection of H's prose writings.

THOMAS, ALFRED, *Hopkins the Jesuit*, London, 1969.

WEYAND, NORMAN (ed.), *Immortal Diamond: Studies in Gerard Manley Hopkins*, London and New York, 1949.
  Studies by Jesuit scholars; although a few of these are poor, this book contains some of the most important essays on Hopkins ever written.

IV OTHER WORKS RELEVANT TO THE STUDY
OF HOPKINS'S LANGUAGE

AUGUST, E. R., *Word Inscapes: A Study of the Poetic Vocabulary of Gerard Manley Hopkins* (unpublished dissertation), University of Pittsburgh, 1964.

AUGUST, E. R., 'The Growth of the Windhover', *Publications of the Modern Language Association* LXXXII (1967).

BERGONZI, BERNARD, *Hopkins the Englishman*, The Hopkins Society: Sixth Annual Lecture, London, 1975.

BOYLE, ROBERT, *Metaphor in Hopkins*, Chapel Hill, N.C., 1961.

BREMER, RUDY, 'Hopkins' Use of the word "combs" in "To R.B.",' *English Studies* LI (April, 1970).

DAWSON, S. W., 'A Note on an Early Poem of Hopkins', *Essays in Criticism* XIX (1969).

EPSTEIN, E. L., 'Hopkins's "Heaven-Haven": A Linguistic-Critical Description', *Essays in Criticism* XXIII (1973).

HARTMAN, G. H., *The Unmediated Vision*, New Haven, 1954.

HARTMAN, G. H., *Hopkins: A Collection of Critical Essays*, Englewood Cliffs, N.J., 1966.
  A selection containing essays by Leavis, Wain, Miller, McLuhan, Ong, Winters, Warren, and others, often with omissions.

HENTZ, ANN L., 'Language in Hopkins' "Carrion Comfort",' *Victorian Poetry* IX (Autumn 1971).

HILL, GEOFFREY, 'Redeeming the Time', *Agenda* X–XI (1972–3).

LEAVIS, F. R., 'Gerard Manley Hopkins' in his *New Bearings in English Poetry* (London, 1932), reprinted in Hartman, *Hopkins*.

LEAVIS, F. R., 'Gerard Manley Hopkins', *Scrutiny* XII (1944), reprinted in his *The Common Pursuit* (London, 1952).

LEAVIS, F. R., *Gerard Manley Hopkins: Reflections after Fifty Years*, The Hopkins Society: Second Annual Lecture, London, 1971.

LEES, F. N., '"The Windhover",' *Scrutiny* XVII (1950).

LEES, F. N., *Gerard Manley Hopkins*, New York and London, 1966.

LILLY, GWENETH, 'The Welsh Influence in the Poetry of Gerard Manley Hopkins', *Modern Language Review* XXXVIII (1943).

McINTOSH, A., 'Linguistics and English Studies' in A. McIntosh and M. A. K. Halliday, *Patterns of Language*: *Papers in General, Descriptive and Applied Linguistics*, London, 1966.

MACKENZIE, N. H., 'The Dragon's Treasure Horde Unlocked', *Modern Language Quarterly* XXXI (1970).

MACKENZIE, N. H., 'On Editing Gerard Manley Hopkins', *Queens Quarterly* LXXVIII, No. 4 (Winter 1971).

MACKENZIE, N. H., 'Gerard Manley Hopkins' "Spelt from Sibyl's Leaves",' *Malahat Review* XXVI (April 1973).

McLUHAN, H. M., 'The Analogical Mirrors', *Kenyon Review* VI (Summer 1944), reprinted in Hartman, *Hopkins*.

MILLER, J. HILLIS, 'Gerard Manley Hopkins' in his *The Disappearance of God*, Cambridge, Mass., 1963, reprinted in part in Hartman, *Hopkins*.

MILROY, J., 'Gerard Manley Hopkins: 'Etymology and "Current Language",' *Critical Survey* V (Winter 1971).

MILROY, J., 'Hopkins' Victorian Language', *Hopkins Quarterly* I (January 1975).

ONG, WALTER J., 'Sprung Rhythm and the Life of English Poetry', in Weyand (ed.), *Immortal Diamond*, reprinted in part in Hartman, *Hopkins*.

RINGROSE, C. X., 'F. R. Leavis and Yvor Winters on G. M. Hopkins', *English Studies* LV (1974).

SCHODER, R. V., 'An Interpretive Glossary of Difficult Words in the Poems' in Weyand (ed.), *Immortal Diamond*.

SONSTROEM, D., 'Making Earnest of Game: G. M. Hopkins and Nonsense Poetry', *Modern Language Quarterly* XXVIII (June 1967).

WAIN, JOHN, 'Gerard Manley Hopkins: An Idiom of Desperation', *Proceedings of the British Academy* XLV (1959), reprinted in Wain's *Essays on Literature and Ideas* (London, 1963) and in Hartman, *Hopkins*.

WARREN, AUSTEN, 'Instress of Inscape', *Kenyon Review* VI (Summer, 1944), reprinted in his *Rage for Order* (Chicago, 1948) and in Hartman, *Hopkins*.

WHITE, NORMAN, 'Harry Ploughman's Muscles', *Hopkins Quarterly* II (April 1975).

WINTERS, YVOR, 'The Poetry of Gerard Manley Hopkins', in his *The Function of Criticism* (London, 1962), a reprint from *The Hudson Review* I (Winter 1949) and reprinted in Hartman, *Hopkins*.